Pelican Books
Electronic Computers

Stuart Hollingdale was born in London in 1910. He was educated at Latymer Upper School, Hammersmith, graduated in mathematics at Christ's College, Cambridge, and did some research at Imperial College, London, for a Ph.D. on the motion of fluids behind moving bodies.

In 1936 he joined the Aerodynamics Department of the Royal Aircraft Establishment at Farnborough. During and immediately after the war he was engaged on a variety of jobs, from operational research on the 'balloon barrage' defence system to helping in the post-war reconstruction of the Scientific Civil Service. In 1948 he returned to Farnborough to become head of the newly formed Mathematics Department; a post he occupied until 1967 when he moved to Birmingham to become Director of the University Computer Centre. He is a Vice-President of the Institute of Mathematics and its Applications.

In 1959 he published *High Speed Computing: Methods and Applications*. In 1962 he was awarded the Bronze Medal of the Institute of Navigation for his work on the mathematics of collision avoidance at sea. Dr Hollingdale is married and has two daughters.

Geoffrey Tootill was born in Oldham in 1922. He went to school in Birmingham, graduated in mathematics at Cambridge, and from 1942 to 1947 worked on the development of airborne radar. After two years of research at Manchester University, he devised the logic design of the first automatic digital computer ever to be put on sale.

He spent six years as a lecturer at the Royal Military College of Science, and then seven years at the Royal Aircraft Establishment. In 1963 he joined the European Space Research Organisation, and after four years in the Netherlands, is now head of the Control Centre Department in Germany.

Mr Tootill was the first chairman of the Terminology Committee of the International Federation for Information Processing. He is married and has three sons.

S. H. Hollingdale and G. C. Tootill

ELECTRONIC COMPUTERS

Revised Edition

Penguin Books

Penguin Books Ltd, Harmondsworth,
Middlesex, England
Penguin Books Inc., 7110 Ambassador Road,
Baltimore, Maryland 21207, U.S.A.
Penguin Books Australia Ltd, Ringwood,
Victoria, Australia

First published 1965
Reprinted 1966, 1967, 1968
Revised edition, 1970
Reprinted 1971
Copyright © S. H. Hollingdale and G. C. Tootill, 1965, 1970

Made and printed in Great Britain by
Hazell Watson & Viney Ltd, Aylesbury, Bucks
Set in Monotype Times

CONTENTS

PLATES

ACKNOWLEDGEMENTS

The authors are indebted to the following for permission to use photographs and figures:
Professor J.Crank, Brunel University (Plate 1). *The Illustrated London News* (Plate 2). Electronic Associates Ltd (Plate 3). Mullard Limited and Ampex Great Britain Limited (Plate 4). International Computers Limited (Plates 5, 6 and 7). British European Airways (Plate 8). IBM United Kingdom Limited (Figure 84). Professor J.G.Hawkes and Mr B.L.Kershaw of the University of Birmingham and Mr R.C.Readett of the Birmingham Natural History Society (Figures 85 (a) and (b)). British Overseas Airways Corporation (Figure 88).

They also wish to thank Messrs H.Haverley and W.Vincer for specialist advice on the draughts program in Chapter 1; Miss J. Clarkson and Miss M.Parker for typing and clerical assistance; many colleagues for suggestions and criticism; and the Ministry of Technology (formerly Aviation) for permission to publish.

1. INTRODUCTION

'The electronic computer has not made the headlines in the same way as nuclear energy, but I believe it is comparable in importance. The ability to apply precise reasoning to very large amounts of data in a reasonable time is something new, and the introduction of computers into science may prove not much less important than the introduction of mathematics in the seventeenth century. ... They can do much to take drudgery out of the office, and can be to the clerk what the bulldozer is to the navvy.'

These words would command general acceptance and indeed excite little interest today. We quote them because they were spoken as long ago as 1956 – by Sir George Thomson, the distinguished physicist, in his presidential address to the Physics and Mathematics Section of the British Association for the Advancement of Science. They certainly make a bold claim for something that was barely ten years old at the time. Since then the computer has become accepted as an indispensable tool in scientific research, engineering design and business administration; about 70,000 of them are now at work and their numbers are growing by about 15 per cent every year. Now, after a mere twenty years, industry and commerce are using computers on a very large scale – to deal economically with large volumes of transactions, to control accurately the quality of products, to evaluate the consequences of alternative policies, and much else besides. Along with space travel, nuclear energy, the genetic code, organ transplant surgery and the contraceptive pill, the computer has become, by common consent, one of the hallmarks of the third quarter of the twentieth century.

In view of this success story it is salutary to point out that a computer can, essentially, do only two things: it can carry out sequences of quite trivial operations, such as copying and adding;

and it can choose between alternative sequences when the need for this has been foreseen.

Perhaps an analogy with another 'marvel' of modern technology may be helpful. The material that issues from a television set is, in its own way, as diverse as the solutions of problems that come from a computer. But all the television equipment really does is to reproduce the original sight and sound patterns at millions of different places. Just as television would be nothing without its artists and performers, so a computer would be nothing without the different specialists who understand the problems and can specify methods of solving them. Television greatly extends the size of the audience the performer can reach; a computer vastly extends the amount of computation that a man can cope with.

Everyone knows that computers work astonishingly fast; they can do simple arithmetic more than a million times as fast as a man. Even more significant is the fact that a computer can perform long connected sequences of operations entirely automatically. This can produce surprising results.

Figure 1 gives the moves in a game of draughts which was terminated by the resignation of White who, being normally a very strong player, realized his position was hopeless. The point is that Black's moves in the game were specified by a computer. It was supplied with the numbers representing the moves of its human opponent, and displayed in reply the numbers representing its own moves. This action was completely automatic, and was based on numerical estimates of the strength of the positions which would result from different alternative moves open to the computer.

Now the significant achievement that this game demonstrates is that of the American computer research worker, Dr A.L. Samuel, who taught the computer how to play. To do this he had to analyse the game of draughts in great detail and reduce its tactics to rules of thumb. Of course these rules are very complicated; they would be uselessly laborious for a human player and an impossible burden on his memory. They provide for the automatic alteration of the relative importance attached to different features of a position in the light of experience of actual games. They allow for the assimilation of published model games

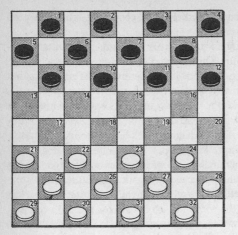

Figure 1.
A Game of
Draughts.

Blk	11–15		Blk	1–10–19–26		Wh.	22–18
Wh.	23–19			takes 3		Blk	27–31 (king)
A Blk	8–11		Wh.	31–22–15		Wh.	18–9 takes
Wh.	22–17			takes 2		Blk	31–22 takes
Blk	4–8		Blk	11–18 takes		Wh.	9–5
Wh.	17–13		C Wh.	30–26		Blk	22–26
Blk	15–18		Blk	8–11		Wh.	23–19
Wh.	24–20		Wh.	25–22		Blk	26–22
Blk	9–14		Blk	18–25 takes		Wh.	19–16
Wh.	26–23		Wh.	29–22 takes		Blk	22–18
Blk	19–15		Blk	11–15		Wh.	21–17
Wh.	19–10 takes		D Wh.	27–23		Blk	18–23
Blk	6–15 takes		Blk	15–19		Wh.	17–13
B Wh.	28–24		Wh.	23–16 takes		Blk	2–6
Blk	15–19		Blk	12–19 takes		Wh.	16–11
Wh.	24–15 takes		Wh.	32–27		Blk	7–16 takes
Blk.	5–9		Blk	19–24		Wh.	29–11 takes
Wh.	13–6 takes		Wh.	27–23		Blk	23–19
			Blk	24–27		Wh.	Resigns

When White resigns, his position is hopeless, for if he plays 5–1, then 19–16, 1–10, 16–7–14, etc. For expert players, we give some notes by H. Haverley of Southampton, a former International player:

    (A) Forms the opening
    (B) 23–19, 15–24, 28–19 my preference here
    (C) 25–22, 18–25, 29–22 best
    (D) 22–17, if E14–18, 20–16, 12–19, 27–23, 18–27, 32–16, draw
    (E) F7–10, 17–13, 2–6, 26–22, draw
    (F) 15–19, 17–10, 7–14, 27–23, G3–7, 23–16, 12–19, 20–16, draw
    (G) 19–24, 26–22, 2–6, 22–17, 6–10, 23–19, 14–18, draw

and, in fact, the first twenty-one moves of the game set out in Figure 1 are the same as those of a game of which an analysis was published by W. Hay in 1838, who concluded that the result should be a draw. It is impressive that the computer played according to the book, and immediately took advantage of White's weak moves at C and D.

Dr Samuel worked out the computer procedure gradually by thinking carefully about one aspect of it at a time, and by making experiments and changes. Indeed, so well has he done the job that this procedure for the most part plays better than he does. This would not be true if Dr Samuel were prepared to spend many months with pencil and paper working out each of his moves, for by this means he could no doubt beat the computer by its own methods. However, the computer's appetite for monotonous and repetitious work is so enormous that it can do in a minute what would be a year's calculation for a man. Between moves in a game of draughts it can therefore conduct an extremely thorough assessment of a number of continuations, even though its methods of analysis would strike a human player as insufferably tedious, and perhaps also rather bizarre.

Many other calculations which would never be attempted without a computer are now carried out as a matter of routine. For example, each day the customers of the German Federal Railways state their requirements for empty wagons to be made available at their nearest railway station for the transport of their products. At some stations there are not enough wagons available and at others there are too many, so empty wagons have to be moved from place to place. A computer, by means of a precise, though laborious, mathematical technique, quickly establishes a schedule for doing this which minimizes the cost and makes substantial savings by comparison with schedules found by other methods.

The impact of electronic techniques on the computational art has indeed been so profound that some people think of computing itself as a branch of electrical engineering, invented about 1944. In fact, of course, man has been calculating since the dawn of history, and has always found it irksome and laborious. He has never ceased making devices to lighten his burden. The electronic computer is the latest exhibit in a line which stretches back for thousands of years to the tally stick, the sand tray and the counting frame.

It is the purpose of this book to explain how computers work, how problems are specified for them by human beings, and what sort of problems they can tackle. In these days of organized scientific research and engineering development, spectacular advances are common; there are many fields in which the technical advances of the last few decades overshadow the progress made in all previous times. This is certainly true with computers: the next chapter is enough to describe the major developments, both in instruments and in the representation of numbers by symbols, up to the early nineteenth century.

Chapter 3 takes the story up to the year 1946, to the arrival of the first computing machines which were genuinely automatic. Since then there has been such proliferation of activity that we devote the remaining four-fifths of the book to it. So many things have been going on at once that chronological treatment is no longer satisfactory.

In Chapter 4 we explain some methods of classifying computers; in Chapter 5 we describe one type (the *analog* computer*) which is particularly useful in engineering design – of aeroplanes and their equipment, atomic power stations, chemical plants, etc. Most of the rest of the book deals with the other important type – the *digital computer*. This is the kind that plays draughts and organizes railway wagons, amongst other things. Chapter 6 introduces the topic of *programming*; that is, of specifying how to solve a problem with the aid of a digital computer. Such a computer, since it works automatically, must be fully instructed in advance. It must be able to 'memorize' these instructions and also the data on which it is to work. How it does this, and what else it consists of besides its 'memory', are explained in Chapters 7 and 8.

By this stage it is clear that the operations that a computer is basically capable of are quite trivial, and Chapter 9 takes up again the specification of sequences of such operations so as to achieve a desired result. In Chapter 10 we turn to the organization and staff needed to enable a computer to give a service to numerous

*The American spelling of 'analogue' has become the international standard.

customers, and in Chapter 11 to some examples of the problems that can be solved. It is sometimes necessary to link together the analog methods of operation of Chapter 5 and the contrasting digital methods of Chapters 7 and 8. This, and some related topics, form the subject of Chapter 12.

In the final chapter we allow ourselves a brief look into the future. There seems little doubt that, if we can avoid a global catastrophe, the present torrent of new ideas will continue and will lead to some spectacular development during the next twenty years or so. Electronic computers are still new, and we are only beginning to learn how to use them properly. Our present achievements, which seem so impressive to us, may well appear to our grandchildren as no more than crude, fumbling, surface-scratchings.

2. FROM THE ABACUS TO THE DESK CALCULATOR

Early man, we may suppose, used the fingers of his two hands to represent numbers. In this way it is comparatively easy to count up to ten, but many primitive peoples find difficulty in getting much further. One method of proceeding, said to be still in use in Africa, is to enlist the aid of a second man. The first man counts the units up to ten on his fingers, while his partner counts the number of groups of ten so formed. The next major step, taken by the first civilizations of Egypt and the Asian river valleys, was to represent numbers by means of pebbles arranged in heaps of ten. This, in turn, led to the development of the *abacus*, or counting frame. This device, in its simplest form, consists of a tray covered with dust or sand in which a number of grooves are made, or of a wooden board with grooves cut in it. A number is represented by pebbles put in the grooves; as many pebbles are put in the first groove as there are units in the number to be represented, as many in the second groove as there are tens, and so on. Objects are counted by placing, for each object, a pebble in the first groove. As soon as there are ten pebbles in that groove, they are removed, and a single pebble is placed in the second groove, and so on. (Indeed, the word *calculation* itself derives from the Latin *calculus*, a pebble.)

The abacus was in use in so many widely separated cultures – in fact it is one of the hallmarks of early civilization – that many authorities believe it was invented independently in several centres. It was to be found throughout the Mediterranean world in the first millennium B.C.: Herodotus, in the fifth century B.C., remarks that the Egyptians reckoned with pebbles 'bringing the hand from right to left, while the Greeks proceeded in the opposite direction'. On the other side of the world, the Spaniards, when they landed in America, found the instrument in common use in the pre-Columbian civilizations of Mexico and Peru. The

Electronic Computers

Aztec form of abacus consisted of a set of parallel rods stuck into a piece of wood, on to which beads could be threaded.

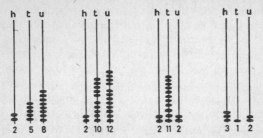

Figure 2. Addition of 54 to 258 on a primitive abacus.

The method of performing addition on a primitive abacus is illustrated in Figure 2, which shows the successive steps in adding 54 to 258. The procedure is well known and the diagrams are self-explanatory. Subtraction was performed by removing pebbles, while multiplication was treated as repeated addition, and division as repeated subtraction.

Several different types of abacus were in use in Rome; the instrument is mentioned, for instance, by Pliny, Juvenal and Cicero. Some Roman abaci were quite elaborate, being provided with a number of additional grooves to facilitate addition of fractions. The early Russian abacus showed a further improvement; the wires were set in a rectangular frame, and ten (or possibly nine) beads were permanently threaded on each wire. The method of using such an abacus will be clear from Figure 3(a) which shows the number 370826 set on the instrument. A number of minor improvements were made in Western Europe during the Middle Ages. One useful innovation – that of labelling the separate beads – is attributed to Gerbert, a remarkable medieval figure who became Pope Sylvester II in the year 999.

An early form of abacus using bamboo rods instead of pebbles or beads was in use in China at the time of Confucius; it survived in Korea until quite recently. The modern form of Chinese abacus, the *suanpan*, came into general use about the twelth century. The frame is divided by a beam into two regions, known as 'heaven' and 'earth'. Instead of ten beads on each wire, there are two on

16

one side of the beam and five on the other. A bead in 'heaven' counts five, while a bead on 'earth' counts one. Calculations are performed by moving beads away from or towards the beam; the rule being that a bead has a numerical value only when it is adjacent to the beam. Figure 3(b) shows a modern Chinese abacus, again set with the number 370826. There is some evidence that the suanpan was introduced into China from Rome; a late Roman abacus embodying the 'heaven' and 'earth' principle is now in the British Museum. The Chinese abacus was probably introduced into Japan in the fifteenth or sixteenth century. It soon attracted the attention of some of the leading mathematicians of the country, one of the most distinguished being Seki Kowa (1642–1708), who developed a form of infinitesimal calculus and so is sometimes called the Newton of Japan. (Newton and Seki Kowa were born in the same year.)

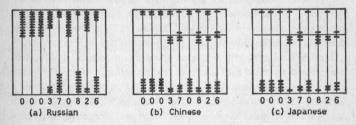

Figure 3. Types of abacus.

A glance at Figure 3(b) will show that two of the beads on each wire of the Chinese abacus – one on either side of the beam – are redundant. The logical simplification was effected in Japan in two stages. About eighty years ago the number of beads in 'heaven' was reduced from two to one, while in 1930 the number in 'earth' was reduced from five to four. The modern Japanese abacus or *soroban* is illustrated in Figure 3(c).

During recent years there has been a marked revival of interest in the abacus in Japan, and operational techniques have been greatly simplified and improved. The Japanese Chamber of Commerce and Industry sponsors an Abacus Research Institute and a Central Committee of Abacus Operators. This latter body lays down methods of training, formulates standards of performance, conducts examinations, and awards certificates of proficiency at various levels.

The Japanese abacus, in the hands of a skilled operator, is certainly a most impressive instrument. As evidence of this we would mention the contest staged on 12 November 1946 between Private T. N. Wood of the Finance Disbursing Section of the U.S. Army, who was elected by a preliminary competition as the most skilled desk machine operator in Japan, and Kiyoshi Matsuzaki, of the Savings Bureau of the Ministry of Postal Administration. Wood used an electric desk calculating machine, Matsuzaki an abacus. The contest covered five types of calculation involving the four basic arithmetic operations, each being judged on speed and accuracy. The result was a victory for Matsuzaki by four to one. The U.S. Service nespaper *Stars and Stripes* commented thus : 'The machine age took a step backward yesterday at the Ernie Pyle Theater as the abacus, centuries old, dealt defeat to the most up-to-date electric machine now being used by the U.S. Government. . . . The abacus victory was complete.' We would only add one remark : an ordinary Japanese abacus costs about two shillings and sixpence.

There can be little doubt that, viewed in the perspective of human history, the humble abacus is the most significant aid to calculation that has ever been invented. For many centuries it was in sole possession of the field ; even today more people probably compute with the aid of the abacus than in any other way – if we exclude the still larger number who rely on their fingers.

Number representations

Computation is a process whereby symbols are altered in accordance with certain rules. If, as is usually but not necessarily the case, the symbols represent numbers and the rules are those of arithmetic, we reach the familiar notion of computing as numerical calculation.

Now clearly there are many ways in which sets of symbols may be used to represent numbers. We shall call each of these ways a *number representation.* To us, of course, the decimal notation is the most familiar, with the Roman a poor second.

In the most primitive number representation, which we shall call the *chalkmark notation*, a number is represented by a series of strokes, the number of strokes giving the value of the number, counting from 1. Here is the number *eighteen* in these three representations:

Decimal	18
Roman	XVIII
Chalkmark	IIIIIIIIIIIIIIIIII
Grouped chalkmark	︳︱︱︱︳ ︳︱︱︱︳ ︳︱︱︱︳ III

In the following passage from *The Trumpet Major*, which is set at the time of the Napoleonic Wars, Thomas Hardy paints a charming little picture of the somewhat uneasy coexistence of two of these number systems.

Behind the wall door were chalked addition and subtraction sums, many of them originally done wrong, and the figures half rubbed out and corrected, noughts being turned into nines, and ones into twos. These were the miller's private calculations. There were also chalked in the same place rows and rows of strokes like open palings, representing the calculations of the grinder, who in his youthful ciphering studies had not gone as far as Arabic figures.

Most of us nowadays have progressed at least as far as the miller!

The characteristic features of the decimal notation are:

(i) a number is represented by an *ordered* set of symbols (known as *digits*); (ii) the numerical *weight* of each digit increases by a constant multiplying factor (i.e. in geometrical progression) as we move along the set of symbols from right to left; (iii) the value of this constant factor, known as the *radix*, is ten.

It follows that the decimal notation requires ten different basic symbols – the ten digits 0, 1, 2 . . . 9.

We should add, for completeness, that if we limit ourselves to whole numbers the weight of the first digit is taken to be unity. (The extension of the number language to deal with fractions is too well known to need comment.) Thus in the number 3037, the weight of the digit '3' on the left is 1000, that of the other '3' is

10, and that of the '7' is 1. The '0' in this number, like any other digit in the set, has a weight depending on its position – in this case a weight of 100. We can say further that this numeral has four digit places but contains only three different digits of the set of 10.

Radices other than 10 are, of course, possible. Indeed, the adoption of a decimal notation is a physiological accident: man happens to have 10 fingers (or digits) on his two hands. Some of the earlier number representations bear traces of radices of 5 (fingers on one hand) or 20 (fingers and toes). A duodecimal notation (radix 12) has many distinguished advocates, its main attraction being that 12 has four divisors (2, 3, 4, 6) as against the two only of the decimal radix.

The smallest possible radix is 2. This gives us the *binary* notation which uses only two different digits – 0 and 1. As electronic digital computers use the binary notation, we shall be meeting it again in Chapter 7.

It is a curious fact that binary representation is used by some very primitive tribes who have not reached the stage of finger counting; they have independent words for 'one' or 'two', composite words for numbers up to six, and everything beyond that is a 'heap'. At the other extreme we find Leibniz, the famous seventeenth-century philosopher and mathematician and co-inventor with Newton of the calculus, being fascinated by the mystic elegance of the binary system. Another distinguished mathematician, Laplace, writing about a hundred years later, comments thus: 'Leibniz saw in his binary arithmetic the image of creation. . . . He imagined that Unity represented God, and Zero the void; that the Supreme Being drew all beings from the void, just as unity and zero express all numbers in his sytem of numeration.'

Some historical number representations

A good choice of number representation is essential for efficient calculation. Try, for instance, to multiply XXVII by XXXIX! For the last few centuries the decimal notation has been the common number representation of the civilized world. Now the point to note is that the abacus provides a concrete means of representing numbers in just this way. Indeed this is precisely what makes it such an effective calculating instrument. All sizeable calculations in the ancient world were performed with the aid of some kind of abacus; a written number representation was needed for record purposes only.

The earliest method of recording numbers – either in writing or by notches in a tally stick – was simply to make the requisite number of strokes; in fact, to use what we have termed the chalk-mark representation. This procedure sufficed for small numbers; it was supplemented as early as the first Egyptian Dynasty (c. 3400 B.C.) by the use of an additional symbol for ten. Further symbols were introduced for 100 and 1000 and the method of grouping by tens was a feature of most of the early civilizations of the Near East. In some cases (Etruscan, early Greek, and Roman) additional symbols for 5 and 50 were incorporated for brevity. The Greeks used two number representations. Some time in the third century B.C. they abandoned their Roman-type notation in favour of another – known as the Alexandrian – which seems to have little to commend it. The numbers 1 to 9 were represented by the first nine letters of the Greek alphabet, the numbers 10, 20 ... 90 by the next nine letters, and the numbers 100, 200 . . . 900 by the next nine letters. (The Greek alphabet contained only twenty-four letters, so three additional symbols were borrowed from other alphabets.) The notation was extended by various artifices to enable numbers greater than 999 to be represented. This system was in fact used for business purposes in the Byzantine Empire until its collapse in 1453.

All such number representations are non-positional; the position of any symbol in the group is without numerical significance. Thus 173, for example, is usually represented in the Roman system as CLXXIII, but the order of the symbols is irrelevant.* The notation merely expresses the fact that 173 is the sum of one hundred, one fifty, two tens, and three ones. Apparently the first people to use a positional system for writing numbers were the

*The late Roman use of the subtractive form (e.g. IV instead of IIII) provides an exception to this statement. The absolute position of the pair of symbols I and V is not important, but the relative position is.

Babylonians. They employed the rather odd radix of 60, which we still retain in our method of expressing angles and time. The Babylonians had separate symbols for 1 and 10, and also one for 100 which was seldom used. The symbol Y for 1 served also for 60, for 60 × 60 = 3,600, and in general for any power of 60; while the symbol ≺ for 10 also served for 10 multiplied by any power of 60. It seems that the number of powers of 60 in any particular case had to be deduced from the context.

The commercially minded Babylonians were the great computers of antiquity, and modern research is enabling us to appreciate the extent of their achievements. For example, they extended the positional notation to deal with fractional numbers and some later Babylonian records even contain a symbol for zero. So far, however, there is no evidence that this symbol was used in computation.

The Mayan civilization of Central America, with its highly developed observational astronomy and its preoccupation with the calendar, also used a positional notation. It was more highly developed than the Babylonian, although it was encumbered with a clumsy mixture of radices: 5, 20, and 360. The Mayas even had a symbol resembling a half closed eye for zero. (The use of 360 as a 'super-radix' is, of course, related to the fact that the Mayan year contained 360 days.)

Although the first steps towards the use of a radix notation were taken by the Babylonians in the third millenium B.C., the logical culmination of this approach was not reached for another 2,000 years. If we leave aside the Mayas on the other side of the world, the credit for this achievement, which cannot be precisely dated but which probably took place during the first or second century A.D., must be given to the Indians. The Hindu mathematicians took the two concepts, both known much earlier, of the positional representation of numbers and the decimal scale, and added their own contribution – the concept of *zero* as one of the basic digits. This recognition of the need to provide a special symbol to represent the empty column in the abacus was a crucial step. It provided the world with a flexible and convenient notation whereby any number, however large, could be represented uniquely by an ordered sequence of symbols drawn from a set of ten. It set the stage for the development of arithmetic during the next few centuries.

The golden age of Hindu mathematics lasted for some seven centuries, from about 500 to 1,200 A.D. The main Indian achievements were in the field of algebra, in marked contrast to the Greeks who excelled in geometry. It will suffice to mention only one of the Hindu mathematicians – Brahmagupta, who lived in the seventh century. He was an astronomer by profession, being head of an observatory at Ujein, but he also wrote some treatises on arithmetic. At this time, practical arithmetical procedures, even with the benefit conferred by the use of positional notation, were somewhat cumbersome, and Brahmagupta enumerated twenty main and eight subsidiary processes. 'A distinct and several knowledge of these,' he stated, 'is essential to all who wish to be calculators.'

The focus of interest now shifts to the Arabs, who by the seventh century had established a vast Muslim empire with its capital at Baghdad. The Arabs had substantial commercial dealings with India : they found the Hindu merchants using the decimal notation and soon adopted it themselves. We know, for instance, that some Indian astronomical tables in which decimal digits were employed were brought to Baghdad and translated into Arabic in the year 773. By the end of the eighth century, the Arabs had absorbed the main body of Indian mathematics; during the following century they became acquanited with the works of the Greek masters.

One of the most distinguished of the many Arab mathematicians was Alkarismi. He lived in the ninth century, and was Librarian to the Caliph who succeeded Haroun Al Raschid. Alkarismi is believed to have visited India, and on his return, about 830 A.D., he wrote his famous book *Al-gebr we'l mukabala*. It was founded on the work of Brahmagupta, and has two claims to our special interest. It gave us the word 'algebra', and it was the main source whereby the decimal notation was introduced, some three centuries later, into the West. At that time no clear distinction was made between what we now know as arithmetic and algebra. The new arithmetic – that is to say, the arithmetic based on the Hindu-Arabic notation instead of the Roman – was indeed known for several centuries as *algorism*, or the art of Alkarismi.

It was, however, not from the Arabic Near East but from Spain that a knowledge of Hindu-Arabic mathematics – and indeed of Greek mathematics as well – first reached Western Europe. The Moorish rule in Spain attained its zenith in the tenth and eleventh centuries, but Islamic culture was carefully guarded from Christians and few breaches were made before the twelfth century. One of the first Christians to penetrate the Muslim curtain was a monk, Adelard of Bath, who disguised himself as a Muslim and studied at the University of Cordova. In about the year 1120 he translated some of the works of Alkarismi and Euclid from Arabic into Latin. A translation of Alkarismi's *Algebra* under the title *Liber Algoritmi De Numero Indorum*, a copy of which is now in the University Library at Cambridge, is usually attributed to Adelard. The earliest known example of the official use of the Arabic numerals in the West also dates from about this time: a Sicilian coin bearing the date 1134.

A pioneer in spreading the new knowledge in Europe was the mathematician Leonardo Fibonacci, who was born at Pisa about 1175. His father was sent by his fellow merchants to control a custom house in Barbary, and Leonardo grew up in an Arab cultural environment and became acquainted with Alkarismi's work. He returned to Italy as a young man, and in 1202 he published his *Liber Abaci* in which he explains the Arabic system 'in order,' as he says, 'that the Latin race might no longer be deficient in that knowledge'. Leonardo was a vigorous propagandist for the use of Arabic numerals in commercial affairs. By the middle of the thirteenth century, a large proportion of Italian merchants were employing the new system alongside the old. The changeover was, of course, not achieved without some opposition. In 1299, for example, an edict was issued at Florence forbidding the bankers to use the infidel symbols.

Outside Italy the new notation gained ground more slowly and merchants in most of Europe containued to keep their accounts in Roman numerals until the middle of the sixteenth century. The Arabic system was, however, in general use for scientific purposes throughout Europe by about the year 1400. While no Arabic numerals are to be found in English parish registers or Manor Court rolls before the sixteenth century, a popular account of the new algoristic arithmetic entitled *The Craft of Nombrynge* appeared as early as about 1300 – one of the first books to be written in the English language. The advantages of the new system were so great that its universal adoption was only a matter of time. The invention of printing hastened the process. The first manual on arithmetic to come off the presses of Renaissance Italy was printed in Treviso, Venice, in 1478. Its opening sentences, quoted below, leave no doubt as to the class of reader at which the book was aimed.

Here beginneth a Practica, very helpful to all who have to do with that commercial art commonly known as the abacus.

I have often been asked by certain youths in whom I have much interest, and who look forward to mercantile pursuits, to put into writing the fundamental principles of arithmetic, commonly called the abacus. Therefore, being impelled by my affection for them, and by the value of the subject, I have to the best of my small ability undertaken to satisfy them in some slight degree, to the end that their laudable desires may bear fruit. Therefore, in the name of God I take for my subject this work in Algorism.

A little later we find the following.

Furthermore, be it known that there are five fundamental operations which must be understood in the Practica, viz. numeration, addition, subtraction, multiplication and division. Of these we shall first treat of numeration and then of the others in order.

Numeration is the representation of numbers by figures. This is done by means of ten letters or figures as here shown, .1., .2., .3., .4., .5., .6., .7., .8., .9., .0. Of these the first figure, 1, is not called a number, but the source of number. The tenth figure, 0, is called cipher or 'nulla' i.e. the figure of nothing, since by itself it has no value, although when joined with others it increases their value.

The sixteenth and seventeenth centuries saw a number of important advances in the technique of practical calculation; mathematical rigour came later. Arithmetical procedures were simplified, additional signs were introduced and the decimal notation was extended to represent fractions. The introduction of the decimal point to mark the gap between the integral and fractional part is attributed to Pelazzi of Nice, about 1492. Stevinus, who was William of Orange's Quartermaster General, was a powerful advocate of the legal use of the decimal system. He was one of the first, in 1585, to develop a decimal notation for fractions; he wrote the number 36.276, for example, as 3 6 ⓪ 2 ① 7 ② 6 ③.

Such, then, is the bare outline of the fascinating story. One of its most arresting features is the length of time that elapsed – at least 3,000 years – between the coming into use of the abacus, a concrete embodiment of the positional decimal notation, and the introduction of the same system for the representation of numbers in writing. The whole sequence of events provides a striking illustration of the importance of notation in mathematics. Even the Greeks, with their unrivalled intellectual powers, could make little progress in arithmetic because of the unsuitable number representations with which they were burdened. We now take the decimal notation so much for granted that it is worth reminding ourselves that the 'invention of zero' must rank as one of the greatest cultural achievements of all time. Laplace, writing at the end of the eighteenth century, summed up the matter thus:

It is India that gave us the ingenious method of expressing all numbers by means of ten symbols, each symbol receiving a value of position as well as an absolute value; a profound and important idea which appears so simple to us now that we ignore its true merit, but its very simplicity, the great ease which it has lent to all computations, puts our arithmetic in the front rank of useful inventions; and we shall appreciate the grandeur of this achievement when we remember that it escaped the genius of Archimedes and Apollonius, two of the greatest men produced by antiquity.

Why did the Greeks miss the crucial idea 'which appears so simple to us now'? A partial answer may be attempted in terms of the social and economic climate of classical Greece, which emphasized the gulf between theory and practice, between the intellectual and the artisan. The point, however, is a wider one, and can be applied to all the ancient civilizations of the Mediterranean and Near East. The very efficiency of the abacus as a computing tool weakened the practical need for an efficient written number representation which would facilitate arithmetical calculations. The calculations of everyday life could be carried on quite satisfactorily with the aid of the abacus. The written symbols were used merely as labels for recording the results. If the records were somewhat cumbersome, no great harm was done. The Greek philosopher with an interest in mathematics could happily devote himself to geometry, with its superior aesthetic and intellectual fascination. So the Greeks missed their opportunity and it was left to the Hindus to take the crucial step. It is interesting to note that the Hindus and the Arabs made comparatively little use of the abacus; so much more acute, therefore, was their need for an effective written number representation.

The utilitarian motive appears, indeed, to dominate the situation throughout. The main stimulus to the spread of the new notation throughout Europe came from the merchants and traders, with the 'establishment', both lay and clerical, usually fighting a rearguard action against the forces of change.

John Napier and the invention of logarithms

By the beginning of the seventeenth century the victory of the Arabic system of numeration – for both calculation and recording – was complete in most of Europe. As a result the abacus went out of use in the countries west of Russia. It was a long time, however, before even the basic processes of calculation became either commonly understood or widely practised. Consider, for instance, the case of Samuel Pepys. On 4 July 1662, when he was in charge of the Contracts Division of the Admiralty, he wrote in his diary:

Up by five o'clock, and after my journal put in order, to my office about my business. . . . By and by comes Mr Cooper, of whom I intend to learn mathematiques, and do begin with him today, he being a very able man. After an hour's being with him at arithmetique (my first attempt being to learn the multiplication table); then we parted till tomorrow.

Now the point to notice is that Pepys was one of the best educated men of his time. He was a senior Civil Servant; he had

27

been to Cambridge; in later life he became President of the Royal Society and a friend of such men as Isaac Newton and Christopher Wren. Yet the poor man had to struggle with multiplication tables at an early hour in the morning!

We may take it that Pepys could add and subtract reasonably well; it was multiplication – and still more division – of large numbers that required the skill of a professional mathematician in his day. The blockage was cleared by two inventions – one quite minor and the other of the very first importance – which effectively reduced all arithmetical calculations to addition and subtraction. Both these inventions were indeed made some years before Pepys was born and both were due to the same man – John Napier of Murchiston, near Edinburgh.

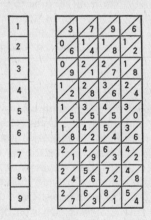

Figure 4. Principle of Napier's Bones.

His minor invention, published in 1617, was a simple mechanical device known colloquially as 'Napier's Bones'. It eases the task of constructing the multiples, from one to nine times, of a number. The equipment consists essentially of a number of rectangular strips of cardboard, bone, metal, or wood, each divided into nine small squares. One of the digits 0, 1, 2, . . . 9 is inserted in the top square of a strip and the results of multiplying this number by 2, 3, 4, . . . 9 are entered in order in the other eight squares. The layout of the strips and their method of use are best illustrated by an example. Suppose we wish to multiply 3796 by 714. The strips relating to 3, 7, 9, and 6 are placed side by side as shown in Figure 4, which also shows an index strip on the left inscribed with the nine different digits.

If we look along the fourth row, we see that the upper and lower rows of figures are 1232 and 2864 respectively. If we now add these two numbers 'diagonally' (from N.E. to S.W.) we get the pattern

$$\begin{array}{c} 1232 \\ \underline{2864} \end{array}$$

giving the sum 15,184, which is four times 3796. The result of multiplying by each digit of the multiplier is obtained similarly, and the required answer by adding the partial products, thus

$$\begin{array}{r} 3796 \\ \hline 15184 \;/\; 4 \\ 3796 \;/\; 1 \\ 26572 \;/\; 7 \\ \hline 2710344 \end{array}$$

The method had in fact been in use in the East for a long time. What Napier did was to replace the strips by 'rods' or 'bones' of square section, each face of a rod being engraved in the same way as one of the strips just described. He also arranged the rods in a box for convenience of handling and positioning.

Napier's major achievement, which really took the sting out of multiplication and division, was the invention of logarithms. He made the first public announcement of his work in a book entitled *Mirifici Logarithmorum Canonis Descriptio*, which was published in 1614 with an English translation a year later. Napier had, however, communicated a summary of his results to the great Danish astronomer, Tycho Brahe, as early as 1594. Today every schoolboy is taught to use 'log tables', and so a brief outline will suffice.[*]

With any positive number, say x, is associated another number, called the logarithm of x and usually written as *log x*. The form of the logarithm relationship (for base 10) is shown in Figure 5

---

[*] A simple and lively account of the basic idéa of logarithms is given in Chapter 6 (How to Forget the Multiplication Table) of *Mathematician's Delight*, by W. W. Sawyer (Pelican).

for values of x between 1 and 10. A simple extension enables us to obtain the logarithm of any number outside this range. Thus, for example, since $log\ 2 = 0.301$, then $log\ 20 = 1.301$ and $log\ 2000 = 3.301$. (The range 1 to 10 in x may be likened to an octave in the musical scale.)

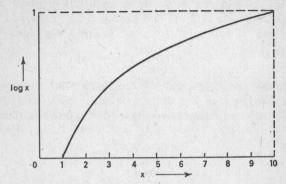

Figure 5. The logarithm of a number between 1 and 10.

The basic property of logarithms – the one which makes them so useful in computation – is expressed in the schoolroom rule: to multiply two numbers, add their logarithms; to divide, subtract. We may put the matter more precisely thus:

$$log\ x + log\ y = log\ (xy)$$
$$\text{and } log\ x - log\ y = log\ (x/y)$$

It follows, therefore, that with the aid of a table of logarithms the processes of multiplication and division are reduced to addition and subtraction. The calculation of square, cube, and higher roots is also simplified.

The slide rule

The importance of Napier's invention was immediately recognized by the practising computers of his day and within a few years the first steps were being taken to mechanize the process. Logarithms were plotted along a straight line and multiplications and divisions were performed by adding or subtracting the corresponding lengths with the aid of a pair of dividers. In 1621, William Oughtred, a mathematically minded English clergyman, used two such lines of numbers sliding by each other to do away with the need for dividers. The first true *slide rule* appeared a few years later. Pepys, not surprisingly, strongly approved of the new instruments. He bought one in 1663 – only a few months after his lessons with Mr Cooper – and found it 'very pretty for all questions of arithmetic'. Pepys' approval has certainly been endorsed by posterity; indeed the slide rule has been the badge of office of the practising engineer for the last hundred years.

The principle of the instrument is illustrated in Figure 6, which shows a strip *AP* marked with the numbers from 1 to 10 in such a way that the number *x* (shown at *B*) is positioned along the strip at a distance from the left hand end (*A*) which is proportional to the logarithm of *x*.

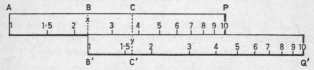

Figure 6. Principle of the slide rule.

To multiply two numbers, *x* and *y*, we need two such strips (*AP* and *B' Q'*). We set the left hand end (*B'*) of the second strip opposite the number marked '*x*' on the first strip (as at BB'). We then find the number marked '*y*' on the second strip (shown at *C'*) and read off the number on the first strip that is opposite to it. This number (shown at *C*) is the required product $x \times y$. The reason is that since $AB = log\ x$ and $B'C' = log\ y$, then $AC = AB + B'C' = log\ (xy)$, by the fundamental property of logarithms.

Now the point to notice is that numbers are represented on the slide rule by *lengths* on a certain scale (in fact, on a logarithmic scale). We set certain lengths on the instrument to represent the numbers we wish to operate with and we *measure* another length to get our answer. A correspondence, or analogy, is set up between the addition (or subtraction) of two lengths and the addition (or subtraction) of the logarithms of two numbers.

Let us consider another simple illustration of this idea of setting up an analogy between physical measurements and arithmetic operations. The well-known Ohm's law in electricity* states that – in certain conditions which need not concern us here – the difference in electric potential (in volts) between two points on a

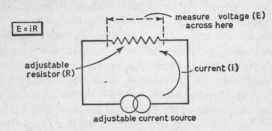

Figure 7. Use of a simple electrical circuit as an analogue of multiplication.

wire is the product of the resistance (in ohms) between the points and the current (in amperes) flowing along the wire (see Figure 7).

Thus we could obtain the product of two numbers (x and y) by arranging for a current of x amperes to flow through a resistance of y ohms, and measuring the voltage difference. In virtue of Ohm's law our simple electric circuit provides us with a physical analogue of the process of multiplication. We set certain physical quantities (in this case resistance and current) and measure another physical quantity (voltage) to give us the answer to our multiplication sum.

Consider, by contrast, the abacus. Here the basic operation is not physical measurement, but counting. The beads on the wires of the abacus are, as it were, a concrete embodiment of the separate decimal digits of a number. A user of the abacus *counts* discrete objects; he can be said to operate directly on numbers in their digital form. An engineer using a slide rule, on the other hand, *measures* continuously variable physical quantities. In this case they are lengths or angles; with another instrument they might be electric voltages, temperatures, or air pressures.

The distinction we have drawn between counting and measure-

* Discussed further in Chapter 5 (p. 89).

ing can be applied over the whole range of calculating devices and leads to the division of calculating machines – or computers, as they are usually called nowadays – into two classes: *digital* and *analog* computers. They will be considered separately in later chapters, but one general point of difference may be noted now.

Digital machines, since they operate directly on numbers in the same way as does a human being when he calculates with pencil and paper, can be used for any kind of computation which can be broken down into arithmetical steps. An analog machine, on the other hand, since it operates by setting up an analogy between a physical process and its mathematical formulation, is restricted in the kind of calculation it does. This is true even of the versatile slide rule – by no means a typical analog machine – which can do multiplication and division (to a moderate degree of accuracy) but cannot help much with addition or subtraction. The more complicated analog machines are also restricted; most of them are designed to deal with specialized calculations such as arise in science and engineering – for example, harmonic analysis or the solution of certain types of differential equations. We shall not pursue the historical development of analog computers in this chapter, but shall return to the topic in Chapter 5. The remainder of this chapter is concerned with the development, during the last 350 years, of digital calculating devices of a mechanical kind.

The mechanical era

The mechanical calculating machine originated in the seventeenth century; indeed, the two crucial inventions were both made during Pepys' lifetime. We have seen that the basic operation of all digital computers is that of counting discrete objects. In the case of the abacus these objects are beads; in mechanical calculators they are teeth on a gear wheel or notches on a bar.

One of the fundamental problems of the machine designer is that of arranging for *carry* from one digital position to the next more significant position. On the abacus this operation is performed by the fingers of the operator, but no mechanical calculating machine is considered worthy of the name unless the carry operation is done automatically by some mechanical arrangement. This can be done in several ways, one of the simplest being the method adopted for recording domestic gas consumption; the direct gearing of successive shafts with gear ratios of ten to one. Another possible scheme, using the stripped gear technique, is illustrated in Figure 8.

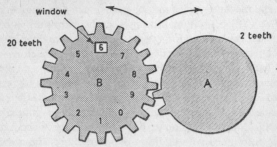

Figure 8. The stripped gear method of carrying.

Gear wheel *B*, which is inscribed with the ten digits as shown, has twenty teeth all round its edge, while gear wheel *A*, of equal size, is stripped of all but two of its teeth. Each time wheel *A* makes a complete revolution, wheel *B* turns through one tenth of a revolution; that is to say, through a distance equal to the space separating two consecutive digits inscribed on the wheel. If we think of wheel *B* as covered up, with a window cut in the cover as shown, the figure visible through the window will increase by unity for each complete revolution of wheel *A*. This arrangement can readily be extended to count beyond nine. Another stripped wheel, *C*, similar to *A*, is attached to the shaft of wheel *B*, and wheel *C* can be geared to a further wheel, *D*, exactly similar to *B*. In this way, if the unit be taken as one revolution of wheel *A*, wheel *B* reads units and wheel *D* reads tens.* The scheme can clearly be extended as far as desired.

The next stage beyond simple counting is the addition of two numbers. A mechanical adder consists of two counters, the process of adding together two numbers *x* and *y* being as follows. (We may suppose that each counter is set to zero initially.) The number *x* is registered on the first counter; the two counters are

---

*The position of wheel *A* gives a decimal fraction.

then locked and their shafts are rotated together until the second counter registers y. The first counter will then register $(x + y)$. Such an arrangement can be achieved by means of a ratchet mechanism; the first counter can move alone, but the second drags the first with it. Subtraction may be performed by adding the second number in, as it were, the reverse direction.

It is usually convenient to set both numbers on one counter, which we may call the *setting counter*, and to have the result registered on the other, which we may call the *result counter*. In this case, the addition operation can be performed, again by means of a ratchet mechanism, by arranging that the two counters are locked (that is rotate together) if the setting counter is turned in an anti-clockwise direction, but are disconnected from each other if the setting counter is rotated in a clockwise direction in order to reset it to zero. If therefore the setting counter is first set with the number x, then reset to zero, and then set with the number y, the required sum $(x + y)$ will be registered on the result counter. We see, then, that a mechanical adding machine, reduced to its simplest terms, consists of a group of setting wheels and a group of result wheels so arranged that each setting wheel is connected to its corresponding result wheel by means of a ratchet device, and that each pair of adjacent result wheels is linked by a *tens carry* mechanism of some kind, such as the stripped gear arrangement just described.

The first mechanical calculating machine on these lines is usually attributed to the philosopher and mathematician Blaise Pascal (1623–62); some of his models are preserved in Paris. He completed his first machine in 1642, having conceived the design at the age of seventeen in order, so the story has it, to assist his father, who was a tax collector. That Pascal had personal experience of the drudgery of computation is suggested by the opening words of his 'advertisement'. 'I submit to the public a small machine of my own invention, by means of which you alone may, without any effort, perform all the operations of arithmetic, and may be relieved of the work which has often times fatigued your spirit when you have worked with the counters or with the pen.'

Pascal's machine, while based on the simple principles just described, is evidence of an inventive ability of a high order; it includes those refinements in design which make all the difference between a paper conception and a working instrument. Figure 9, based on one of Pascal's own drawings, illustrates the general layout of the top of the machine. Each of the setting wheels can be rotated by means of a stylus or peg from 1/10 to 9/10 of a turn, the rotation being transmitted by gearing to the corresponding result wheel. To get his tens carry Pascal used, not a stripped-gear mechanism, but a weighted-ratchet device between each pair of result wheels. The ratchet is gradually raised as the number being registered approaches nine. As the result wheel passes from nine to nought, the ratchet is released and in falling advances the next result wheel by one unit. One of the problems that confronts a designer of calculating machines is to arrange matters so that a reasonably small load applied to a setting wheel will suffice to

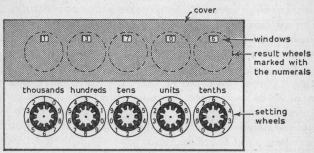

Figure 9. Schematic of Pascal's calculating machine.

propagate the 'carry' as far forward as desired. The worst case is when all the result wheels are in the ninth position, and a one is added at the units end. In Pascal's design only a slight lifting remains for each ratchet in such a case. Pascal was justifiably proud of his solution. 'It is just as easy,' he says, with pardonable exaggeration, 'to move one thousand or ten thousand dials, all at one time, if one desired, as to make a single dial move, although all accomplish the movement perfectly.'

Another interesting feature of Pascal's design is that subtraction is performed by the addition of complements,* thus enabling the

*The complement of 13706, the number shown set in Figure 9, is 86294. This idea is explained fully on page 182.

setting wheels always to be rotated in the same direction, whichever of the four arithmetic operations is being performed. 'I have
devised it,' said Pascal, 'that although the operations of arithmetic are in a way opposed the one to the other – as addition to
subtraction, and multiplication to division – nevertheless they are
all performed on this machine by a single unique movement.'

It will be appreciated that Pascal's machine was essentially an
adding (and subtracting) device; multiplication had to be treated
as repeated addition, the number to be added at each step being
set separately. The next major advance was due to Leibniz (1646–
1716), whom we have already met as the binary enthusiast. Pascal
had mechanized the process of addition; Leibniz took the logical
next step and mechanized multiplication. His first machine was
constructed about 1671; he made several others, one of which is
preserved at Hanover, where Leibniz lived during his later years.

Leibniz describes his machine, in an account written in Latin in
1685 and now preserved in the Royal Library at Hanover, thus:

There are two parts of the machine, one designed for addition (subtraction) and the other for multiplication (division) and they should fit
together. The adding (subtracting) machine coincides completely with
the calculating box of Pascal. Something, however, must be added for
the sake of multiplication. . . .

He then describes how his machine has three kinds of wheels:
'the wheels of addition, the wheels of the multiplicand and the
wheels of the multiplier.' He continues as follows:

The wheels which represent the multiplicand are all of the same size,
equal to that of the wheels of addition, and are also provided with ten
teeth which, however, are movable so that at one time there should
protrude 5, at another 6 teeth, etc., according to whether the multiplicand is to be represented five times or six times, etc. For example, the
multiplicand 365 consists of three digits 3, 6, and 5. Hence the same
number of wheels is to be used. On these wheels the multiplicand will
be set, if from the right wheel there protrude 5 teeth, from the middle
wheel 6, and from the left wheel 3. In order that this could be performed
quickly and easily a peculiar arrangement would be needed, the exposition of which would lead too far into details.

The 'peculiar arrangement', known as the Leibniz stepped
wheel, is the crucial feature of the whole design. Indeed, this

37

elegant device is still used, essentially in the form Leibniz left it, in some contemporary calculating machines.

The Leibniz stepped wheel consists of a cylindrical drum containing nine teeth of varying length, as shown in Figure 10. A

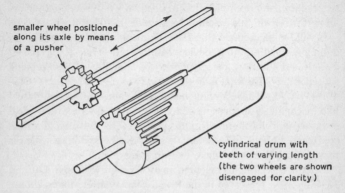

smaller wheel positioned along its axle by means of a pusher

cylindrical drum with teeth of varying length (the two wheels are shown disengaged for clarity)

Figure 10. The Leibniz stepped wheel.

smaller pinion wheel engages a varying number of teeth, depending on its position. The two wheels are mounted on parallel axles and the pinion wheel can be displaced along its axle by means of a pusher. We may assign a length of nine units to the longest tooth on the cylinder, eight units to the next longest, and so on, in decreasing sequence. Thus one revolution of the cylinder will cause the pinion wheel to engage 0, 1, 2, etc., up to 9 teeth, depending on its position as determined by the pusher. We have in effect, therefore, a gearwheel containing a variable number of teeth.

The 'wheels of the multiplicand' consist, then, of a set of Leibniz stepped wheels mounted on a common axle; the digits of the multiplicand are set by moving the pushers associated with the appropriate wheels. Each stepped wheel is connected to the corresponding 'wheel of addition'. It is clear that multiplication by an arbitrary multiplier can be achieved with this device by rotating the stepped wheels, for each digit of the multiplier, a number of times corresponding to that digit, and moving these wheels one position to the left at each digital stage. This procedure is, in fact, adopted in most of the simpler calculating machines today. Leibniz, however, went a step further in the direction of fully automatic operation. His machine contains a third set of nine wheels, 'the wheels of the multiplier'. Each wheel represents one of the decimal digits, 1 to 9, its diameter being proportional to the value of the digit. The two sets of wheels forming the multiplying part of the machine are connected by sprocket chains, the appropriate connexions being made when the multiplier number is set on the machine. The mechanism is so contrived that the result of multiplying the complete multiplicand by any digit of the multiplier can be transferred to the result register (i.e. the set of 'wheels of addition') by means of a single turn of the appropriate multiplier wheel. To multiply by more than one digit requires only a single shift-and-turn operation for each digit of the multiplier, the final answer being obtained as the sum of the various partial products, just as in a pencil-and-paper calculation.

Leibniz goes on to describe how his machine may be used for division, and concludes his account – not forgetting to direct a side thrust at Pascal – in the following terms.

Pascal's machine is an example of the most fortunate genius but while it facilitates only additions and subtractions, the difficulty of which is not very great in themselves, it commits multiplication and division to a previous calculation so that it commended itself rather by refinement to the curious than as of practical use to people engaged on business affairs.

And now we may give final praise to the machine and say that it will be desirable to all who are engaged in computations which, it is well known, are the managers of financial affairs, the administrators of others' estates, merchants, surveyors, geographers, navigators, astronomers, and those connected with any of the crafts that use mathematics.

The crucial steps were taken, then, by Pascal and Leibniz in the seventeenth century. Since then the story has been one of continuous improvement in detailed design to give greater convenience of use, increased speed and improved reliability. During the eighteenth century, many attempts were made to design a machine which could be made in quantity, but the degree of mechanical precision needed was beyond the capabilities of the production engineering techniques of that time. It was not until 1810 that the first successful commercial machine was made by

Charles Thomas of Colmar, Alsace. Some 1,500 machines to his basic design, which embodied the Leibniz stepped wheel mechanism, are believed to have been made over a period of about sixty years. Addends or multiplicands are set on the Thomas type machines by moving a set of pointers in slots in a fixed coverplate. The ten possible positions of each pointer correspond to the digits 0 to 9, and the movement of any one of the pointers causes a small pinion wheel to slide along an axle parallel to that of the associated Leibniz stepped wheel. The 'wheels of the multiplier' are dispensed with, but instead an additional register is provided to count the number of turns of a hand crank. A variant of the Leibniz wheel – a wheel with a variable number of protruding teeth – was patented by F. J. Baldwin in 1875, and a number of machines using Baldwin's device were made by W. T. Odhner a little later. A vast number of Odhner type machines have been made in many countries since then, a familiar example being the well known Brunsviga desk calculator.

Today desk calculators are familiar objects in commercial, technical, and scientific establishments, and the more recent developments need not be described here. Suffice to say that in most contemporary machines numbers are set by means of a keyboard, as in a typewriter; so-called 'automatic' multiplication and division facilities are often provided; and the adding mechanism may be actuated by electric power, instead of manually. In the most recent desk calculators, electronic devices have wholly replaced mechanisms, except for the keyboard.

3. THE PIONEERS OF AUTOMATIC COMPUTING

The various calculating devices discussed in the last chapter are *non-automatic* in the sense that they require the frequent attention of a human operator. Consider, for example, what happens when a calculation is done by pencil and paper, with the aid of a desk calculator. At each step the operator must set the necessary numbers – by pressing keys or moving levers – and must then stimulate the machine – by pressing a further key or cranking a handle – to perform the desired arithmetical operation. From time to time he will also need to read some of the numbers shown on the face of the machine and write them down on a sheet of paper. He must, in fact, exercise continuous and detailed control throughout the course of the calculation.

This method of working clearly sets a severe limit to the speed of calculation. Even with a calculator than can add or multiply two numbers in a small fraction of a second, little time is saved overall since the operator has to set the numbers each time by hand. Such a situation prompts the question: is it possible to make an *automatic* calculating machine; that is to say, a machine that can carry out extensive calculations without human intervention?

Charles Babbage and the analytical engine

The first man to put forward detailed proposals for an automatic calculating machine was Charles Babbage (1791–1871). From 1828 to 1839 he held the post of Lucasian Professor of Mathematics at Cambridge – but without delivering a single lecture in the University. He was busy enough in other directions, however. Not only did he attempt to reform the Royal Society, Greenwich Observatory, and the teaching of mathematics at Cambridge – all very proper activities for a Professor of Mathematics – but he also found time to analyse the operation and economics of the Post Office, the pin-making industry, and the printing trade; to publish one of the first reliable actuarial 'life tables'; and to make some of the earliest dynamometer measurements on the railways, running a special train on Sundays for the purpose.

In 1812 Babbage conceived the idea of constructing what he called a *Difference Engine*, a mechanical device for computing and printing tables of mathematical functions. The idea occurred to him, so the story goes, while he was sitting in his room at Cambridge, looking at a table of logarithms, which he knew to be full of mistakes. To see what this idea was, we must explain what is meant by a *difference table*. Consider by way of illustration the function $y = 2x^2 + 3x + 4$. The difference table for this function, for unit steps of x, is:

x	y	First Differences	Second Differences
			(4)
		(1)	
0	4		(4)
		5	
1	9		4
		9	
2	18		4
		13	
3	31		4
		17	
4	48		4
		21	
5	69		4
		25	
6	94		

The column labelled 'first differences' consists of the differences between successive values of the function, y; 'second differences' are formed from the first differences in the same way. In our example, the second differences are constant, so the third and all higher differences must be zero. The function is a simple example of an important class of mathematical functions, known as *polynomials*. The difference table of any polynomial, if carried sufficiently far to the right, eventually yields a column of constant differences. A fifth degree polynomial, for example, has constant fifth differences. What this means is that a table of values of any polynomial – and most functions can be represented to sufficient accuracy, at any rate over a limited range, by means of polynomials – can be constructed by simple additions only. It was this process that Babbage, with his Difference Engine, proposed to mechanize.

Such an Engine must consist of a set of registers, linked together by some mechanism whereby additions from one register to the next may be performed according to a fixed cycle. Provided the registers are set with the correct initial values, successive values of a polynomial function can be built up, step by step, by continued repetition of a short sequence of simple addition operations. In our example, only three registers are needed (we may number them 1, 2 and 3 to contain respectively y, the first difference, and the second difference). The cycle of operations for computing one function value consists of two additions: first, add the number in register 3 to the number in register 2; and secondly, add the number now in register 2 to the number in register 1. If the numbers 4, 1, and 4 are set on the registers initially, then their contents at successive stages will be the numbers shown in the table, on lines sloping upwards from left to right. Thus after four cycles, register 1 will contain the number 48 and register 2 the number 17. Register 3 will, of course, still contain the number 4.

The 'method of differences' can also be used to detect errors in mathematical tables. Here we work across the difference table the other way – from left to right. Suppose, for instance, we had written 32 instead of 31 in the fourth row, then the column of second differences would read 4, 5, 2, 5, 4 instead of a sequence of fours. The error would stick out like a sore thumb!

Babbage constructed a small machine with three registers which would tabulate quadratic functions, like the one in our illustration, to eight decimal places. This he demonstrated in 1822 to such effect that he secured the support of the Royal Society and of the Government of the day for the construction of a full size machine to compute and check tables of sixth-degree polynomials to no less than twenty places of decimals. This machine was never completed: twenty years later, after the Government had spent some

£17,000 on it, official support was withdrawn and the project was abandoned. A part of the machine is now in the London Science Museum.

Some years later, a Swedish engineer, Georg Scheutz, stimulated by some published accounts of Babbage's ideas, started to experiment on similar lines. He succeeded, with the help of his son, in building a working machine which would tabulate fourth degree polynomials to fourteen decimal places. A copy of Scheutz's differencing machine was made for the British Government and used in the Registrar-General's office to prepare a set of life tables which was published in 1864. This machine is also in the Science Museum.

Several types of mechanical Difference Engine have been built commercially during the present century. One of the best known is the National Accounting Machine, which has six twelve-decimal digit registers, a printing mechanism, and a keyboard for making the initial settings. Differencing can also be performed very conveniently by means of punched-card machinery, which will be discussed later in the chapter.

In 1832 Babbage largely lost interest in the Difference Engine, although the project was not finally abandoned until ten years later. His imagination had been fired by a much more ambitious scheme for the construction of what he called an *Analytical Engine*. This machine, like the earlier one, was, alas, never built. Nevertheless, Babbage's ideas are of the greatest interest today because the Analytical Engine was conceived as a completely automatic *universal* computer, with all the essential facilities such a machine must have. By a universal computer (the usual term today is *general purpose*) we mean one that is capable of doing any kind of calculation whatsoever. The Difference Engine, by contrast, can carry out only a fixed sequence of operations: it is a *special purpose* calculating device.

What, then, are the essential constituent parts of an automatic general purpose computer? We may list them as follows:

(i) a *store* (called a *memory* in the U.S.A.) for holding numbers – both those forming the data of the problem and those generated in the course of the calculation;

(ii) an *arithmetical unit* – a device for performing arithmetic operations on those numbers (Babbage called this part the *mill*);

(iii) a *control unit* – a device for causing the machine to perform the desired operations in the correct sequence;

(iv) *input devices* whereby numbers and operating instructions can be supplied to the machine;

(v) *output devices* for displaying the results of a calculation.

For storage Babbage proposed to used columns of wheels, each wheel being capable of resting in any one of ten positions and so of storing one decimal digit. Transfer of numbers between the store and the mill was to be accomplished by means of an elaborate mechanism of gears, rods, and linkages. The store itself was to accommodate 1,000 numbers, each number being represented to no less than fifty decimal places. It seems that Babbage intended that numbers would normally be set on the storage wheels or on the mill by hand, but he also envisaged supplying mathematical tables to the machine in punched-card form. Several alternative kinds of output were envisaged: direct printing, the production of moulds from which printers' blocks could be cast, and punched cards.

Babbage's ideas for controlling the operation of his machine are of particular interest in the light of contemporary practice. He proposed to adapt the method that was employed to control the Jacquard looms which were used for weaving fabrics of complicated design. Now in order to produce a desired pattern, it is necessary, during each throw of the shuttle which carries the weft threads, to lift certain of the warp threads, in accordance with the requirements of the pattern, so that the shuttle may pass underneath. Early in the nineteenth century, Joseph Marie Jacquard (1752–1834) invented a system of controlling the threads by means of punched cards. His arrangement may be briefly described as follows. All the threads which move together are fastened to a single rod. Sets of cards, each card being punched with a pattern of holes, are arranged in sequence on a string and pass over a drum. During each throw of the shuttle one of the cards – the next in sequence – is pressed against the whole set of rods. Those rods

45

which are opposite a hole in the card remain at rest, the other rods are lifted. The ingenuity of this invention fired Babbage's enthusiasm. 'The Jacquard loom,' he wrote, 'weaves any design which the imagination of man can conceive. The patterns designed by artists are punched by a special machine on pasteboard cards and when these cards are placed within the loom, it will weave the desired patterns.'

A portrait of Jacquard, woven on one of his own looms at Lyons a few years after his death, hung on the wall of Babbage's drawing room. No less than 24,000 punched cards were needed to produce the portrait, and the details were so fine that most people took it for an engraving. The Prince Consort, who saw it when visiting Babbage with the Duke of Wellington, was one of the few who recognized the picture for what it was.

Babbage proposed to use two sets of Jacquard cards, which he called the *operation cards* and *cards of the variables*. The former would control the action of the arithmetic unit and specify the kind of operation to be performed (addition, multiplication, etc), while the latter would control the transfer of numbers to and from the store. It is interesting to note that the operation of many modern electronic computers is controlled in just this way. The instructions for a calculation are supplied to the machine on punched cards, although it is usual nowadays to combine Babbage's two kinds of cards into a single set of *program cards*, as they are called.

Another of Babbage's innovations is still widely used today. When two numbers are added together, 'carry digits' may arise. Since, as illustrated in the example below, the addition of a carry digit may in turn cause a carry into the next higher place, it might be thought that any carry digits in a mechanical adding device would have to be added in sequentially, one place at a time, starting at the least significant end. Babbage invented an ingenious system, known as *anticipatory carry*, which enabled carry into all stages to take place simultaneously, thereby effecting a substantial saving of time in the process of mechanical addition.

His method was based on the fact that if, in any digit position, the sum of the two digits to be added together is 9, and there is a carry in from the right, then the sum digit must be changed to 0, and the carry passed on to the left. In the example shown, this occurs in four digit places, those having weights of 10, 1,000, 10,000, and 100,000. In fact, as the example below shows, there is still an element of consecutiveness in the logic of the process, but for any reasonable total number of digits, in a mechanical device, the carries can be made, for practical purposes, simultaneously. This is not true for electronic devices; see page 180.

5	312	945	
1	687	958	
6	999	893	
	1	1	carry digits
6	000	803	nines changed to noughts and
1		1	carries passed on
7	000	903	final addition of carries

The Analytical Engine, as we have said, was never completed, although Babbage continued to work on it almost until his death in 1871. The basic trouble was that Babbage's schemes were far too ambitious (consider, for instance, his idea of working with numbers to fifty decimal places!) and the techniques of precision engineering in the mid-nineteenth century were quite inadequate to meet his demands. At that time even simple desk calculators were far from reliable mechanically and could not be made in any quantity.

As time went on the frustrated inventor became increasingly embittered by a sense of failure. He quarrelled with many of his contemporaries, from his own craftsmen to the Astronomer Royal; he became even more intolerant of criticism, more caustic in his judgements, more out of sympathy with his time. 'He spoke,' said a friend after a visit to him, 'as if he hated mankind in general, Englishmen in particular, and the English Government and Organ Grinders most of all.' Lord Moulton, speaking at the Napier Tercentenary Celebrations in Edinburgh in 1914, drew a poignant picture of the brilliant but unhappy genius in his later years.

One of the sad memories of my life is a visit to the celebrated mathematician and inventor, Mr Babbage. He was far advanced in age, but

47

his mind was still as vigorous as ever. He took me through his work-rooms. In the first room I saw the parts of the original Calculating Machine, which had been shown in an incomplete state many years before and had even been put to some use. I asked him about its present form. 'I have not finished it because in working at it I came on the idea of my Analytical Machine, which would do all that it was capable of doing and much more. Indeed, the idea was so much simpler that it would have taken more work to complete the calculating machine than to design and construct the other in its entirety, so I turned my attention to the Analytical Machine.' After a few minutes' talk we went into the next workroom, where he showed and explained to me the working of the elements of the Analytical Machine. I asked if I could see it. 'I have never completed it,' he said, 'because I hit upon the idea of doing the same thing by a different and far more effective method, and this rendered it useless to proceed on the old lines.' Then we went into the third room. There lay scattered bits of mechanism but I saw no trace of any working machine. Very cautiously I approached the subject, and received the dreaded answer, 'It is not constructed yet, but I am working at it, and will take less time to construct it altogether than it would have taken to complete the Analytical Machine from the stage in which I left it.' I took leave of the old man with a heavy heart.

Poor Babbage! He suffered the unhappy fate of the misunder-stood genius who is too far ahead of his time. It has taken the world a century to catch up with him. Today, when his germinal ideas are bearing so rich a fruit, we can appreciate the magnitude of his achievements and the depth of his prophetic insight.

Lady Lovelace: the first programmer

Although Babbage wrote extensively on many topics, he left no systematic account of the Analytical Engine. Fortunately, we are well served from other sources. In 1840 Babbage gave a series of lectures in Turin. Among his audience was L. F. Menabrea, a young engineer officer on the staff of the Military Academy in that city. Menabrea wrote an account of Babbage's ideas and pub-lished it in a Geneva journal in 1842. The paper was translated into English by Lady Lovelace, who added extensive notes of her own, and was published in Taylor's *Scientific Memoirs* in 1843.

Augusta Ada, Countess of Lovelace (1815–52) was the only

child of Lord and Lady Byron. She had considerable mathematical talent – in this she followed her mother, who was described by her husband as the 'Princess of Parallelograms' – and frequently visited Babbage while he was working on his engine. She had a remarkable grasp of Babbage's ideas, which she explained far more clearly than Babbage himself ever seems to have done. Her lucid notes make fascinating reading after an interval of more than a century.

Both Menabrea's paper and Lady Lovelace's notes (which are three times as long) are mainly concerned with what we should now call the subject of programming for the Analytical Engine; that is to say, the formulation of a schedule of instructions (the program) which will enable the machine to carry out a desired calculation automatically. Lady Lovelace goes into the subject in considerable detail and illustrates her points by describing several programs for performing advanced mathematical calculations, some of them of considerable sophistication. It will therefore be convenient to defer discussion of her work until we come to the subject of programming in Chapter 6.

Hollerith punched-card machines

Our story now moves to America, where the next major advance was made about twenty years after Babbage's death. This was the invention of electromechanical punched-card calculating machines by Herman Hollerith, a statistician on the staff of the U.S. Bureau of the Census. American law required that a census be taken every ten years. In 1886 the returns of the 1880 census were still being counted and sorted and it was clear that, with the methods then existing, the job would still be unfinished in 1890, when the next census was due. Hollerith saw that the solution lay in some measure of mechanization and set about the task of devising suitable equipment. He was familiar with the punched-card system of control used on the Jacquard looms, and realized that the answer to many census questions, which are of the 'yes' or 'no' type (for example, 'Are you a householder?') could be represented by the presence or absence of a hole in a particular position on a Jacquard type card. The answers to more complex questions (for example, 'What is your age?') could be represented in coded form by the presence or absence of holes in a group of positions. He also realized that the positions of holes in a card could be detected by electrical means. The presence of a hole would allow a current to flow through; the absence of a hole would stop it.

Hollerith experimented with devices working on this principle for sorting and counting – the main census operations – and some of his machines were used for analysing the U.S. Census in 1890. (Punched-card machines were first applied in Britain to the Census of 1911). Thereafter progress was rapid; the range of 'Hollerith' machines was extended to deal with most of the operations of office arithmetic. During the last fifty years punched-card equipment has been extensively applied to the ever increasing mass of clerical work in commerce, industry, and administration – and to a lesser extent, to scientific and technical calculations.

A typical punched-card installation consists of a number of self-contained machines, each of which can perform a single type of operation, or possibly a small number of related operations. Information to be processed is first converted into patterns of holes in standardized cards – still often called Hollerith cards. (Such cards are also used for permanent storage of information.) A typical card is illustrated in Figure 11. The length of a card is divided into eighty columns; the width into twelve rows or levels, referred to as the 12, 11, 0, 1 . . . 8, 9 rows respectively. A total of $12 \times 80 = 960$ binary digits can thus be stored on a single card, a 1 in any position being represented by the presence, and a 0 by the absence, of a hole in that position. To record ordinary decimal numbers, the usual practice is to punch one decimal digit in each column; in this way one 80-digit decimal number – or alternatively ten 8-digit numbers, for example – can be punched on one card. The actual digit stored in any column is indicated by the position of the hole punched in that column. Thus the card illustrated in Figure 11 holds the number 384 in columns 26 to 28. Punchings in the 12 and 11 rows are normally used to give special instructions to the machine; sometimes for indicating the sign (positive or negative) of the numbers punched on the other ten rows. Alphabetic information may also be represented on Hollerith cards in coded form by punching more than one hole in a column. In one common

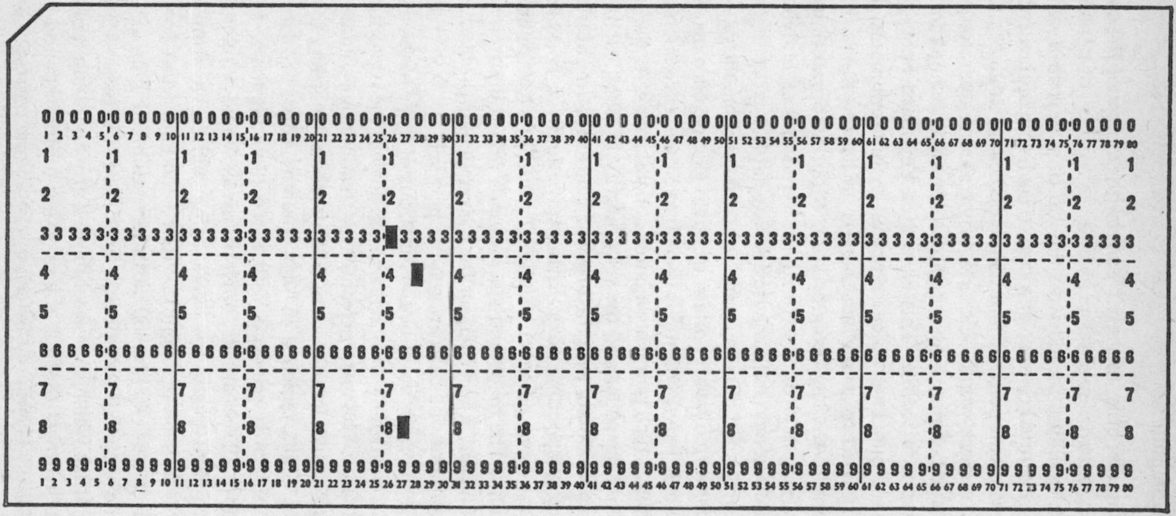

Figure 11. A punched card.

code, for example, holes in the 12 row and the 6 row of the same column represent the letter F.

Cards are usually punched with the aid of a *keyboard punch*, which has a separate key to correspond to each row of the card. A skilled operator can punch about 250 to 500 cards in an hour. In most cases the work would be checked by a second operator who may be regarded as punching the cards over again using another device known as a *verifier*. This is really a keyboard punch but with the sharp punching knives replaced by blunt plungers. The verifier is arranged to stop when there is no hole in the position corresponding to the key being pressed. More elaborate punching and verifying devices, electrically powered and embodying a number of additional facilities, are also available.

When a card is fed into any punched-card machine the pattern of holes is converted into a pattern of timed electric currents. The reading of a hole in any column is done by a brush, corresponding to that column, which is pressed against a metal roller. As the card passes between the roller and the set of eighty brushes, each row in turn comes in contact with the brushes. The exact time at which the circuit corresponding to a particular column is completed determines the row, and hence the digital value, of a hole punched in that column. The machine then responds according to its design and to the way it has been set for the particular problem. All the eighty columns of a card are read in parallel.

We shall now briefly describe the functions of three of the more widely-used punched-card machines: the sorter, the reproducer, and the tabulator. The *sorter* selects cards, reading one column on each run, and places them in numbered pockets according to the values of the digits punched in that column. Thus, to place in order a set of cards punched with three digit numbers, three separate runs of all the cards through the sorter would be required, one for each digit place, the cards being withdrawn from the pockets and the pack reassembled after each run. Most sorters work at speeds from 400 to 800 cards per minute. Figure 12 is a diagrammatic sketch of the sorter. Cards are fed between a brass roller and a brush which can be set to read any one column of the cards. They then pass through the selecting mechanism and into the card pockets. There are thirteen of these; one corresponding to each of the twelve rows of a card and a reject pocket corresponding to an unpunched column. The sorting mechanism consists of a set of spring-steel tongues resting on a plate which is the armature of an electro-magnet underneath. The magnet is energized, and the armature pulled down, as soon as the circuit is completed through a hole in the card. The timing of this event, which depends on the row in which the hole is punched, serves to guide the card into the desired pocket. Some sorters are also provided with a set of counters which display the number of cards in each pocket, and the total number of cards sorted.

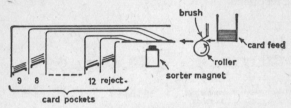

Figure 12. Sorter.

The *reproducer* consists of two independent parts, the reading and the punching units. Each unit has one card feed and one output pocket, and contains sets of brushes and punching knives as shown in Figure 13. The various component parts of the reproducer are connected to the back of a plugboard; plug and socket connexions may be made on the front. The reproducer has four distinct uses, known as reproducing, comparing, gang punching, and summary punching.

Reproducing is the operation of copying the holes on one set of cards on to a second, blank set, either in the same or different columns. The cards to be copied are fed to the reading unit and the blank cards to the punching unit. The comparing brushes on the former are used to check that the cards are correctly punched.

Comparing is the operation of testing whether the punchings in two sets of cards agree. Here again, both the reading and punching units of the machine are used, but the latter is set so that the punching knives are inoperative.

Gang punching is the operation of transferring common patterns

53

from master cards to groups of what are called 'detail cards'. The master cards are identified by an '11' punching in one column. Gang punching only involves the punching unit. The punch brushes are connected through the plugboard to the punching knives, so that any card under the brushes transfers its pattern of holes to the following card, which is passing under the knives. This latter card, now punched, then passes under the punch brushes and transfers its newly-punched pattern to the card immediately following. The process continues until a punching in the 11 row of a following master card is read by one of the 11-brushes. The cycle is then repeated.

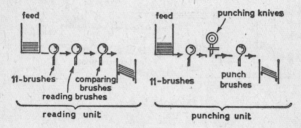

Figure 13. Reproducer.

Summary punching is the operation of punching on to blank cards information stored in the registers of another punched-card machine, the tabulator, which we shall consider next. The two machines must be connected together by a multi-wire cable so that electrical signals can pass from the tabulator to the reproducer. Once, again, only the punching unit of the reproducer is used.

The *tabulator* can perform the operations of card reading, adding, subtracting, and printing. A typical tabulator, illustrated in Figure 14, consists of six eleven-digit registers (called counters), three plug boards, and a print unit. The registers are in fact accumulators, since numbers can be added or subtracted from one register into another. Connexions between the component parts, and for addition or subtraction between registers, are again made on plugboards. A double set of reading brushes, which enables the punching in selected columns of one card to be compared with those in the following card, is used for dealing with such matters as the printing of sub-totals (for instance, after every hundred cards) and the layout of the printed copy (for instance, a double space after every tenth line). The print unit, unlike a typewriter, is a parallel operating device. Up to eighty characters (usually either decimal digits, signs or letters of the alphabet) can be printed across the sheet of paper in one stroke, at a maximum rate of about two lines a second. Information may be printed from any of the registers or direct from cards.

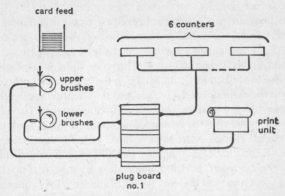

Figure 14. Tabulator.

Two other punched-card machines in common use are the *multiplying punch*, which can form and punch the sixteen-digit product of two eight-digit numbers, all three numbers being punched on the same card; and the *collator*, which is essentially an electromechanical filing clerk. Its function is to arrange cards in one or more sequences by actions controlled by comparisons between different cards. It is used for selecting, matching, and merging cards, and to some extent may be regarded as an extension of the sorter. The operating speed of punched-card machines depends on the complexity of the operations being performed; in most cases cards would be read or punched at rates of between 100 and 400 cards a minute.

These machines, although still in common use today, were developed in the period between the two world wars. In recent years the manufacturers of punched-card machinery have not only extended the scope of their electromechanical equipment but have entered the electronic computer field on a large scale.

The punched-card installation, with its multiplicity of separate single purpose machines each set up manually by means of plug-and-socket connexions, operates to best advantage when a large quantity of numerical material has to be treated in the same way; when the emphasis is on *data processing* rather than on computing, to use the current terminology. This is the normal situation in the business office; it is the exception in the scientific laboratory. Even so, punched-card machinery has proved extremely useful for some kinds of scientific calculation. Now, however, the electronic computer has almost entirely superseded the punched-card machine for scientific and technical work. The same thing is happening, but more slowly and less completely, in the commercial office.

One of the earliest – and most successful – scientific applications of punched-card machines was in the astronomical field. This is not surprising in view of the labour of computing – and checking – astronomical tables. Astronomers have had, for centuries, the best of reasons for exploiting any mechanical aids which might lighten their burden, and it is interesting to note that in 1832 Babbage was awarded the gold medal of the Royal Astronomical Society for his invention of the Difference Engine. The President of the Society, in making the award, said: 'In no department of science or of the arts does this discovery promise to be so eminently useful as in Astronomy and its kindred sciences . . . The practical astronomer is interrupted in his pursuit and is diverted from his task of observation by the irksome labour of computation.' He went on to express the hope that the aid 'which mechanism has made possible through Mr Babbage's invention' would be exploited 'to the utmost extent'. His hopes, as we shall see, remained unrealized for more than a century.

In 1926, Dr L. J. Comrie, of the British Nautical Almanac Office, found that the Burroughs accounting machine, which was designed solely for commercial work, could be used as a 'difference engine' to perform the tasks of subtabulating, printing, and checking astronomical tables. Two years later he took the next step towards full mechanization when he adapted the Hollerith punched-card system to the work of the Office. The first big job to be handled in this way was the calculation of the future position of the moon; one of the most exacting problems of classical astronomy. The moon's position was computed at twelve-hourly intervals (noon and midnight) from the year 1935 to the year 2,000. The basic information was taken from E. W. Brown's *Tables of the Moon*; 20 million holes were punched in half a million Hollerith cards and some 100 million figures were operated on during the course of the work. The computed results were printed in about seven months. Following this initial success, Comrie rapidly expanded the use of punched-card machines. Indeed, they were used for most of the computational work of the Office until a short time ago, when electronic computers began to take over the job.

The first automatic computer (A.S.C.C.)

The fully automatic 'universal' calculating machine was conceived, as we have seen, in Cambridge, England, in 1832; it was born in Cambridge, Massachusetts, one hundred and twelve years later.

In 1937, Howard H. Aiken of Harvard had the idea of using the techniques and components developed for punched-card machines to produce a fully automatic calculating machine. To this end he approached the International Business Machines Corporation, one of the largest manufacturers of punched-card machinery. The result of their collaboration was the Automatic Sequence Controlled Calculator (A.S.C.C. for short) which was completed in 1944 and presented to Harvard University in August of that year. Babbage's dream had at last come true!

In the A.S.C.C., as in the Analytical Engine, numbers were stored in registers consisting of sets of wheels. Each wheel – termed a counter wheel – could take up ten positions and so could store one decimal digit. A group of twenty-four such wheels (corresponding to twenty-three decimal digits plus a sign digit) made up a storage register, there being seventy-two such registers in all. An interesting feature of the A.S.C.C. is that each storage register was fitted with a full adding mechanism so that a number in one register could be directly added to (or subtracted from) the number in another register. Each register was in fact an *accumulator* and performed a dual function – as a store for numbers and as an arithmetic unit, so far as additive or subtractive operations were concerned. Multiplication and division were dealt with in a separate unit. Additional storage for sixty constants – that is to say, numbers whose values are known before the start of a calculation – was provided by sets of switches which could be set by hand.

With each group of counter wheels was associated a continuously rotating shaft. Any counter wheel could be connected to this shaft for any desired fraction of a revolution by means of an electromagnetic clutch controlled by a relay such as is used in automatic telephone exchanges. A brush wiping over ten contacts was fitted to each counter wheel to give an electrical indication of its position. The addition of one number to another was effected by making the appropriate connexions between the brushes of one accumulator, A, and the clutch mechanism of another, B. The counter wheels of accumulator B were thus caused to rotate by amounts which depended on the number stored in accumulator A.

Operating instructions were supplied to A.S.C.C. as patterns of holes, not on cards as Babbage proposed, but on lengths of paper tape. The holes were read electromechanically, one row at a time, there being twenty-four positions across the tape in which holes might be punched. An A.S.C.C. instruction consisted of twenty-four binary digits. Some of these specified the type of operation to be carried out (for example, addition); the others served to tell the machine where to find the numbers to be operated on and where to put the result. Thus the functions of Babbage's two kinds of cards (the operation cards and the cards of the variables) were combined in A.S.C.C. in a single instruction. In this matter – as, indeed, in many others – Aiken established the pattern for the future.

The input and output arrangements were quite elaborate. Numbers – apart from constants set on switches – were supplied to the machine on punched cards, and answers could be given out either in punched-card or typewritten form. In all, two card readers, one card punch, and two typewriters were provided. Special mechanisms were also provided for evaluating some of the commoner functions, such as sines, cosines, and logarithms, while tables of other functions could be supplied to the machine on special tapes known as function tapes.

The A.S.C.C. was built on a lavish scale and – very wisely at that time – no attempt was made to economize on space or cost. The complete machine contained more than three quarters of a million parts and used more than five hundred miles of wire. Addition or subtraction of two numbers took three tenths of a second, multiplication about four seconds and division about ten seconds. Although an extremely slow machine by electronic standards, it has a special claim to fame as the first fully automatic computer to be completed. It remained in continuous use, night and day, at Harvard for about fifteen years.

The first electronic computer (ENIAC)

The next major advance – the application of electronic techniques to computer design – followed very quickly. The first electronic digital computer – the famous ENIAC (Electronic Numerical Integrator and Calculator) was completed in 1946, only two years after the A.S.C.C. Indeed, it started to do useful work in the summer of 1945. Its designers were J. P. Eckert and J. W. Mauchly, of the Moore School of Electrical Engineering of the University of Pennsylvania. Although ENIAC was a completely 'universal' machine, it was primarily designed to meet a specialized military need: the calculation of trajectories of bombs and shells.

In saying that ENIAC is an electronic computer we mean that the storage and manipulation of numbers inside the machine, and also the control of the sequence of operations, were done by means of electronic circuits. Indeed, apart from the input and output mechanisms, the machine had no moving parts. The use of electronic techniques enabled the operating speed to be increased enormously, although the innovation had some disadvantages. The electronic circuits of ENIAC contained 18,000 valves, most of them being double triodes. To maintain so many circuits in working order at the same time was in those days a considerable feat. If this could be achieved for a single hour, however, it was possible to do what would be more than a week's work for A.S.C.C., or for the other non-electronic automatic computers that were being built in the U.S.A. at the time. With the success of ENIAC the victory of the thermionic valve over the relay and the counter wheel became almost complete. Nearly all the automatic computers built since 1950 have been electronic, although the valve was ousted in its turn by the more reliable and compact transistor, which is now giving way to integrated circuits.

It is interesting to compare ENIAC with its contemporary, the A.S.C.C. Although the two machines made use of radically different techniques, much the same range of facilities was provided on both. For instance, in both machines numbers were stored in decimal form, either on hand-set switches or in accumulator registers; input and output of numbers was by means of punched cards, and special facilities were provided for supplying the computer with tables of mathematical functions. (In ENIAC the values were set on switches; in A.S.C.C. they were punched on tape.)

In ENIAC, furthermore, a decimal digit was represented in a manner that can be thought of as the electronic equivalent of a counter wheel. The circuit is called a *ring counter* and has ten different stable states, in each of which only one out of ten similar valves conducts current. When a pulse is received by the circuit, the valve which is 'on' is put 'off' and the next valve in order is put 'on'. In this sequence, when valve 9 is put off and valve 0 is put on, a signal is given to indicate that a carry is required, in the same way as when a counter wheel turns from position 9 to position 0. An ENIAC accumulator – of which there were twenty in all – consisted of ten such ring counters, one for each of the ten digits of the number being stored, together with one additional device to store the sign of the number. Again, as in A.S.C.C., each accumulator included complete carry arrangements, so that a number stored in one accumulator could be added directly to that stored in another.

A number in transit from one part of ENIAC to another was represented by trains of electric pulses along a group of eleven wires, a separate wire being allocated to each decimal digit of the number and another to the sign indication. When an accumulator was stimulated to emit in pulse form the number stored in it, each separate ring counter emitted a number of pulses equal to the decimal digit stored therein. An electrical pulse generator supplied a continuous stream of timing pulses to all parts of the machine at the rate of 100,000 pulses per second, that is, a pulse every ten microseconds. From these pulses, various electronic circuits provided a set of standard waveforms. These were used both to control the sequence of operations and to build up trains of pulses representing the different decimal digits. These standard waveforms were repeated at intervals of one five-thousandth of a second (200 microseconds). This was the period needed for the addition or subtraction of two numbers, known as the *addition time*. Every operation took a whole number of addition times; multiplication about fourteen and division about thirty.

A problem had to be set on ENIAC by hand; this usually entailed making a great many plug-and-socket connexions and setting a great many switches. (It should be remembered that it was originally designed as a special-purpose computer.) There were two quite separate sets of connexions; one to route *digit pulses* (that is, pulses representing numbers) and the other to route *control pulses* from one part of the machine to another. The purpose of the latter was to stimulate the various units of the machine to operate in the desired sequence. Thus, while the actual setting-up process was a most tedious and lengthy business, once it had been done the whole program for the calculation was, so to speak, stored in the machine. This meant that the sequence of operations could be obeyed much more rapidly than was possible, for instance, on A.S.C.C., where instructions were punched on tape, which had to be stepped on, one row at a time, as each operation was performed.

ENIAC, like A.S.C.C., was built on a grand scale; it consumed about 150 kilowatts of electric power, all of which was eventually turned into heat, since the computer did no mechanical work. Its main limitations were the small storage capacity (twenty numbers) and the difficulty of changing from one problem to another. Even so, this famous pioneer machine constituted a most impressive feat of electronic engineering. Its fine record of performance over many years – notwithstanding its size and complexity – is a striking tribute to the skill and tenacity of purpose of its designers.

In the summer of 1946 two events – both, as we now see, of cardinal importance – took place at the Moore School of Electrical Engineering in Philadelphia. The first was the completion of ENIAC; the second, the delivery of a course of lectures on 'The Theory and Techniques of Electronic Digital Computers'. Looking back on the situation in the light of our knowledge of subsequent events, we can see that the design principles expounded in these lectures fixed the functional pattern of the electronic computer as we know it today.

The new ideas had been worked out by a group of mathematicians and engineers led by John von Neumann. They first analysed the computer-design problem in logical terms and then put forward specific proposals for a new type of machine which would be at once considerably smaller and much more powerful than ENIAC. The construction of such a computer was put in hand in the same year, but its completion took longer than had been expected and several other machines designed on the new principles were, in the event, finished first.

The year 1946 may thus be taken as marking the end of the pioneer stage of automatic computer development. We shall therefore conclude our historical survey at this point and not continue chronologically, but by dealing with one subject at a time.

4. THE DIFFERENT KINDS
OF COMPUTERS

In previous chapters we have been concerned only with calculations where close timing is not important – that can be carried through on a piece-work basis at a speed convenient to the human operator. Not all computations are done like this; indeed, in some computers* the actual passage of time is utilized to represent a variable in the problem which is being solved. Answers are produced in a continuous flow process, and the passage of time during the computation usually represents the passage of time in the real situation to which the problem relates. (This may not be at the rate of one second's computation for each second in the real situation – *real time operation*; faster and slower rates both have advantages for different purposes.)

This technique is useful in many contexts; for example, during the design of equipment intended to work continuously in changing circumstances, such as an aeroplane automatic pilot, or an atomic power station subjected to changing demands for power. Predictions can be made of how the equipment would work if it were to be constructed in each one of a number of different possible ways. Moreover, it may be necessary to incorporate computing units in the equipment itself when it is constructed (in which case they must obviously work in real time). This is frequently done nowadays, for example, to improve the control of chemical processes.

A computation involving time

As an illustration, we consider how to compute the up-and-down movement of a car going along a rough road. As the car moves along, the irregularities in the road surface force the wheels

---

* In this, and following, chapters the term *computer* implies automatic operation in the sense explained at the beginning of Chapter 3.

to move up and down. The road springs and shock-absorbers transmit some of this movement to the chassis and body of the car; we want to know how the body will move in response to a given road surface at different speeds. Figure 15 illustrates the essential features of the system. We can analyse the diagram to obtain a mathematical representation of the elements of the problem, which in turn will lead on to a description of a computer to give the required solution.

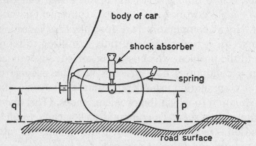

Figure 15. Diagram of car suspension.

A designer of vehicle suspensions does in fact use a computer in this way, but to obtain a suitable explanation we must simplify the problem to basic essentials. We imagine that the car body is balanced on only one wheel. The distance p in Figure 15 is the height of the centre of the wheel above the average level of the road surface. The centre of the wheel will trace out approximately the road profile as the car moves, on the further simplifying assumption that the tyre is hard and rigid and that the irregularities in the road have less curvature than the outside of the tyre. A graph of p against distance travelled will therefore be a copy of the road profile. The distance q is the height of a point on the car body above the average level of the road surface. This point is chosen to be on a level with the wheel centre when the car and wheel have ceased moving up and down, so that $p = q$ when this has happened. The spring, in this case, will have flexed just enough to support the weight of the car, and this steady load can be ignored. When relative movement of the wheel and body takes place, the change in upward force exerted by the spring on the body is taken to be proportional to $(p - q)$; in other words, the spring is assumed to obey Hooke's law.*

To simplify the behaviour of the shock-absorber, we assume that it exhibits purely viscous friction. In this case, the upward force it exerts on the car body is proportional to the rate at which it is being compressed, no force being exerted when the compressive motion ceases. If u is the rate of change of p, i.e. the speed up and down of the wheel centre, and v is the rate of change of q i.e. the speed up and down of the body, then the shock absorber upward force is proportional to $(u - v)$.

The remaining mathematical element of the problem is the response of the car body to the total force. The body moves so that upward acceleration, f (which is the rate of change of v), is proportional to the total upward force, by Newton's second law of motion.

A diagram (Figure 16) can now be drawn describing the necessary computations. These may conveniently be thought of as taking place at the same speed as the phenomena to which they relate.

The arrows in the diagram indicate the sequence of cause and effect, and show something which is typical of this technique: paths which loop back to their starting point. For example, a value of q must first be assumed in order to compute $(p - q)$. This quantity determines the present spring force, which contributes to total force, which in turn yields acceleration, all in a negligibly short space of time. On the other hand, the present value of the acceleration (f) does not determine the speed (v) itself but only its rate of change. The present value of the speed has in fact been determined by all the previous values of f. Similarly, the present value of q has been determined by all the previous values of v. Thus, once this loop of operations has been working long enough, we can see that it will continue to work correctly. The method of starting the process uses the obvious solution to a special case of the original problem, namely, that when p is constant (that is, when the road is flat) q becomes constant and equal to p, while f and v become zero. These mutually consistent values are used

*This law is explained more fully in Chapter 8 of Sawyer (op. cit.).

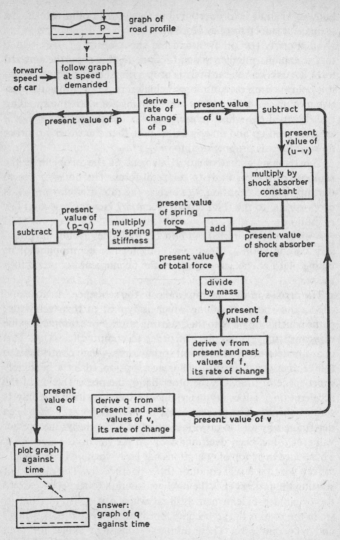

Figure 16. Calculation of movement of car body in response to a rough road.

before p is allowed to start varying; that is to say, the calculation is made to start from equilibrium values which correspond to the equilibrium condition of the mechanical system.

The operations represented in Figure 16 are, of course, intended to be performed by computing equipment. Each block in the diagram implies the need for a particular computing unit with interconnexions from its output to the inputs of the other computing units as shown by the arrowed lines. It can be seen that two *subtractors* are required, one to form $(p - q)$ and the other to form $(u - v)$; one *adder* to give the total force; two units to multiply by constants, one to give the spring force and the other the shock-absorber force; one unit to divide by a constant, the car mass* (M); an input device for road profile, and an output device for the vertical motion of the car. The process of deriving a quantity, (for example q or v) from present and past values of its rate of change is well known mathematically as 'integration with respect to time', and the two units which do this are called *integrators*. The converse process of deriving the rate of change of a quantity (for example u) is known as 'differentiation with respect to time', and the unit which does this is a *differentiator*.†

There are several different principles which can serve as a basis for the operation of these various computing units. They may be mechanical, electronic, or even pneumatic, and either analog or digital representation of the various quantities may be used. More information on computing units, and on complete computers made up from such units, is given in later chapters. The rest of this chapter sums up the difference between the computers of Chapter 3 and a computer organized like Figure 16; it ends with some general comparisons between computers of different types.

Simultaneous and sequential computers

The computing units in Figure 16 are of about half a dozen

---

*In fact, a unit to multiply by a constant would be used, the constant being $1/M$.

†Integration is discussed further in the next chapter (p. 82). We would also refer the non-mathematical reader to Sawyer (op. cit.). (Differentiation is simply explained in Chapter 10; integration in Chapter 12.)

different standard types. We may think of a computing laboratory as containing a stock of units of each type from which sufficient numbers are drawn to meet the requirements of the particular problem to be solved. In practice it often happens that all the stock is permanently incorporated in the computer equipment. The units which are not needed are not connected up and stand idle during the computation. The distinguishing feature of the particular problem being solved is embodied in the interconnexions between the computing units, known as the *set-up* for the problem. Figure 16 is an example of a *set-up diagram*. The interconnexions are made with shafts, wires, or even pipes, depending on how the computing units operate.

A computer of this kind is called a *simultaneous computer*, since the various computing units do all the portions of the computation at the same time. It is characteristic of a simultaneous computer that several specimens of a particular type of computing unit are needed; in fact as many as the number of times that the problem calls for the particular computing operation. A further characteristic is that a given interconnecting path in the set-up carries signals representing successive values of the same quantity (e.g. values of shock absorber force), and at different times during the computation never carries values of different quantities.

The contrasting type of computer, which is more familiar, is called a *sequential computer*. Here the same equipment does different portions of the computation one after the other, one adding unit being provided, for example, to do all the additions needed in the solution of the problem. A further characteristic is that the interconnecting paths in the computer carry, at different times, signals representing different quantities. This method of working means that equipment must be provided in the sequential computer to *store* intermediate results until they are needed again; this is not necessary in the simultaneous computer.

Babbage's Analytical Engine, A.S.C.C., and ENIAC are examples of sequential computers. A wages clerk, using pen, paper, and a simple desk calculator, provides an analogy of the way they work. The pen, paper, calculator, and the clerk herself are to be regarded as part of a composite computing system. She uses the calculator to multiply hours worked by hourly rate of pay, to calculate bonus, to add it in, and to subtract income tax and other deductions. She writes down intermediate results – that is, she stores them temporarily – and the interconnecting paths of the system are mainly provided by the clerk herself. She reads the dials of the machine and the figures on the paper, presses keys on the machine and writes on the paper. We can identify here items corresponding to three of the five components listed on page 44 as being essential in a general purpose sequential computer. The sheets of paper correspond to the store, the calculator to the arithmetic unit, and the young lady's brain to the control unit. The other two components – the input and output organs – have no counterparts here. This is because their function in the computer is to interpret between human beings and the computer; a necessary thing for an automatic device, but not for a system incorporating a human being. Such non-automatic systems are almost always sequential in nature, and the main use of the terms 'simultaneous' and 'sequential' is to classify automatic computers.

If it is possible to solve a problem either on a simultaneous computer or on a sequential one, the solution is, naturally, obtained more quickly, in general, by a simultaneous computer. Since speed of operation is a major preoccupation of computer designers, it is strange, at first sight, that they are concentrating more and more on sequential computers. There are two reasons for this. First, the sequential computer is cheaper for extensive computations, since its size does not increase with the size of the job, as does that of a simultaneous computer. Secondly, the sequential computer is more adaptable to a wide variety of problems, as will be explained in Chapters 6 and 9. Although a particular simultaneous computer may be capable of performing many diverse computations – relating, for example, to the internal conditions of an atomic pile, to the performance of an aircraft auto-pilot, or to the road-holding of a motor car – simultaneous computers as a class are certainly less versatile than sequential ones. For this reason, the words *general purpose computer* are usually taken, rather unfairly, to mean a sequential computer.

Analog and digital computers

Another pressing requirement nowadays is for very high accuracy of computation. Accuracy, as such, is not relevant to the choice between the simultaneous and sequential modes of operation, but it dominates the choice between digital and analog computers. The essential difference between these two classes lies in the way in which numerical variables are represented inside the computer. This has already been briefly explained in Chapter 2, but it is worth while pursuing a little further. In an analog computer we have a continuously varying physical quantity corresponding to the continuous variation of the variable which is represented. In a digital computer, on the other hand, the representation of a variable quantity does not change continuously. When the variable changes by more than a certain minimum amount, its representation jumps discontinuously to a new value. A smaller change than this minimum produces no effect on the representation. Figure 17 shows the two stages in the conversion of a continuously changing variable to its digital representation.

First, the continuous variable is replaced by a *quantized variable* (Figure 17(a)); that is to say, the value of the continuous variable is replaced by the nearest value selected from the finite number of different values that the quantized variable can take (the 'chalk-mark' representation of Chapter 2). Second, the value of the quantized variable is replaced by the serial number of this value, counting from 0, and using the particular digital representation of the serial number that is required (usually a fixed-radix notation). Figures 17(b) and (c) show, for the particular case of a representation using two decimal digits, how these digits change as the continuous variable changes. The *quantum* of the representation is the smallest possible change in the quantized variable, and is shown in Figure 17(a).

If more than two decimal digits are provided, the number of distinguishably different values of the quantized variable increases, and if the total range of the variable is kept the same, the size of the quantum decreases. Since the maximum error in the quantized variable is half a quantum, the accuracy of the digital representation increases correspondingly. The important point is that higher accuracy is not needed in the apparatus used to represent the extra digits; this apparatus is of exactly the same nature as that used for the first two digits. Furthermore, once the digital representation is obtained, the operations of arithmetic can readily be performed without appreciably increasing the error.

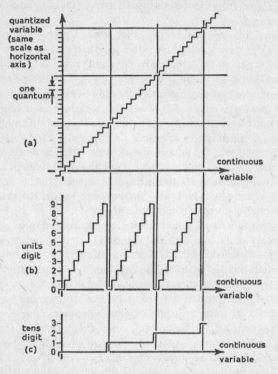

Figure 17. (*a*) Graph of the quantized version of a variable against the variable. (*b*) and (*c*) Units and tens digits in the decimal digital representation of the variable.

That is to say, by providing enough extra digits, the additional errors due to digital computing operations can be kept as small as desired. In analog computation, by contrast, errors can be reduced only by using more refined computing apparatus. There is a practical limit to the attainable accuracy; with present-day apparatus this limit corresponds to errors of about 1 part in 10,000. Moreover, less accurate equipment with errors of 1 part in 1,000 (say) is much cheaper and has other advantages as well. In fact analog computers suffer from the operation of a severe law of diminishing returns in the increased accuracy that can be obtained for extra cost.

In digital computers, on the other hand, an error of 1 part in 1,000,000 can be obtained for rather less than twice the cost of an error of 1 part in 1,000 merely by providing twice as many digital places. This is an example of a rare law of increasing returns – one thousand times the accuracy for only twice the cost.

We thus have a pair of two-way classifications; simultaneous/ sequential and digital/analog. This gives four classes of computers in theory, but only two in practice. On the one hand sequential analog computers are almost non-existent. The reason for this is that a sequential computer needs a store, and the error in an analog store usually increases with the time of storage, whereas no error occurs in a digital store. The consequence is that for practical purposes all sequential computers are digital.

On the other hand, simultaneous computers need quite a lot of computing units, and a digital computing unit has always been much more expensive than its analog counterpart. Although the cost difference has lessened, the demands for higher speed combined with higher accuracy that might have been met by simultaneous digital computers have in fact been met in other ways; in some cases by faster sequential digital computers, and in others by combinations of digital and analog computers – termed *hybrid* computers, and discussed briefly in Chapter 12. The next chapter describes the simultaneous analog computer, and Chapters 6 to 11 concentrate on the nowadays ubiquitous sequential digital computer.

5. ANALOG COMPUTERS

The distinguishing feature of analog computing is the use of a physical quantity, called the *representation* or *analog*, to represent a variable in the problem being solved. This physical quantity – for example, the angular position of a part of a mechanism, or the electrical voltage between two points in a circuit – is made directly proportional to the value of the variable that is to be represented. In the case of the slide rule (p. 31), to take another example, the distance moved by the slide or the cursor is proportional to a variable that is equal to the logarithm of some number.

When a scientist or engineer wishes to study a natural phenomenon, or a device that he has designed, he usually prefers to do so directly, by making measurements and recordings of the real thing. It this is too difficult or too expensive, he seeks a less direct method of obtaining the information that he needs, but he keeps his method as close as possible to the direct one. This is why he is often led to a simultaneous analog computer, with which he can make a conceptual model (or analog) of his phenomenon or device in such a way that the model mirrors the real thing quite directly. He can then say to himself, for example: 'Although I know that this voltmeter reading is really just a reading of the output voltage of an integrator, I will pretend it is a reading of the vertical position of the body of a car moving along a rough road.' This sort of pretence is easy and rewarding because of the direct proportionality between a variable and its analog representation, and because one can have enough analog computing units to depict nearly all the features of the real thing.

In explaining analog computers, we are therefore bound up much more closely with the facts of physics and engineering than we need be when, in later chapters, we come to explain digital computers. We encounter the standard method of describing and explaining such facts, namely mathematics – in our case, algebra and calculus. To those of our readers who anticipate this with pleasure, we apologize immediately for the fact that we propose to dilute the equations with explanations in words of how they arise and what they mean. To those who take the opposite view, we can only say that equations, for their devotees, sum up the alternative verbal explanation in the simplest possible way, without missing anything out; that is why we include some equations here.

Apart from the rather special case of the slide rule, the most useful analog in practice is either electrical voltage or mechanical angular position. That is to say, we represent a variable, x, by generating a voltage ax, or by turning a shaft through an angle bx. Here a or b is the *scale* of the representation; that is, the number of volts or degrees, which represents one unit of magnitude of x.

In fact angular position, and indeed all mechanical representations, are now out of favour. This is because wholly electrical computing units can work much faster. Nowadays angular position usually occurs in some incidental way, for example as the original representation of a variable that is to be an input to a computer. Mechanical analog computers, although obsolete, nevertheless have many interesting features, and some of the principles involved in using them are still important. Furthermore, many people find them easier to understand than purely electronic devices. Before turning to electrical analog computers we shall therefore describe a mechanical computer, dealing first, for both types, with some of the more important component units, and explaining how they would be used in the car suspension computation of the previous chapter.

Mechanical computing units

One of the simplest computing operations is the multiplication of a variable by a constant. This is required three times in the car suspension set-up of Figure 16. In a mechanical computer, where variables are represented by shaft angles, a pair of gears does this operation. The multiplying constant is simply the ratio of the number of teeth on one gear to the number on the other. When none of the gears available in stock gives the desired ratio, it is possible to use a mechanical integrator instead. This is explained a few paragraphs further on.

The operation of adding two variables together (for example, spring force and shock absorber force in Figure 16) can be done by a mechanism known as a differential gear. This works on the same principle as a motor-car differential (usually part of the back axle). The input rotations (*u* and *v* in Figure 18) are, however,

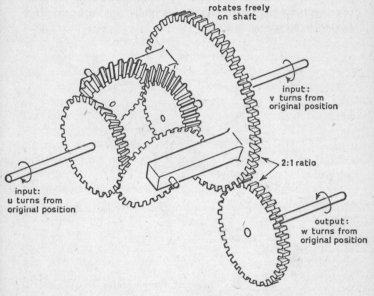

Figure 18. A differential gear.

applied to the shafts that would turn the driving wheels of the car and the output rotation (*w*) is taken from the shaft corresponding to the drive shaft from the engine. The *u* and *v* shafts can turn quite independently.

Two special cases are helpful in understanding the mechanism. First, suppose that the *u* and *v* shafts are turned to the same extent in opposite directions; then the large gear in the figure, and hence also the output shaft, will remain stationary. That is to say,

75

$w = 0$ when $v = -u$. Secondly, suppose the u and v shafts are turned to the same extent in the same direction; then the large gear and the bevel gears will rotate together as a unit, and the output shaft will turn twice as much. That is to say, $w = 2u$ when $v = u$. The general relationship is, in fact, $w = u + v$.

A differential gear can also perform subtraction if, say, the u and w shafts are used as input shafts, and the v shaft as output shaft; this is because it is possible to change the direction of flow of power through the device. Two differential gears are needed for the two subtractions in Figure 16.

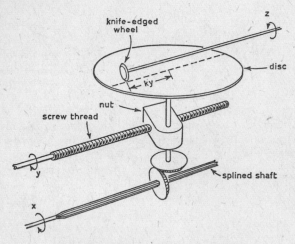

Figure 19. Wheel and disc integrator.

Any gearing with a ratio that can be varied continuously, and that can be set accurately to a desired value, can perform the operation of integration (see p. 82). In 1876, James Thomson, the brother of Lord Kelvin, designed one of the many known mechanisms for this purpose, and another, the 'wheel and disc integrator', is shown in Figure 19. An input shaft (the angular position of which is x) rotates a large horizontal disc about a vertical axis. On this disc rests a knife-edge wheel. The rotation of the disc causes the wheel to rotate by friction, and the wheel in turn drives a horizontal shaft (angular position z), carried in very light bearings. In principle, this is the output shaft. If, however, it is to do anything more than move a pointer over a scale, a power follow-up device is necessary, to rotate the output shaft proper under the control of the knife-edge wheel and exactly in step with it. A second input shaft (angular position y) can move the carriage (which supports the disc) horizontally, by means of a screw thread, thus moving the point of contact of the wheel with the disc radially on the disc to a precise distance (ky) from the centre of the disc. If no slipping occurs at the point of contact, the gear ratio between the x- and z-shafts is ky/a, where a is the radius of the wheel.

It follows that if the x-shaft is turned at a constant speed by a governed motor, then the speed of the z-shaft is proportional to y, i.e. z is proportional to the integral of y with respect to time. This is what is required in Figure 16 for the derivation of v from f and of q from v. The variable y can have positive or negative values, with the z shaft turning forwards or backwards to correspond. When $y = 0$, that is when the wheel is resting at the centre of the disc, the z-shaft is stationary. It is in this position, incidentally, that the amount of sliding of the wheel on the disc, as opposed to rolling, is the greatest. A central rough spot, due to wear, can sometimes be seen on the steel disc of an integrator of this type which has had a lot of use.

The general case is when the x-shaft turns to represent a variable x, and not at a constant speed; z is then proportional to the integral of y with respect to x. In the special case when y is constant, i.e., when the y-shaft remains stationary with the value of y the same as the original setting made by the operator, the value of z is merely that of x multiplied by a constant.

The power follow-up device, which forms part of a wheel and disc integrator in a complete computer, is called a *torque-amplifier*. Its function is to provide the considerable turning-force (or 'torque') needed to rotate extensive shafting and gearing in the computer in step with z, while demanding only the very small torque that the knife-edged wheel can supply without slipping. It works on the principle of the capstan; a drum is rotated steadily by a motor, a tape or string being wrapped loosely in a helix round the drum. An arm on the same shaft as the knife-edged wheel pulls tangentially on one end of the tape, in the direction of drum rotation, to tighten it on the drum, and the other end of the tape then pulls on another arm to turn the output shaft of the torque amplifier with increased force. When this shaft has turned into alignment with the first shaft, the tape slackens again, and the drum turns freely inside the encircling tape. The mechanism is self-adjusting, so that the amount of slipping of the tape on the drum is exactly right to keep the two shafts in synchronism at any speed from zero up to nearly the speed of rotation of the drum itself. In order to allow also for rotation of the z-shaft in the opposite direction, the torque-amplifier contains a second specimen of the same mechanism, with the drum rotating in the opposite direction.

The differential analyser

A computer which uses the mechanical units just described is called a *differential analyser*. A number of such machines – ranging from small laboratory-made instruments to massive engineering structures – were built between 1920 and 1950. They were mainly used to obtain solutions of what are called 'ordinary differential equations', of which the car suspension problem is a simple example.

The central portion of the differential analyser (Plate 1) is, in principle, merely an elaborate gearbox in which shafts and other items can be installed, Meccano-fashion, to suit the problem to be solved. The longitudinal shafts can transmit rotations from one end of the machine to the other, or as far as necessary, and carry the gears and differential gears demanded by the problem. Each of the cabinets in the photograph contains two integrators and their torque amplifiers. The input shafts of the integrators and the output shafts of the torque amplifiers extend transversely across the longitudinal shafts at a lower level, and a drive can be provided between any transverse and any longitudinal shaft by installing a pair of helical gears at the place where they cross. These pairs of helical gears are available in two varieties, which produce opposite directions of rotation.

The large boards seen in the photograph are known as *input tables* and *plotting tables* (or *output tables*); they can be connected to the longitudinal shafts in the same way as the integrators. Each table is provided with two long screw threads which move a carriage over its surface independently in two directions at right angles. For a plotting table, the carriage holds a pen (nowadays a ball point), and the two shafts which drive the carriage are both driven by the rest of the machine, so that a graph is drawn of one variable against another as the solution of the problem proceeds. This is how the answer is obtained in the car suspension problem.

For an input table, a prepared graph is fastened to the table, and the carriage has cross-wires and a lens instead of the pen. The carriage is driven across the table by a drive from the rest of the machine, while an operator moves the carriage up and down by turning a handle, so as to follow the graph. The up-and-down movement of the carriage provides a drive to the rest of the machine, so that a dependent variable corresponding to the graph is available in the set-up. This is how road profile is supplied to the car suspension set-up (Figure 16). A development of this system, known as a *curve follower*, uses photoelectric cells to control a motor, thus dispensing with the human operator.

The x-shafts of the two integrators in Figure 16 must be driven at a constant speed, since both integrations are to be performed with respect to time. A motor is provided in the machine expressly for this purpose. It drives one of the longitudinal shafts, known as the *time-shaft*, at a constant speed, and the time-shaft drives the two x-shafts. The horizontal drive to the carriage of the plotting table also comes from the time-shaft, as does the horizontal drive to the input table, through gearing chosen to correspond to the desired road speed. The remainder of the set-up corresponds in a straightforward way to the diagram, except for one unit, the differentiator, which obtains u from p.

The operation of differentiation is awkward to deal with in mechanical computers and is avoided whenever possible. The next section includes an explanation of how this is done in the case in point.

The name 'differential analyser' is unfortunate on two counts: the operation of differentiation is very uncommon, and the problems are set up on the machine by building up mathematical expressions term by term, which is hardly a process of analysis. A counter-proposal is 'integrating synthesizer', but it is too late to carry pedantry this far. It is better to reserve the name 'differential analyser' for the mechanical computer, and to disallow it for the more modern electrical analog computers, as we do in this book.

The principle of the differential analyser (including the loops mentioned on p. 65) was proposed by William Thomson (later Lord Kelvin) in a paper in the *Proceedings of the Royal Society* for 1876, no doubt stimulated by his brother's interest in the mechanical integrator. The proposal was unfortunately neglected, and not until fifty years later was a workable machine constructed by Vannevar Bush and his colleagues at the Massachusetts Institute of Technology. This was the start of renewed activity, a prominent figure in England being the late Professor D. R. Hartree, who was later one of the first to use the ENIAC as a general-purpose computer. He thus set an excellent early example in avoiding narrow specialization on either analog or digital computers.

Simulation or equation-solving

We obtained the set-up diagram of Figure 16 by analysing into constituent elements the physical system we were considering. Interconnexions in the diagram correspond directly to interactions between elements in the physical system, and the nature of the computing units is specified mainly by the behaviour of the elements. There is no need for mathematical manipulation of equations, and the interconnexions in the diagram are labelled with quantities having a direct physical interpretation. This technique is known as the *simulation* of a physical system by means of an analog computer. It has many advantages, of which the most important are the ease and directness of deriving the computer set-up from the physical system, and the directness with which the behaviour of all parts of the system can be studied on the computer. The technique is also applicable to some problems which do not arise in a physical context; to the study of an economic or biological process, for example.

The alternative method, which cannot always be clearly distinguished from simulation, can be called *equation-solving*. It starts with the same analysis of the system into elements and the writing down of a simple equation to represent the behaviour of each element. The next stage is more mathematical, however. The equations are combined, by the elimination of as many variables as possible, and the resulting much smaller number of equations may then be manipulated mathematically to simplify them still further. The computer gives the solution of the simplified problem, which by this time may be superficially unrecognizable as an alternative formulation of the original problem. The computer solution must then be translated back into the original terms. The advantages of this technique are that details disappear and the problem is generalized; it may be found to be related to some known theory, perhaps in some other subject, but in any case one gets a much better insight into the class of similar problems. Furthermore, the computer needed to solve the simplified problem is simpler. The disadvantages are the greater human effort required, the danger of introducing unwarranted assumptions, and the danger of eliminating and overlooking important secondary aspects of the system. There is no doubt that simulation and equation solving are both useful, and neither can be discarded.

Mechanical differential analysers, in particular, were usually used as equation solvers, because in practice they did not contain sufficient computing units to solve interesting problems by direct simulation. The extreme simplicity of the car suspension problem, as we have posed it, is non-typical, and the problem is indeed easily soluble without any computer. We shall give the first step in the equation-solving approach, because a similar step is usually possible with more complex problems. We shall first derive a single equation which summarizes the behaviour of the car suspension, and then, instead of continuing with the mathematical solution, shall use this equation as the basis of a computer set-up which is an alternative to Figure 16.

From the analysis given on p. 65, we obtain

$$\text{Spring force} = k_1 (p - q)$$
$$\text{Shock absorber force} = k_2 (u - v)$$
$$\text{Total force} = Mf.$$

We now use the fact that Total force is Spring force plus Shock absorber force to eliminate the forces from these equations. This gives

$$Mf = k_2 (u - v) + k_1 (p - q). \qquad (1)$$

This equation means that knowing p and q, the vertical positions of the wheel centre and of the car body, and also u and v, the vertical speeds of the wheel centre and of the car body, we can evaluate f, the vertical acceleration of the car body, by computing the right-hand side of the equation, and dividing it by M. Unfortunately, to assume we know u means, as we have just noted, that we need a differentiator to obtain it from p. This is inconvenient, so what we do is to modify equation (1) so as to remove u. This is achieved by the process, mentioned on p. 67, of integrating the equation with respect to time. It gives equation (2) on p. 83, to which some of our readers will wish to skip directly.

The basis of the process of integrating an equation with respect to time is simple. If the speeds of two objects, A and B, are always identical, and they are known to be at the same position at one particular instant, then it follows that they will always be at the same position. If we have an equation which states 'speed of A equals speed of B' and we also know that A and B start from the same position at the same instant, then we can replace the equation by another equation which states 'position of A equals position of B'. This does not gain or lose us any information; we replace a statement about one aspect of the situation with an equivalent statement about a closely related aspect.

Now, in fact, we can regard any variable as the rate at which a related variable is changing. Sometimes this related variable means something easily understandable; for example, speed is the rate at which position is changing, and acceleration is the rate at which speed is changing. Sometimes the related variable is difficult to correlate with real life; for example, position is the rate at which a rather artificial variable, that does not have an ordinary name, is changing. All we can call this variable is 'integral of position'. The essential point is that, in all cases, the operation of integration replaces a variable by the related variable of which it is the rate of change. The actual operation of integration is always the same, just as the operation of multiplication is always the same; for example, we must use the same operation in passing from acceleration to speed as in passing from speed to position. Furthermore integration can be applied individually to terms which are added or subtracted, and the algebraic sum of the integrals is the integral of the same algebraic sum of the terms.

We can now apply these ideas to equation (1). The integral of the acceleration f is the speed v, and therefore the integral of Mf

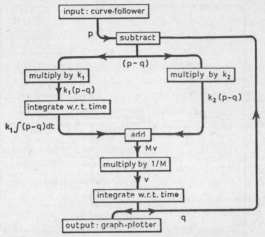

Figure 20. Set-up for solving equation (2) (w.r.t. = with respect to).

is Mv, since M is a constant quantity. Similarly, the integral of the difference in speeds, $(u - v)$, is the difference in positions, $(p - q)$. The integral of the difference in positions fortunately does not need to be interpreted as anything else; all we are going to do is to form $(p - q)$, and present it to an integrator. The artificial quantity which the output of this integrator represents is normally written as shown on the right of equation (2) below,* which is the result of integrating the equation (1) we started with.

$$Mv = k_2 (p - q) + k_1 \int (p - q) \, dt. \tag{2}$$

This equation specifies the set-up of Figure 20 in a reasonably straightforward way.

*The integration sign, '$\int$', is an old fashioned S for 'Sum' (see Sawyer, op. cit., Chapter 12).

There is now no need for a differentiator, and only one subtractor is needed instead of two. The price to be paid for this improvement is that all the interconnexions can no longer be labelled with quantities having direct physical interpretations. It is this set-up that would have been used in practice with a mechanical differential analyser. The important point is that by suitable

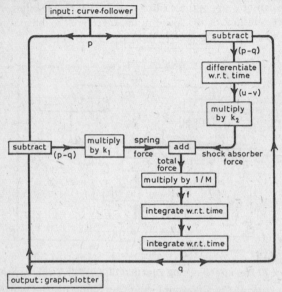

Figure 21. Modified set-up for simulation of car suspension.

manipulation of the equations to be solved, it is usually possible to avoid using a differentiator, as in this case.

We can show how the simulator set-up (Figure 16) can be turned by successive manipulations into the equation-solving set-up (Figure 20). This approach to the problem may be looked upon as a non-mathematical alternative to the process of deriving equation (2) and hence the set-up of Figure 20. The first step is to move the differentiator to the output side of the subtractor at the top of Figure 16. To compensate, the input with the negative sense must now be q instead of v. The set-up is now as in Figure 21, and the representation of u has been removed so that the vertical velocity of the wheel is not directly available from the simulation.

Since the two subtractors are now doing the same computation we can remove one of them, and draw the set-up as in Figure 22.

The positions of the differentiator and the unit for multiplying by the shock-absorber constant can be interchanged, since k_2 does

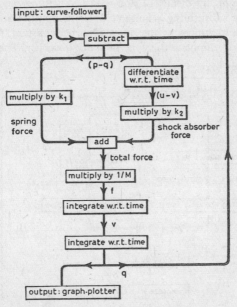

Figure 22. Simplification of previous figure.

not vary. Similarly, the positions of the integrator with input f and the unit for multiplying by $1/M$ can be interchanged, since M does not vary. The integrator is now fed directly from the output of the adder. We can therefore replace it by two integrators, one in each input connexion to the adder, to obtain Figure 23. Neither the total force nor the car body acceleration, f, is now represented in the set-up. Finally, since the integrator that is fed directly from the differentiator recovers perfectly (in theory, if not with practical computing units) the input to the differentiator, we can replace both units by a direct connexion. This gives Figure 20 and removes the representation of shock-absorber force from the diagram.

These simple examples of simulation and equation-solving illustrate one further point. Practical shock-absorbers do not have idealized viscous friction as we have assumed. For one thing the performance on the rebound is usually made different from that on the bump by means of non-return valves. By a change to Figure 16, substituting a more complex computing unit for the one which multiplies by the shock-absorber constant, the set-up can correctly simulate this type of shock-absorber. The assump-

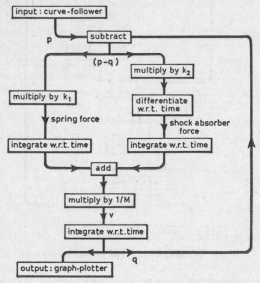

Figure 23. Modification of previous figure.

tion made in deriving Figure 20, that k_2 does not vary with time, is then no longer legitimate, and, in fact, the more realistic shock-absorber cannot be accommodated in the simplified set-up. This illustrates the general point already made that simulation, being more directly related to the original problem than is equation-solving, allows more detailed and realistic conclusions to be drawn, at the price of using more equipment.

Applications of the computing amplifier

Since about 1940, scientists and engineers have increasingly used electrical analog computers in their research and design work; much more indeed than they ever used mechanical analog computers. This is because the electrical computer is easier and quicker to set up for most problems, and can be bigger in terms of number of computing units, thus permitting more elaborate problems to be solved.

In the electrical analog computer, the variables of a problem are represented by voltages, measured with respect to the earth terminal of the equipment, instead of by angular positions of shafts. A voltage is positive, zero, or negative according as the variable itself is positive, zero, or negative. Wholly electrical (or electronic) equipment performs well – with high accuracy and speed – in *linear operations*; that is, in those operations in which a change in one of the input quantities causes a proportional change in the output quantity. With non-linear operations it is a different story, as we shall see later.

The simplest operation, as in the mechanical computer, is again multiplication of a variable by a constant, for which in this context it is convenient to have a special name, *scaling*. The unit which does this is called a *scaler* in contrast with a *multiplier*, which multiplies a variable by another variable, a much more difficult operation in both electrical and mechanical computers. The constant multiplying factor in a scaler is called the *scaling constant*.

Two resistors, connected as in Figure 24, can perform scaling. This circuit is known as a *potential divider*. The connexion of the resistors across the source that supplies the voltage u is assumed not to alter this voltage; that is to say, in the jargon of the electrical engineer, the unit which supplies u is assumed to have a negligibly small output impedance. The scaler output voltage, v, is a fraction $S/(R + S)$ of u. Two remarks must be made about this simple device: the first, that it can only be used if the scaling constant is less than one (unlike a pair of gears) and the second, that the output impedance is not small enough to be negligible for many practical purposes.

To multiply by a constant greater than one, voltage amplification is required. The electronic amplifier which is used to provide this must meet rather special requirements, and is the product of a great deal of development work. It is correctly described as a *high-gain directly-coupled amplifier* (but this is usually abbreviated to *amplifier*), and is represented by the triangular symbol in Figure 25. The sense of the amplification, or *gain*, is negative; that is, if the potential difference (w) between the input terminal and earth becomes more positive, then the potential difference (v) between the amplifier output terminal (which is effectively the same as the output terminal of the complete circuit in the figure) and earth becomes more negative. It does this to a very much

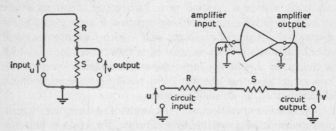

Figure 24. Potential divider as a scaler.

Figure 25. Amplifier connected as a scaler.

greater extent; that is, the gain is very high. Another important feature is that when w changes to a new steady value, then v changes to its corresponding new value, and remains at this value as long as w does not change again. The description 'directly-coupled' implies this behaviour to an electronic engineer; it contrasts with the way in which, say, an audio amplifier would behave. The performance of the high-gain directly-coupled amplifier is therefore summarized by the equation

$$v = -Aw. \tag{3}$$

where A (the gain) is very large, values of 100,000 being commonly achieved in practice.*

These characteristics fit the amplifier for use with what is called

---

*Very much higher figures are obtained at the very low frequency end of the range of operating frequencies, and these alone are sometimes quoted in sales literature.

negative feedback. This is a well-known electronic technique for reducing the effect of imperfections in an amplifier, and reducing its output impedance, at the expense of reducing the gain available. In the present case, negative feedback makes the performance of a computing unit depend almost entirely on the characteristics of its passive components – resistors and capacitors – and not very much on the characteristics of the valves or transistors in its amplifier, which are very much less stable and linear. The remainder of this section is a catalogue of the principal uses of this technique.

The gain of the amplifier being so large, it follows that whatever output voltage the amplifier is called on to deliver, the input voltage, *w*, will be practically zero by comparison. This idea, although elementary, is the basis of a very powerful simplifying technique that applies to explanations of the uses of the high-gain amplifier for computing. The name *virtual earth* is given to the live amplifier input terminal, because it remains approximately at earth potential even though not connected to earth. Because of the negative sense of the amplification, the presence of the resistor *S* in Figure 25 results in negative feedback. Accepting that this implies stable behaviour, we can obtain the relationship between the output voltage *v* and the input voltage *u* of the complete circuit, by the aid of a little elementary electrical theory.

The reader who is not familiar with this should think of a resistor as similar to a narrow-bore pipe, an electrical current through the resistor as equivalent to a current of water through the pipe, and the difference in the voltage with respect to earth of the two ends of the resistor as equivalent to the difference in water pressure at the two ends of the pipe. This simple analogy will help him to keep in mind that rate of current flow is determined by voltage difference between the ends of the resistor. In fact, current flow is voltage difference divided by resistance, a constant of the resistor in question. This is usually known as Ohm's law, and is not applicable to water in pipes – the equivalent law is more complicated. A line joining two points in a circuit diagram indicates a wire of zero resistance, and corresponds to a large-bore pipe which produces no pressure drop. Clearly when several wires join in a point, we expect all the current that flows into the junction to flow out again by another path. This holds good, and the reader may care to know that it is called Kirchhoff's first law.

We now apply these ideas to Figure 25. Because no current flows into or out of the input terminal of the amplifier, the same current must flow through resistors R and S. But the junction of the resistors is at approximately zero voltage with respect to earth, so the voltage difference across resistor R is simply u. We now use R not only as a label for the resistor in the diagram, but also to stand for the magnitude of its resistance. Thus, by Ohm's law, the current through this resistor is u/R. This current also flows through resistor S, so the voltage difference across S must be uS/R with the right-hand end of the resistor at a lower voltage than the left-hand end. Since the left-hand end is at zero, the right-hand end must be at $-uS/R$. Thus we have

$$v = -uS/R. \qquad (4)$$

The circuit is therefore a scaler, the scaling constant being $-S/R$, which is inherently negative, and can be greater or less than one according to whether S is greater or less than R. Normal values range from -10 to -0.1. Because of the negative feedback the output impedance of the circuit is very low and it is often used because of this property alone, in which case it is called a *buffer amplifier*.

The name *see-saw circuit* is sometimes given to this circuit. The pivot of the see-saw is the junction of R and S, and the lengths of the two arms are the resistances of R and S; as the input terminal end of the see-saw is raised or lowered by the input voltage, the output terminal end is lowered or raised to a proportionate extent by the action of the circuit.

A circuit very similar to that of Figure 25 performs addition. In this case, shown in Figure 26, there are two inputs, u_1 and u_2. Again, the virtual earth concept makes analysis of the circuit very simple: since w is approximately zero, the currents in the two input resistors are u_1/R_1 and u_2/R_2. Since the input terminal of the amplifier does not draw any current, a current equal to the sum of the input currents must flow through resistor S. Now the total current through S is again $-v/S$, whence it follows that

$$u_1/R_1 + u_2/R_2 = -v/S,$$
$$\text{or } v = -(u_1 S/R_1 + u_2 S/R_2). \tag{5}$$

If R_1, R_2, and S are equal in value, v is equal to minus the sum of u_1 and u_2, so the circuit can perform addition. Once again there

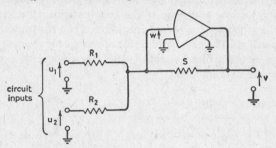

Figure 26. Amplifier connected as an adder.

is an inherent reversal of the sign of the answer, which cannot be avoided. This does not, in practice, cause much difficulty, since the set-up can usually be arranged to allow for it (see the paragraph on subtraction below). Occasionally, however, it turns out that one or another quantity inevitably has the wrong sign. In this case an extra amplifier must be used, connected as in Figure 25, with R and S equal in value, to obtain a sign-reversal pure and simple (eqn 4).

Equation (5) shows that the circuit can perform scaling at the same time as addition. By choice of R_1 and R_2 the scaling constants associated with u_1 and u_2 can be chosen independently, in which case the circuit performs a weighted addition. The addition circuit, like the scaling circuit, has a low output impedance.

If it is desired to subtract u_2 from u_1, an extra amplifier must be used for a preliminary sign reversal. Unlike the differential gear, the adder circuit does not permit the input and output terminals to exchange functions. If the sign of u_2 is changed, an addition circuit can then generate $-(u_1-u_2)$, the quantity required, with the usual sign reversal. If instead the sign of u_1 is first changed, the addition circuit generates $+(u_1-u_2)$, so that either alternative sign of output can be obtained with the same number of units.

Circuits for performing integration and differentiation with respect to time are shown in Figures 27 and 28. One of the limitations of the analog computer using amplifiers with feedback, as compared with the differential analyser, is that it cannot easily do integration and differentiation with respect to a variable other than time. In less technical language, this means that it is not easy to deal with the rate of change of one quantity with respect to another (for example, rate of fuel consumption in a road vehicle per mile travelled). The only natural rate of change for the computer is the speed with which a quantity varies (for example, rate of fuel consumption per minute).

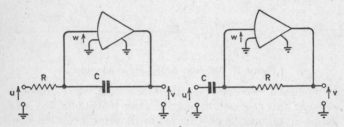

Figure 27. Amplifier connected as an integrator.   *Figure 28.* Amplifier connect as a differentiator.

The operation of the integrator and differentiator circuits depends on the behaviour of an electrical capacity. On the analogy with water in pipes, an electrical capacitor is equivalent to a sealed tank, full of water, with inlet and outlet pipes at opposite ends, closed off from each other by a stretched rubber sheet across the middle of the tank. The pressure difference between inlet and outlet pipes is related to how much the sheet has been forced away from its central position by the water. We can express the state of affairs more conveniently by performing the operation of differentiation – which, it will be recalled (p. 67), is the opposite of integration. This tells us that the rate of change of pressure difference is related to the rate at which water is entering one pipe and leaving the other (the rates in the two pipes are the same, since the tank remains full of water). In the electrical capacity, the current flow at either terminal is equal to the rate of change of voltage between the terminals, multiplied by the magnitude of the electrical capacity.

In Figure 27, the virtual earth approximation means that the rate of change of voltage between the capacitor terminals is simply minus the rate of change of v, which is written as $-dv/dt$ in the normal notation of the calculus.* The current through the capacitor is therefore $-Cdv/dt$, and since this is equal, as before, to the current in the input resistor, u/R, we obtain

$$u/R = -Cdv/dt. \qquad (6)$$

By integrating both sides of this equation and dividing by $-C$, we transform it to

$$v = -\int u \, dt/CR. \qquad (7)$$

That is to say, v is equal to minus the integral of u with respect to time, divided by the quantity CR. In other words, the rate of change of the output voltage of the circuit with respect to time is equal to minus the input voltage divided by CR.

This result is not strictly true in all circumstances, as may be seen by considering u to be constant at a negative value. In this case v will be increasing steadily, and sooner or later will reach the maximum output voltage which the amplifier can give. The voltage will then remain at this maximum value as long as u remains negative, and in this condition the circuit is no longer integrating correctly. When the maximum amplifier output voltage (termed the *limiting* output voltage) is attained, the gain of the amplifier falls to zero, so the assumption on which the analysis is based – that the amplifier gain is very high – is no longer true. A similar effect occurs if u is maintained at a steady positive value, in which case v eventually reaches the negative limiting output voltage. The same trouble can occur when a computing amplifier is used other than as an integrator. It is possible to demand by mistake an output voltage higher than the amplifier can give, and precautions must be taken to avoid this. For the integrator, the time over which correct integration can be expected is in any case limited by an effect which is not revealed in our simple analysis. Within this time, amplifier output voltages must be kept inside the limiting values. This is done by making CR (equation (7))

* See Sawyer, op. cit., Chapter 10.

sufficiently large, usually by trial and error. Even so one of the commonest faults when a set-up is being put together is that an integrator reaches its limiting voltage. This is often due to a wrong algebraic sign somewhere in the analysis, which results in a runaway system being simulated instead of the desired system. In the set-up of Figure 16, a sign reversal in the loop comprising spring force, total force, f, v, q, and $(p - q)$, would produce this effect, and would correspond to the simulation of a spring of negative stiffness, which would tend to flip hard over one way or the other.

In the differentiator circuit of Figure 28, the current through the capacitor is Cdu/dt. The current is also equal to $-v/R$, giving

$$v = -CRdu/dt. \tag{8}$$

That is, the output voltage of the circuit is equal to minus the rate of change of the input voltage with time, multiplied by the quantity CR.

The use of this circuit is avoided wherever possible. The reasons for this are outside the scope of this book, and have to do with the fact that the differentiator is more likely than other computing units to generate or enhance spurious signals. Thus, once again, the differentiator is a weak link in the set-up, and the same techniques for eliminating it are used as with the differential analyser.

Application of the potentiometer

We now turn to the *non-linear* computing operations of multiplication, division, and function generation.* These operations cannot be done both accurately and economically by wholly electrical units; a mixture of mechanical and electrical components is needed.

Provided that one variable is represented by a voltage and another by a shaft rotation, they can be multiplied together by what is known as a *potentiometer*, such as the one shown in

* By 'function generation' we mean the derivation of a dependent variable equal either to a nominated mathematical function of another variable, e.g. the sine, the logarithm, or perhaps an arbitrary or empirical function.

Figure 29(a). This comprises, first, the *element*, which consists of a fine wire of high resistance, r, wound uniformly on a hollow cylindrical former, the ends of the wire being connected to the terminals A and B for the purpose of external connexions. Secondly, there is the *slider*, which is an arm carried on the central shaft. The slider makes contact with the element at a point that can be moved, by turning the shaft, from one end of the element to the other. A diagrammatic representation of the potentiometer is shown in Figure 29(b), the resistor, r, being the element, and the arrowhead the slider.

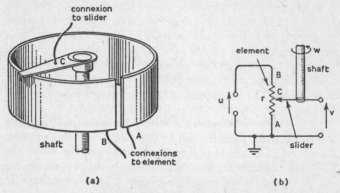

Figure 29. The potentiometer.

The simplest potentiometer multiplier uses nothing but the potentiometer itself. A voltage representing one input variable, u, is applied to the element. We assume that the resistance between the bottom end, A, of the element and the point, C, at which the slider makes contact, is proportional to the mechanical input, w. That is to say, we assume that the slider is positioned so that C is at A when $w = 0$, and that the potentiometer is constructed so as to ensure a constant rate of increase of resistance from A to B. The extent to which this latter requirement is met is a figure of merit of a potentiometer for computing purposes, and is known as the *linearity* of the potentiometer. Discrepancies between measured resistance, and resistance as predicted by the assumption of proportionality, can be kept below one ten thousandth of the total resistance of the element by refinement in design and manufacture.

Now provided no current is drawn from the output terminals of the device, the fraction of the voltage u that is developed across these terminals will be accurately proportional to the distance of the slider from A, and hence to w. This means that v is proportional to the product of u and w, as required for a multiplier; in fact that

$$v = uw/a. \tag{9}$$

where a is the value of w when the slider reaches the upper end, B, of the element. It should be noticed that the circuit of Figure 29(b) works for positive and negative values of u, but for positive values only of w. If negative values of w must be provided for, a centre-tapped potentiometer must be used, with the centre tap connected to earth, and an additional input voltage $- u$ (which is negative when u is positive and vice versa) must be generated, to be applied to the opposite end of the element from the input voltage $+u$.

Although this arrangement achieves the desired multiplicative action, the potentiometer must be followed by a buffer amplifier for general purpose use as a multiplier in a computer, otherwise its output impedance is too high. A suitable circuit is the scaling unit of Figure 25. The resistance R must be large compared with the total resistance, r, of the potentiometer element, since the current taken from the slider (which is determined by R) causes in Figure 29(b) a departure of v from proportionality to w. For the highest possible accuracy, various tricks can be used to compensate for this error.

Another disadvantage of the simple potentiometer multiplier of Figure (29(b)) is that one of the input variables is represented by a shaft rotation. Now if mechanical and electrical representations are both to be used in the same computing system, methods of converting from one to the other must be available. Conversion from mechanical to electrical representation is done by the potentiometer as a special case of multiplication. The input voltage u is taken from a constant voltage supply and v is then proportional only to w, so that v can be taken as an electrical representation of the same variable as w. This method is used extensively in automatic control systems to obtain an electrical signal representing a mechanical motion, and the device is often called a *pick-off potentiometer*.

The other conversion, from electrical to mechanical representation, is much less direct, involving the use of the reverse conversion and negative feedback. The device which does this is shown in Figure 30, the potentiometer inside the dotted line and the caption to the figure being irrelevant for the moment. Applying equation (9) to the pick-off potentiometer we have

$$y = ew/a, \tag{10}$$

where e is a constant voltage. This means that the voltage y is proportional to w, which is the angular position of the output shaft of the device. This voltage is subtracted from the voltage x, the input which is to be converted to mechanical representation. The *difference signal*, $(x - y)$, is amplified and causes the motor to run forwards or backwards depending on the sign of this signal. The motor thus turns the w shaft in a direction which is arranged to reduce the difference between x and y. This goes on until y becomes so nearly equal to x that the amplifier delivers insufficient excitation to the motor to turn it. In this condition, putting $y = x$ in equation (10) and re-arranging it, we have

$$w = ax/e. \tag{11}$$

That is to say, the angular position of the shaft is proportional to the input voltage x, as required. This input is called the *demand voltage*; when it changes the motor runs, and w is automatically altered to correspond. The complete device is called a *position-control servomechanism*. In practice, it must have an extra feature, not shown in the diagram, to prevent 'hunting'; that is, the continuous oscillation of w about the demanded value, due to the inertia of the moving parts. The prevention of hunting is called *damping* the oscillation, and could, for example, be done by deliberately adding viscous friction. A great deal of standard theory and practical knowledge exists on this topic, but for the present purpose enough has been said.

The servomechanism is not usually embodied in a computer as a general purpose electrical to mechanical converter, because this would imply that some of the interconnexions made between units of the computer to suit the problem being solved would be made by mechanical shafts as in the differential analyser. To restrict interconnexions between different units to electrical connexions only, the servomechanism is incorporated in a multiplier or a function-generator unit. In this case, the output shaft drives several other potentiometers as well as the pick-off potentiometer, such as the multiplying potentiometer shown inside the dotted line in Figure 30. Equation (9) applies to this potentio-

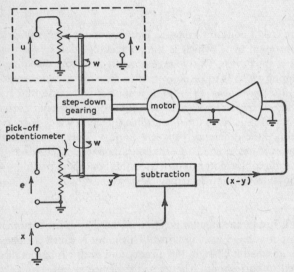

Figure 30. Consistent electrical multiplying unit using a servomechanism.

meter, and since it is as nearly as possible identical in its characteristics to the pick-off potentiometer, equations (9) and (11) apply with the same value of the constant a (using the notation of Figure 30). On eliminating w from these equations we obtain

$$v = ux/e, \qquad (12)$$

that is, the output voltage, v is proportional to the product of the two input voltages u and x. This multiplier is called a *consistent* computing unit, because the inputs and outputs are all in the same representation – namely, voltage.

In practice, more than one such multiplying potentiometer is usually driven by the w shaft because it is frequently required to multiply several quantities u_1, u_2, etc., by the same quantity, x, to obtain several products u_1x, u_2x, etc., for different purposes. Each output requires its own buffer amplifier, as explained in connexion with Figure 29.

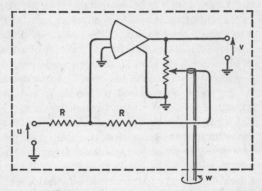

Figure 31. Modification to previous figure to perform division.

A rearrangement of the connexions to one of these multiplying potentiometers and its buffer amplifier provides one method of doing division. The circuit is shown in Figure 31 and can be substituted for the portion of Figure 30 enclosed by the dotted line. The angular setting of the shaft is still ax/e, as given by equation (11), so by analogy with equation (12) the voltage with respect to earth of the slider of the potentiometer in Figure 31 is vx/e, since the amplifier output voltage v is connected to the element of this potentiometer. The see-saw action of the circuit makes the currents in the two resistors R equal, so we have

$$u/R = -vx/eR$$

$$\text{or} \quad v = -ue/x, \tag{13}$$

that is, the output voltage v is proportional to the quotient of the input voltages u and x. What this means is that the effect of putting the potentiometer in the feedback path of the scaling amplifier, as in Figure 31, is to multiply the input voltage by the quantity e/x, whereas with the potentiometer in the input circuit the input voltage is multiplied by the quantity x/e.

There are important restrictions on the utility of this circuit, as indeed there are for any divider. If the quotient u/x becomes too large, the amplifier will reach its limiting output voltage. Furthermore, if the input x becomes so small that the quantity e/x becomes large enough to be comparable with the gain of the amplifier (even though u is also very small so that the quotient u/x is not too large), the accuracy of the circuit will become very low, because the effective gain of the amplifier, for feedback purposes, will be seriously reduced. The circuit works correctly with positive and negative values of u, but even if correct operation for values of x near zero is not required, the modification of the circuit to accept negative values of x is not straightforward.

The final topic in this section is the use of special types of potentiometer for function generation. One such type is the *shaped-card potentiometer*, in which the resistance from one end of the element to the slider is not made proportional to the angular setting of the slider, but to a specified mathematical function of the variable represented by this angle. This can be regarded as a method of storing, inside the potentiometer, a table of values of the function. The principal use of the shaped-card potentiometer is for sine and cosine functions. Other functions are not required often enough in practice to warrant the manufacture and stocking of special potentiometers each of which can only be used for one particular function.

A much more versatile arrangement is to use a linear potentiometer with numerous fixed connexions to the element (*taps*) spaced evenly along its length (Figure 32(a)). This device is called a *tapped potentiometer*, and is used as follows. On a graph of the required function the full movement of the slider of the potentiometer is taken to represent the range of the independent variable over which the function is required. Ordinates are marked on the graph at the positions which correspond to the positions of the taps on the element, and in each space between two ordinates a straight line is drawn approximating to the curve of the desired function, as shown in Figure 32(b). This is termed a *piecewise linear* approximation. The lengths of the ordinates to the intersections of these lines are read off, and a set of proportionate voltages, of practical magnitude, is calculated (e_1, e_2, e_3, and e_4). Each tap is then maintained at a voltage with respect to earth equal to the appropriate one of this set, with the result that the voltage variation along the element is exactly the piecewise linear function which was worked out. When the slider is moved over

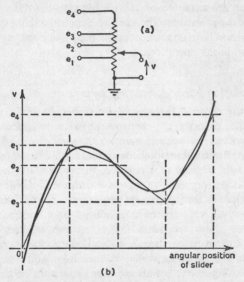

Figure 32. Tapped potentiometer function generator.

the element by a position-control servomechanism, the voltage between slider and earth therefore approximates to the required function of the angular position of the slider.

The accuracy of this device can, of course, be increased by increasing the number of taps. In practice, up to about fifteen are usually provided – sufficient to give surprisingly high accuracies when, as usually happens, the graph of the required function is not very sharply curved. The sources of the constant voltages for the taps must be adjustable, and if each source has a low output impedance, setting up is straightforward. This arrangement is usually too expensive, however, and it is usual not to use low-impedance sources. This means that setting up has to be done by repeated readjustment of each tap voltage in turn.

The electro-mechanical computing units described in this Section are slower in action than the wholly electronic units of the previous Section. On the other hand, the various wholly electronic units which have been devised to perform non-linear operations are either less accurate or more expensive than their electro-mechanical equivalents. The user of electrical analog computers thus has usually to choose between speed and accuracy when he needs non-linear operations.

Electronic non-linear computing units

One of the cardinal features of electronic devices is a lack of accurate reproducibility – between different specimens of nominally identical devices, and even for the same device on different occasions. Electronic analog computing started in the early 1940s when it was realized that negative feedback could be used to make the performance of active electronic devices nearly as reproducible as that of passive components (p. 89). As we have seen, however, this approach produced only linear computing units. For about ten years many research workers tried, in general without much success, to make reproducible non-linear units. They used a wide variety of principles, and a tremendous amount of ingenuity, but always failed to obtain either speed or accuracy, or both. Devices using cathode-ray tubes (including many using specially constructed cathode-ray tubes) were not accurate enough. A device using the heating effect of an electric current was much too slow. Devices using a magnetic field were not quite accurate or fast enough.

The simplest non-linear electronic component is a diode, which has a very high resistance when its anode is negative to its cathode, and a low resistance when positive. Modern diodes approximate an open circuit or a short circuit respectively, and the transition occurs over a very small range of voltage. The ratio of back-resistance to forward-resistance can be as high as 10^7. Such diodes or other equivalent semi-conductor devices, are used quite directly to simulate phenomena like mechanical stops to a movement, and backlash in gearing. In the early 1950s a circuit was invented in the U.S.A. for using diodes to alter the effective input and feedback resistances in a computing amplifier circuit, according to the value of the input voltage. This gave a piecewise linear relationship between output and input voltages that could be made to approximate to a desired function. This idea was developed further and incorporated in *diode function generators*; the graph of output versus input voltage of such a device resembles Figure 32(b), except that the *corners* – that is the transition from one slope to another – need not necessarily be spaced equally in terms of input voltage. Both the speed and accuracy of diode function generators can be comparable with those of linear computing units. Diode function generators can have manual controls on their front panels to allow the operator to set up the slopes and corners that he requires. They are also very useful when constructed to give a fixed square-law or parabolic relationship between input voltage (u) and output voltage (v). Two such square-law function generators, together with adders and subtractors, can in fact perform multiplication, by virtue of the formula:

$$xy = \tfrac{1}{4}(x+y)^2 - \tfrac{1}{4}(x-y)^2.$$

Here x and y are the input voltages to the multiplier. We generate $u_1 = x + y$ and $u_2 = x - y$, whereupon we have $xy = \tfrac{1}{4}(u_1{}^2 - u_2{}^2)$. Such a multiplier is called a *quarter squares multiplier*, and is nowadays widely used.

Using an electrical analog computer

A modern analog computer (Plate 3*) might comprise 250 amplifiers, 75 quarter-squares multipliers and other diode-function generators, one or two electrically operated plotting tables, and 250 manually adjustable potentiometers, called *coefficient potentiometers*, for use in scalers. Clearly, it is essential to have a systematic method of connecting together all this equipment into the

*Items E and G to L together on Plate 3 constitute an analog computer.

set-up for a particular problem. This is provided by a device called a *plugboard* or *patchboard* which is similar in principle to a manual telephone switchboard, and also to the plugboards used in punched-card equipment (pp. 53–56). A typical plugboard has several thousand sockets which are connected to the inputs and outputs of all the amplifiers, multipliers, etc. These sockets can be interconnected, as dictated by a particular set-up, by plugs and wires. For a problem which uses most of the available computing units, making these interconnexions is a lengthy business, so plugboards are often constructed so that they can be detached from the computer. The interconnexions can then be prepared on the plugboard at leisure, without immobilizing the computer, and the plugboard put into position on the computer in one operation. Furthermore, automatic methods of setting coefficient potentiometers are sometimes provided, again to reduce the time spent in changing from one problem to the next.

Another feature that is necessary in practice is a means of setting the variables in the set-up to their initial values before the start of a run.* The only initial values in the set-up that can in fact be assigned arbitrarily are in general those of integrator output voltages, and if the set-up is correctly designed, they correspond to the real disposable initial conditions of the problem. Each integrator is provided with a switch with two positions 'set initial conditions' and 'compute', and also with a potentiometer on which the operator can set the desired initial values. All the switches for the different integrators are operated together to start the run, and if it is arranged to do this automatically and to alternate repeatedly between the two positions, the run is repeated over and over again, and the behaviour of different variables can conveniently be examined in turn on a single voltmeter, or on a cathode-ray tube if the repetition is fast enough.

We conclude this chapter with a practical example. The problem is to investigate how a building would behave in an earthquake, a subject which has been studied in the Dominion Physical Laboratory in New Zealand. For our purposes, the problem has the advantage of being easily intelligible, and of illustrating the fact that simulation can be easy when experiments with the real

*We were able to evade this requirement on p. 65.

thing are very difficult. Furthermore, the computer set-up divides into a series of similar portions, one for each storey of the building, and we need only explain one typical portion.

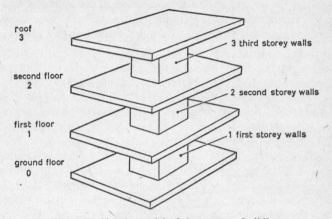

roof
3

second floor
2

first floor
1

ground floor
0

3 third storey walls

2 second storey walls

1 first storey walls

Figure 33. Simple model of three-storey building.

In most places affected by an earthquake, provided they are not too near the epicentre, the ground remains horizontal and moves sideways, carrying the foundations of buildings bodily with it. The building vibrates as a result, the motion being different at different heights from the ground, with various forces and moments being developed. These latter are, of course, of particular interest to the structural engineer, as they show whether or not the building will break up.

A multi-storey building, whose outer walls carry the load of the floors and roof, can in some cases be adequately represented as a series of columns and floors fastened together, as in Figure 33. The floors are massive and do not bend, whereas the walls are comparatively light and do bend. The four walls of one storey can therefore be lumped together into a single column of equivalent stiffness, as shown.

The ground moves sideways (say, parallel to one pair of walls), its distance from its starting point being x_0 at any instant of time, t. The centres of the floors thereupon move, through distances x_1,

105

x_2, etc., and the floors tilt through angles w_1, w_2, etc., all at time t, as shown in Figure 34, where the motion of the ground is to the right. A sideways force F_1 is exerted on the foot of the first storey walls by the ground, and because the mass of the walls can, to a sufficient approximation, be neglected, the walls exert the same force, in the same direction, on the first floor. Forces F_2 and F_3

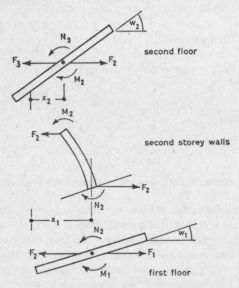

Figure 34. Specimen of notation for analysis of previous figure.

are similarly transmitted by the second- and third-storey walls, the forces and reactions being in the directions shown. The various parts of the building also exert turning moments on one another; for example N_2 at the foot of the second-storey walls, and M_2 at the top of them. The variables in the problem thus consist of a displacement x, an angle w, a force F, a moment M at the top of the walls and a moment N at the base of the walls, for each storey. The relationships between these variables, all changing with time, are expressed by numerous equations.

First, there are the equations of linear and angular motion of the floor. Taking the second floor as a specimen, they are

$$m\frac{d^2x_2}{dt^2}=F_2-F_3, \tag{14}$$

$$I\frac{d^2w_2}{dt^2}=N_3-M_2, \tag{15}$$

where m is the mass of the floor, I its moment of inertia about a horizontal axis through the centre of gravity, and the differential coefficients* on the left of the equations represent linear and angular acceleration, in the normal notation of the calculus.

Secondly, there are equations relating the force and moments developed by, say, the second-storey walls to their deformation. The walls of each storey are treated as a beam, and the theory of beams gives

$$M_2=N_2-hF_2 \tag{16}$$
$$\tfrac{1}{2}(M_2+N_2)=e(w_2-w_1)/h \tag{17}$$
$$h^3F_2/12e=x_1-x_2-h(w_1+w_2)/2 \tag{18}$$

where h is the height of the storey, and e is a constant depending on the elasticity, size, and shape of the walls (it is in fact the product of Young's modulus for the material of the walls and the second moment of area of the plan view of the walls).

Equation (16) arises from taking moments for the beam (ignoring its mass) about a horizontal axis. Equation (17) states that the average bending moment developed by the beam is proportional to the amount by which it is bent. Equation (18) is more complicated, and expresses the extent to which the beam is bent into an S-shape.

A set of equations similar to (14) to (18) applies to each storey. Each storey is influenced by the displacement and tilt of the storey below, and by the force and moment exerted on it by the storey above. At the bottom there will be an arbitrary input, x_0, the displacement of the ground, with w_0 zero, since the ground remains horizontal. At the roof (say, the third floor) F_4 and N_4 will

* $\dfrac{dx}{dt}$ is the rate of change of x with time; $\dfrac{d^2x}{dt^2}$, which is shorthand for $\dfrac{d}{dt}\left(\dfrac{dx}{dt}\right)$, is the rate of change of $\dfrac{dx}{dt}$ with time.

be zero, since there is nothing above to influence the roof. These considerations, together with the desire to avoid using any differentiators in the computer set-up, have led to the equations being

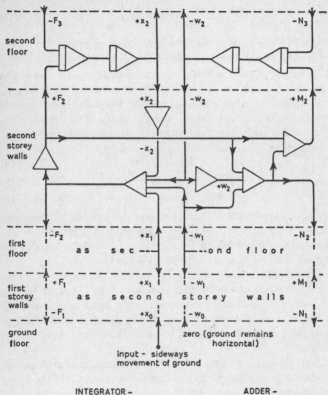

Figure 35. Simulation of response of a building to an earthquake.

formulated in the way they are set out above, with the intention that each right-hand side be synthesized to give the value of the variable on the left. All, that is, except (17), from which M_2 is best eliminated by the use of (16) to give

$$N_2 = e(w_2 - w_1)/h + hF_2/2. \tag{17a}$$

A computer set-up to solve these equations, with (17) replaced by (17a), is given in Figure 35. As noted in the legend, new symbols are used for integrators and adders, while input and feedback components (and earth connexions) do not appear explicitly. Con-

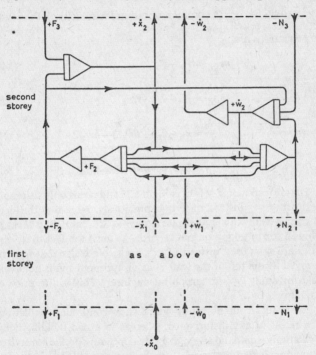

Figure 36. Simplified version of previous figure.

stant multiplying factors would, in practice, be set by the operator on potentiometers, but these are not shown in order to improve the clarity of the diagram. Input and output devices are also necessary, but again are not shown. The input signal could be obtained from a unit generating an arbitrary function of time, set up to reproduce x_0 for a typical earthquake. The output would be obtained by connecting one or more plotters to the signals in the set-up representing quantities of interest, that is, x_n, w_n, F_n, M_n, N_n.

As is to be expected, we can simplify the set-up by manipulating the equations. The objective is to make the integrators do more of the addition, to eliminate some of the adders, and also to remove as many sign-reversing amplifiers as possible. If we write $\dot{x}_2$ for $\frac{dx_2}{dt}$ and $\dot{w}_2$ for $\frac{dw_2}{dt}$ (a common notation for velocities), the resulting equations are

$$m\frac{d\dot{x}_2}{dt} = F_2 - F_3 \tag{14b}$$

$$I\frac{d\dot{w}_2}{dt} = N_3 - N_2 + hF_2 \tag{15b}$$

$$\frac{h^2}{6e}\frac{dN_2}{dt} = \dot{x}_1 - \dot{x}_2 - 2h\dot{w}_1/3 - h\dot{w}_2/3 \tag{17b}$$

$$\frac{h^3}{12e}\frac{dF_2}{dt} = \dot{x}_1 - \dot{x}_2 - h(\dot{w}_1 + \dot{w}_2)/2. \tag{18b}$$

The corresponding set-up is Figure 36 and needs only six amplifiers per storey instead of ten, as previously. Note that the signs of signals dealt with in alternate storeys are reversed; this must be allowed for in taking output records, as must the fact that velocities are now used instead of positions. Note also that M_2, the moment at the top of the walls, has disappeared and is not available for study by the structural engineer. This is the price of economy.

The results from this set-up would show continuing oscillations as a result of any disturbance, whereas in a real building, such oscillations would die away, at a rate depending on the amount of damping inherent in the structure. In fact, one of the objectives of the New Zealand simulation work is to investigate the nature of structural damping, and various possible damping mechanisms can be incorporated in the set-up of Figure 36.

We shall now leave the analog computer, pre-eminently a tool for scientific and technical work and pass to the digital computer, which is not restricted to these fields.

6. HOW A DIGITAL COMPUTER IS PUT TO WORK

The remaining chapters, with the exception of Chapter 12, deal with the design and use of sequential digital computers. Nowadays such computers are almost always electronic, which means that they can calculate – that is, manipulate electrical signals – extremely rapidly. Most of them are designed as general purpose machines; they can do any kind of calculation that can be broken down into a sequence of elementary steps. Furthermore, they can be switched rapidly from one task to another; many modern computers habitually perform scores of different calculations in the course of a single day.

The five basic functional component parts of a digital computer have been listed on pp. 44–5. Figure 37 shows, in schematic form, the relationships between them.

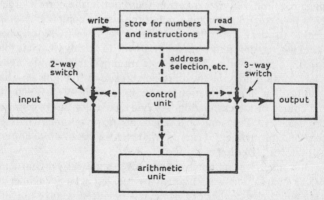

Figure 37. Block diagram of a general purpose sequential digital computer.

Full lines denote channels carrying number signals. Such signals may be sent *to* the store from either the input unit or the arithmetic unit; they may be sent *from* the store to the output unit, the arithmetic unit or the control unit. The selection of the source and destination is made by what are called *control signals* (broken lines) which set the two switches shown on the diagram. (In practice these are electronic switches, which can operate at high speed.) The control unit also specifies what arithmetic operation is to be performed next and has certain functions to perform in the store. Each of the units in Figure 37 will be discussed in more detail in later chapters. The way they work will be more easily understood after the explanation, in this chapter, of how the complete computer is told how to perform a desired calculation.

The program for a calculation

A computer, since it operates automatically, must be supplied in advance with both the instructions and all the numerical data it needs for the complete calculation. The schedule of instructions that must be so supplied is called the *program* for the calculation. (The American spelling is now established usage.) The program must ensure not only that the computer performs all the operations required, but that it carries them out in the correct order. Now the computing machine, unlike the human computer, is quite unable to make the smallest extension to its instructions when faced with an unforeseen situation; it will do exactly what it is told to do, no more and no less. The programmer, then, must foresee every contingency, and must provide precise instructions on what is to be done in any situation that might conceivably arise during the course of the calculation. As Lady Lovelace put it with her usual clarity: 'The Analytical Engine has no pretensions whatever to originate anything. It can do whatever we *know how to order it* to perform.' (Her italics.)

How, then, is a computer so ordered? In some early digital computers instructions were inserted by making a large number of plug and socket connexions by hand – as indeed is still done with most electrical analog computers. The disadvantage of this procedure is the length of time it takes to set up a problem or to change to the next. With a general-purpose machine we want to be able to switch rapidly from one calculation to another. Plugged connexions have now been almost entirely superseded, and the general practice is to *store* the complete program of instructions inside the machine before the calculation starts. Any numbers needed to specify the desired calculation must also be stored in the computer beforehand, and some extra storage space must be provided for numbers that may be generated during the course of the calculation.

Provision must be made, then, for the storage of both instructions and numbers. Some machines, particularly those designed for special purposes, are provided with two separate storage units, one for numbers and one for instructions. With a general-purpose machine, however, such an arrangement is wasteful of storage space. Some computations require a large number of instructions but only a small storage capacity for numbers; while in others a few instructions suffice to manipulate a large amount of numerical material. For this and other reasons, most computers are designed so that numbers and instructions are stored together; the storage unit of the machine holds both kinds of data. (This is why the storage box in Figure 37 is labelled 'Store for numbers and instructions'.) This being so, it is clearly convenient to represent instructions and numbers inside the machine in the same way; in fact, to *code* an instruction as a number, that is, as a set of digits. We shall use the term *word* to denote a standard length set of digits, which can represent either a number or an instruction coded as a number. The store of a computer may be thought of as consisting of a set of pigeon holes, or *registers*, each of which can hold a single word.

The programmer does his job with pencil and paper in his office away from the computer. Indeed, he need know little of the engineering features of his machine; what he must know is how to 'order it to perform'. Clearly, any computer must be so designed as to be able to perform a certain number of basic operations – such as adding two numbers together – when suitably stimulated to do so. Each time an instruction in a program is executed, the computer is caused to perform the corresponding basic operation. The schedule of the available basic operations is known as the *computer instruction set*.

The basic operations are, so to speak, built into the hardware of the computer. The larger their number, the more complicated and expensive the computer will be. On the other hand, the programmer will be inconvenienced if his repertoire of instructions is too restricted, and, more important, his computation will take longer to perform. As an example, consider a computer for which multiplication is not a basic operation. In this case, the programmer must write a program which imitates the long multiplication process we all learnt at school. Admittedly he can then use the program again and again without further effort, but at a heavy price in extra computing time. It might take 100 times as long to execute a multiplication program as it would to multiply two numbers together on a computer having a built-in multiplier unit. A compromise must be reached on many such points between cheapness and operating speed; the point at which the balance is struck varies a good deal from one computer to another.

Reducing matters to bare essentials, we may say that the programmer thinks of the computer as a large and possibly rather mysterious black box,* having certain properties that he can make use of. The two most important of these are, first, the computer can be instructed to perform simple operations, as specified by its instruction set, and second, the computer contains a set of storage registers, each capable of holding a single word.

In most computers an individual storage register is not a separate entity, either physically or conceptually, and the term *storage location* is more appropriate. It is convenient to number the storage locations sequentially, starting from 0. The number (or numerical label) which designates a particular storage location is called its *address*. We shall use (n) to denote the storage location whose address is n, and $C(n)$ – which stands for the *contents of* location (n) – to denote the word stored there. The reader will find these distinctions helpful: n is the number marked on the pigeon hole; $C(n)$ is the different number that is currently stored in the pigeon hole; while (n) is the pigeon hole itself, and is not a number.

Most of the steps in a calculation involve the transfer of one or

---

*In modern jargon, a 'black box' is any process or device the external properties of which are relevant and important, but the internal means by which these properties are achieved, irrelevant and unimportant.

more words along the number-channels of Figure 37. Most computers are so designed that the contents of a storage location are not affected when a transfer is made *from* it to another part of the machine; the original word stored in that location remains available there for later use. On the other hand, when a word is transferred *into* a storage location from elsewhere, the new word replaces and erases the one previously stored there. When the word in a storage location consists entirely of zeros, that location is said to be *empty*, or clear.

The way in which an automatic computer is 'instructed' to carry out a desired calculation cannot be presented convincingly in general terms, and so we shall now discuss the construction of three very short programs for a hypothetical computer having a simple basic instruction set.

A program for evaluating squares of integers

Let us first consider the program needed to cause the computer to evaluate the squares of all the positive integers from 1 up to a specified number, N.

We shall assume, to begin with, that the computer can perform only a small number of basic operations; more will be introduced as they are needed. Addition clearly qualifies for inclusion; a convenient instruction might be:

'Add $C(X)$ to $C(Y)$ and send the result to (Z)',

where X, Y, and Z denote the addresses of storage locations. Some computers are indeed designed to respond to instructions of this form. They are said to have a three-address instruction format, since three separate storage locations are specified in each instruction. A more common practice, however, is to arrange matters so that only one storage location is specified by an instruction (a single-address format). This considerably simplifies the job of the designer, and usually leads to a cheaper machine. The price to be paid, however, is that more instructions are needed to enable the computer to carry out a desired calculation – the program is longer. For example, an addition operation of the kind just described would require, in a single-address format computer, three separate instructions:

$$\begin{cases} \text{Send C}(X) \text{ to } A \\ \text{Add C}(Y) \text{ to C}(A) \\ \text{Send C}(A) \text{ to } (Z) \end{cases}$$

where A denotes a special register called the *accumulator*, which forms part of the arithmetic unit of Figure 37. The instruction 'add C(Y) to C(A)' means that the new value of C(A) is C(Y) plus the old value of C(A); it is therefore possible by repeated use of this operation to 'accumulate' the total of successive incident numbers.

The basic instruction set of our single-address computer must also provide for numbers to be subtracted from the contents of the accumulator. We must also be able to transfer numbers in both directions between the accumulator and the store. We thus require at least the following instructions:

	New contents of accumulator	New contents of location (n)
Add C(n) to C(A)	C(A) + C(n)	C(n)
Subtract C(n) from C(A)	C(A) − C(n)	C(n)
Copy C(n) in A	C(n)	C(n)
Copy C(A) in (n)	C(A)	C(A)

C(A) is the content of the accumulator before the instruction is executed. The two columns on the right show respectively the contents of the accumulator and the relevant storage location *after* the operation has been performed. Since the original contents of the destination register are obliterated automatically, it is not necessary in a program to specify explicitly the erasure of a number before a different number is written in the same place. We have used the word 'copy', rather than 'send' or 'transfer', to emphasize that a number, when transferred, also remains available in the original register for subsequent use.

We have already pointed out that the process of programming entails the preparation of a schedule of instructions which effectively describes the desired computation. A good programmer will try to reduce the number of his instructions to a minimum – to save both labour and storage space. If follows, therefore, that the sequence of operations describing the computation should be as repetitive as possible, the same instruction being used again and again with different numbers during the course of the calculation.

We shall adopt this principle in our squares program and shall arrange matters so that the same group of instructions is used for each stage; that is, for evaluating $(i + 1)^2$, having already evaluated i^2, whatever the value of i may be. Let us therefore assume for the moment that i is stored in (3) and i^2 in (4) and see what instructions are needed to compute the next square, namely $(i + 1)^2$, and place it in (4). We shall also assume that before the calculation starts the number 1 has been put in (1) and N in (2), as illustrated in Figure 38. (Location (5) may be ignored for the moment.) It is also convenient to keep location (0) always empty.

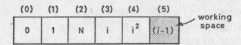

Figure 38. Contents of storage locations at end of ith cycle of squares program.

The following set of instructions will achieve our objective.

		C(A)	C(3)	C(4)	C(5)
100	Copy C(3) in A	i	i	i^2	
101	Copy C(A) in (5)				i
102	Add C(1) to C(A)	$i + 1$			
103	Copy C(A) in (3)		$i + 1$		
104	Add C(5) to C(A)	$2i + 1$			
105	Add C(4) to C(A)	$i^2 + 2i + 1$ $= (i + 1)^2$			
106	Copy C(A) in (4)			$(i + 1)^2$	

The columns on the right show the contents of the accumulator, A, and registers (3), (4), and (5) after each instruction has been obeyed (only changes of contents are explicitly indicated).

The effect of these seven instructions is to replace i by $(i + 1)$ in storage location (3), and to replace i^2 by $(i + 1)^2$ in (4). Note that location (5) is used as working space for the temporary storage of a number needed during the computation.

117

The program must now cause the computer to proceed to the next step of the calculation – that is, to evaluate $(i + 2)^2$, then $(i + 3)^2$, and so on. We have already indicated the objections to the direct procedure – that of writing down seven separate instructions for evaluating each square. What is needed, in accordance with the principle of maximum repetition, is some method of instructing the computer to return to the first of the above instructions after the seventh one has been obeyed. An instruction which does this is called a *jump* instruction. We may specify it thus:

'Take $C(n)$ as the next instruction' or, more concisely, 'Jump to (n).'

The point to notice is that the next instruction to be obeyed is specified by the *address* of the storage location in which it is held. It follows, therefore, that before the jump instruction can be incorporated into our program, we must decide where each of the instructions is to be stored. Any of the storage registers other than those needed to store numbers may be used; we shall arbitrarily allot addresses 100 to 106 to the seven instructions already listed (as shown on the left of the program), and address 107 to the jump instruction, which must transfer control back to the instruction in location (100).

The execution of this program, with the jump instruction at the end, will cause the set of eight instructions to be obeyed repeatedly, an additional square being evaluated each time. While a cycling process of this type is taking place, the computer is said to be in a *loop* of the program.

The next question that arises is: how do we tell the machine when to stop; or, to be more precise, how do we tell it when the loop of instructions has been cycled N times and no further computation is required?

The question has two parts:

(1) how do we arrange to count the number of cycles round the loop of instructions, and

(2) how do we cause the machine to vary its performance – in fact to come out of the loop – when the count has reached a certain value – in this case N?

The answer to the second part of the question brings us to one of the most important instructions in the repertoire of any computer. This is the *conditional jump* instruction, which enables the machine to decide, at any stage in a computation, which of two alternative instructions it will obey next, the decision being taken as a result of applying some numerical test. The numbers to which the test is applied may be supplied to the computer in advance or, more usually, may be generated by the machine itself during the course of the calculation.

Conditional jump instructions may take a variety of forms. In a single address computer of the kind we are considering here, a suitable form would be:

'If the number in the accumulator is negative, take as the next instruction the one stored in location (n); otherwise proceed in the usual way and obey the next instruction in sequence' or, more concisely, 'Jump to (n) if $C(A)$ is negative.'

The existence of the conditional jump instruction clearly makes a separate plain jump (or *unconditional jump*) instruction unnecessary. If a programmer needs an unconditional jump, he can use a conditional jump instruction provided he ensures that $C(A)$ is in fact negative. We shall, therefore, for brevity, use 'jump' to mean 'conditional jump'.

We now turn to the other part of our question; how do we arrange for the machine to *count* the number of cycles round the loop of instructions? Now a glance at our program will show that such counting is in fact already being done – in location (3), which holds the current value, i, of the number being squared. This must be regarded as a fortunate accident; in most programs one or more separate storage locations must be allocated for the specific purpose of cycle counting.

The number held in (3) is, as we have seen, augmented by 1 each time the loop of instructions is traversed. If this location is cleared before the computation starts, then $C(3) = 1$ after the first cycle, $C(3) = 2$ after the second, and so on. After the ith cycle, when i^2 has been evaluated, $C(3) = i$; at the end of the calculation $C(3) = N$. To terminate the calculation at the correct point – when N^2 has been evaluated during the Nth cycle – we must arrange matters so that, at the end of each cycle, the accumulator contains the difference between $C(3)$ – the current count of the number of cycles – and the number N, which is always available in location (2). If this is done, the required jump instruction, which replaces the previous one at the end of the list of instructions, is:

'Jump to (100) if $C(A)$ is negative.'

The effect of this instruction is to cause the loop of instructions to be obeyed again so long as $C(3)$ is less than $C(2)$. At the end of the ith cycle, $C(3) = i$ and $C(2) = N$, and so a further cycle will be ordered so long as i is less than N, During the Nth cycle. $C(3)$ is increased from $(N - 1)$ to N. The value of $[C(3) - C(2)]$, which is equal to $C(A)$, is now no longer negative, but has become zero. At this point the jump instruction causes the other route to be chosen, and the next instruction in sequence is obeyed. This instruction causes the machine to *stop*. (We may suppose there is an instruction which does this.)

The set of instructions forming the loop now consists of the seven instructions listed on p. 117, followed by these four further instructions:

> Copy $C(3)$ in A
> Subtract $C(2)$ from $C(A)$
> Jump to (100) if $C(A)$ is negative
> Stop.

It should be remembered that $C(0) = 0$, $C(1) = 1$ and $C(2) = N$ throughout, while $C(3)$ and $C(4)$ change during the course of the calculation and must be cleared initially.

This set of instructions, together with the preliminary instructions needed to set the correct starting numbers in certain locations, would indeed cause the machine to carry out the prescribed calculation; that is, to compute 1^2, 2^2, ... up to N^2 and then stop. However, this in itself would be of little value unless the answers could be recorded in a convenient form.

We thus need an *output instruction*. The arrangements for recording answers vary considerably from one computer to another, and to fix ideas we shall suppose that the computer is connected to a printing device of some kind – for example, an electric typewriter so arranged that it can operate automatically when the appropriate electrical signals are sent to it. We shall further suppose that the machine will print out an answer when ordered to do so by an output instruction of the following form:

'Print the number stored in location (n)' or, more concisely, 'Print $C(n)$.'

If we wish to print a table of squares in the form shown in the table below, then two output instructions must be inserted at appropriate points in the program. Arrangements must also be made to give the desired layout of the printed numbers on the page; this might be done by special instructions supplied to the computer or by manual settings made on the printing device itself.

i	i^2
1	1
2	4
3	9
4	16
5	25
.	.
.	.

Finally, we need an *input instruction* to enable numbers or coded instructions to be supplied to the computer and stored there until required. Again, the exact method of doing this varies considerably. In this chapter we shall assume that the words to be fed into the machine are represented physically by patterns of holes punched on a length of paper tape. The situation is illustrated diagrammatically in Figure 39, where A, B, C, D denote susccessive words on the tape. These patterns of holes are 'read', one word at a time, under the control of the input instruction, by means of a reading device forming part of the input unit of the computer. We shall suppose the input instruction may be expressed thus:

'Read the next word on the tape and send it to storage location (n)' or, more concisely, 'Tape to (n).'

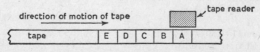

Figure 39. Punched tape input.

Let us suppose that the computer receives an input instruction when the word A on the tape is under the reading device. The sequence of events is then as follows. First, the pattern of holes representing the word A is sensed in some manner by the reading device; this causes a corresponding set of electrical signals to be sent to the storage location specified in the instruction – that is to say, the word A is stored in this location. Secondly, the tape is caused to move past the reading device so that the next word on the tape, say, B, is in the correct position to be read when the computer is next instructed to do so.

Before the computer starts to obey the instructions comprising the main repetitive loop of our squares program, a few setting-up operations must be performed. These are done by means of input instructions. On most computers there are special arrangements for clearing all the storage registers before starting a fresh calculation, so separate instructions for clearing locations (0), (3), and (4) need not be included in the program. We do, however, need input instructions to read the numbers 1 and N from the tape and to send them to locations (1) and (2).

The final squares program, including input and print instructions, then appears as follows:

		Contents during $(i + 1)$th cycle			
		$C(A)$	$C(3)$	$C(4)$	$C(5)$
98	Tape to (1)				
99	Tape to (2)				
→100	Copy C(3) in A	i	i	i^2	
101	Copy C(A) in (5)				i
102	Add C(1) to C(A)	$i + 1$			
103	Copy C(A) to (3)		$i + 1$		
104	Print C(3)				
105	Add C(5) to C(A)	$2i + 1$			
106	Add C(4) to C(A)	$i^2 + 2i + 1$			
107	Copy C(A) in (4)			$(i + 1)^2$	
108	Print C(4)				
109	Copy C(3) in A	$i + 1$			
110	Subtract C(2) from C(A)		$(i + 1) - N$		
└111	Jump to (100) if C(A) is negative				
112	Stop				

One further general point may be mentioned at this stage. In addition to the numerical data needed for a calculation, the set of coded instructions which constitutes the program itself must also be punched on tape, read into the computer, and stored away. Clearly some, at least, of the program must be read in before any calculation can start.

Now, the computer cannot read anything from the tape unless instructed to do so. How, then, is the input process started? There are in fact several ways of doing this, but we shall mention one only. This is to have a small 'start program' permanently stored in the computer – we may think of it as being built in by the designer. This program is obeyed when the operator gives a start signal – say by operating a switch on the control desk. The execution of the start program causes the main program of instructions for the particular calculation to be read from the tape and stored in the computer. The calculation proper can then begin.

It is sometimes convenient, before programming a calculation in full detail, to prepare a schematic chart showing the main operations that must be performed and the relations between them; to draw, as it were, a picture showing the general organization and the broad flow of the computation. Such a chart is known as a *flow diagram*; Figure 40 shows one for the squares program. For an intricate calculation involving many repetitive loops, the preparation of a flow diagram is an essential preliminary stage in the programming process.

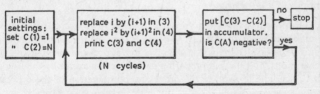

Figure 40. Flow diagram of squares program.

Two features of this program deserve special emphasis in view of their importance in programming technique: the use of repetitive cycles, whereby the same set of instructions is obeyed over and over again; and the use of a jump instruction to enable the calculation to take one or other of two alternative paths. Lady

Lovelace had a clear understanding of the importance of both these ideas. 'The engine is capable', she writes, 'under certain circumstances of feeling about to discover which of two or more possible contingencies has occurred, and then of shaping its future course accordingly.' In one of her more elaborate programming examples she introduces a number in a certain register for the specific purpose of counting the number of repetitions of a group of instructions. This number is arranged to change sign when the desired number of cycles has been executed, and a jump instruction is inserted to cause the machine to move out of the loop at this point to the next part of the calculation.

She also discusses the mechanism whereby such a transfer of control is to be effected. It will be recalled that Babbage proposed to use Jacquard-type punched cards to control his Analytical Engine. Now the punched cards in the Jacquard loom pass through the mechanism in a fixed order which cannot be varied once the loom is set up. Lady Lovelace explains why an additional facility – known as *backing* the cards – must be provided in the Analytical Engine, and she describes the mechanical arrangement needed. The drum over which the train of cards passes must be able to rotate in the reverse direction, the occasion and extent of the backward motion being determined by the program. 'The object of this extension', she writes, 'is to secure the possibility of bringing any particular card or set of cards into use *any number of times successively* in the solution of one problem.' She continues in a later note.

The power of repeating the cards reduces to an immense extent the number of cards required. It is obvious that the mechanical improvement is especially applicable wherever *cycles* occur in the mathematical operations, and that, in preparing data for calculations by the Engine, it is desirable to arrange the order and combination of the processes with a view to obtain them as much as possible symmetrically and in cycles, in order that the mechanical advantages of the *backing* system may be applied to the utmost.

She then illustrates her point by discussing a highly repetitive procedure for solving a set of mathematical equations.

Lady Lovelace wrote in the year 1842. It is sobering to find that the Automatic Sequence Controlled Calculator, as originally built in 1944, had no jump instruction in its basic set. An equivalent facility, of a rather rudimentary kind, had in fact to be added later.

Before leaving the subject of squares it is perhaps worth telling a story for which we are indebted to Lord Bowden. In 1837 Babbage posed the following problem to illustrate the power of his Engine. What, he asked, is the smallest number whose square ends in 269,696? (He thought the answer was 99,736.)

A small extension of our squares program would suffice to enable the computer to solve the puzzle. Only two extra steps would need to be added to the main loop of instructions: the first to subtract each square, when computed, from 296,696; the second to test if the last six digits of the number so formed were zero. If they were not, the cycle would be repeated for the next square; if they were, the number whose square satisfied the condition would be printed out and the calculation would stop. On most modern computers the calculation itself, with the cycle of operations being repeated 99,736 times, would not take more than a minute or two. We ought to allow about twenty minutes, however, to prepare the program, punch it on tape, and feed the tape into the machine. These times are quite impressive, but the story is not yet finished.

Some years ago the problem was propounded to William Klein of the Mathematisch Centrum of Amsterdam, one of the most remarkable calculating prodigies of this century. Klein solved the problem entirely in his head; it took him just three minutes to show that the correct answer is 25,264, and that Babbage had been wrong! (The reader is invited to check the result for himself.)

An iterative square root program

For our second program we move from squares to square roots. Most of us were taught at school how to evaluate square roots, digit by digit, by a procedure similar to that of long division. A bit later we learnt to use log tables and promptly forgot the long division method! We shall now consider yet a third method: that of successive approximation – or iteration, to give it its mathematical name. We start by making a rough guess at the answer we want, and then proceed to compute a sequence of numbers, called *iterates*, which approach ever nearer to the true answer. The process is stopped when a sufficiently close approximation is achieved. An essential feature of iterative processes is that the same procedure must serve to compute any term of the sequence (other than the first) from the preceding one.

For our specific problem, we may let N be the number whose square root is required, and let $y_1, y_2 \ldots y_n$ be successive terms in the sequence of approximations to $\sqrt{N}$. To evaluate any term, say, y_{i+1}, from the preceding one, y_i, we shall use the formula

$$y_{i+1} = \tfrac{1}{2}(y_i + N/y_i). \tag{1}$$

The first approximation, y_1, may be obtained from tables, or simply from inspection. A numerical example will illustrate how the process works. Suppose we wish to find the square root of 79.532. Since $9 \times 9 = 81$, we know that the number we want is a bit less than 9. If we take 9 as our first approximation, we get

$$y_1 = 9$$
$$y_2 = \tfrac{1}{2}(y_1 + 79.532/y_1) = 8.9184$$
$$y_3 = \tfrac{1}{2}(y_2 + 79.532/y_2) = 8.91807$$
$$y_4 = \tfrac{1}{2}(y_3 + 79.532/y_3) = 8.91807.$$

Now the value of $\sqrt{79.532}$, correct to five decimal places, is in fact 8.91807 and we see that the successive approximations quickly settle down to this value. This will always be the case provided that our first guess is not too far out. If, for example, we start with 8 instead of 9 (a much poorer guess), only one more iterate need be calculated. (In this case the successive iterates are 8, 8.971, 8.91823, 8.91807, 8.91807.)

We will now construct a program for this calculation. First, however, we need to introduce two more basic instructions to deal with the arithmetical processes of multiplication and division. We shall specify these as follows:

Multiply $C(A)$ by $C(n)$	New $C(A) = C(A) \times C(n)$
Divide $C(A)$ by $C(n)$	New $C(A) = C(A)/C(n)$

With any approximate process, the accuracy to which the result is required must always be specified. We shall denote by E the maximum error that can be tolerated in the computed value of $\sqrt{N}$; that is, we want to be sure that the final approximation lies between $\sqrt{N} + E$ and $\sqrt{N} - E$. The quantity E must be supplied to the computer as part of the data of the problem. For example, if we want the result to be accurate to five places of decimals, we would take $E = 0.000\,005$. Now with the formula we have chosen, it so happens that successive iterates (from y_2 onwards) steadily decrease and approach $\sqrt{N}$ from above, and that the required accuracy will be attained as soon as the difference between successive approximations becomes less than E. To avoid having to make special arrangements to get the process started properly, we shall take for our first guess (y_1) a number which we know to be greater than $\sqrt{N}$. This ensures that $(y_i - y_{i+1})$ is always positive. Our program will compute this quantity at each step of the approximation process, then test whether $(y_i - y_{i+1})$ is greater than or less than E, and finally terminate the process as soon as $(y_i - y_{i+1})$ becomes less than E. The value of y_{i+1} at this stage will be the value of $\sqrt{N}$ to the required accuracy.

A program for the calculation is given below. It should be noted that the formula (1) may be written as

$$y_i - y_{i+1} = \tfrac{1}{2}(y_i - N/y_i). \tag{2}$$

Storage locations for both numbers and instructions are allocated on similar lines to those adopted for the squares program. In practice, of course, it would not be worth while to enlist the aid of a high speed computer to calculate a single square root.

(0)	(1)	(2)	(3)	(4)	(5)
0	$\frac{1}{2}$	N	E	y_i	$(y_i - y_{i-1})$

Figure 41. Contents of storage locations in square root calculation at the start of the ith iterative cycle.

The set of instructions given on p. 128 is therefore to be regarded as forming part of a program for a larger computation, and so input and output instructions are not included.

The following initial settings are required:

$C(1) = \frac{1}{2}$, $C(2) = N$, $C(3) = E$, $C(4) = y_1$. (See Figure 41.)

The columns on the right of the program show the contents of the specified locations during the ith cycle of the loop of instructions. Location (4) holds the values of successive iterates, eventually the final result. Location (5) holds the differences between successive iterates.

An interesting feature of iterative calculations of this kind is that the programmer cannot forecast the course of the calculation in full detail; he does not know how many iterations will be needed in any particular case, nor how long the machine will take to complete the job. What the programmer does is to provide the machine with criteria on the basis of which it 'decides', so to speak, between alternative courses of action. Which choice is made on a particular occasion depends on certain numbers that are generated by the machine during the course of the calculation.

		Contents during ith cycle		
		$C(A)$	$C(4)$	$C(5)$
→100	Copy C(2) in A	N	y_i	$y_i - y_{i-1}$
101	Divide C(A) by C(4)	N/y_i		
102	Subtract C(4) from C(A)	$N/y_i - y$,		
103	Multiply C(A) by C(1)	$\frac{1}{2}(N/y_i - y_i)=$ $y_{i+1} - y_i$		
104	Copy C(A) in (5)			$y_{i+1} - y$
105	Add C(4) to C(A)	y_{r+1}		
106	Copy C(A) in (4)		y_{i+1}	
107	Copy C(3) in A	E		
108	Add C(5) to C(A)	$E + (y_{i+1} - y_i)=$ $E - (y_i - y_{i+1})$		
109	Jump to 100 if C(A) is negative			

The programmer does not know what these numbers are and so cannot predict what 'decisions' the machine will make. Dr Samuel's draughts program of Chapter 1 is a much more impressive example of the same kind of thing. This 'power of decision' has led some people to speak of computers as being endowed with a faculty of judgement, and even of possessing rudimentary powers of thought. This topic will be taken up in the last chapter. It suffices here to make the point that what the computer does is to apply a set of rules: the rules themselves are prescribed by the programmer.

A statistical program

As our final example we consider a program for performing the following small calculation. We are given two sets of numbers, with n numbers in each set, and wish to calculate the quantity, S_n, formed by multiplying together corresponding numbers of the two sets and adding up the resulting products. If the two sets of numbers are denoted by a_1, a_2, $a_3 \ldots a_n$ and b_1, b_2, $b_3 \ldots b_n$, we wish to calculate

$$S_n = a_1 b_1 + a_2 b_2 + a_3 b_3 \ldots + a_n b_n.$$

This calculation arises in many contexts. Engineers will recognize S_n as the scalar product of two vectors; statisticians as one of the terms in the expression for the coefficient of correlation between two variables – for example, the heights and weights of a group of men. (We shall meet this concept again in Chapter 9.)

To fix ideas, we shall assume that the numbers a_1, $a_2 \ldots a_n$ are stored in consecutive storage locations starting at (200), and that b_1, $b_2 \ldots b_n$ are stored similarly starting at (300). (See Figure 42.)

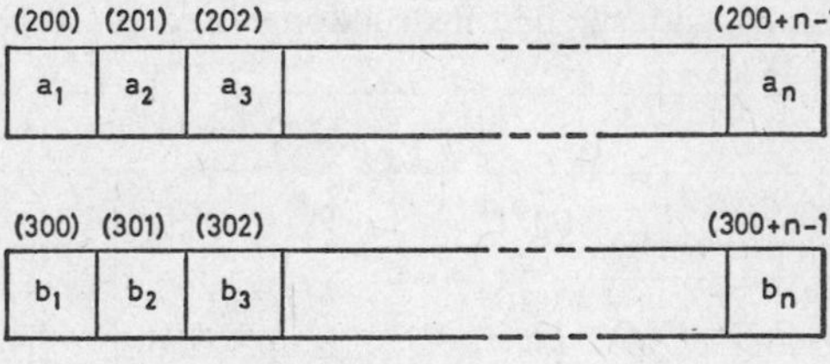

Figure 42. Locations of the two sets of numbers in the statistical program.

Once again, the calculation will be cast in repetitive form, and we shall first consider the group of instructions forming the loop. This loop is to be traversed n times, and a count must be kept of the number of cycles.

We need some initial settings; let us suppose that C(1) has been set to 1 and C(2) to n, and that locations (3) and (4) have been cleared. The successive products will be accumulated, as they are computed, in location (3), which will eventually hold the final answer, S_n. After the first cycle it will hold a_1b_1, after the second $(a_1b_1 + a_2b_2)$, and so on. After r cycles, location (3) will hold $a_1b_1 + a_2b_2 \ldots + a_rb_r$, which it will be convenient to denote by S_r. The cycles will be counted in location (4) and the jump instruction used to stop the calculation when the loop has been traversed n times. (See Figure 43 – ignoring (5) for the present.)

(0)	(1)	(2)	(3)	(4)	(5)
0	1	n	S_{r-1}	$(r-1)$	W

Figure 43. Contents of storage locations in statistical program at the start of the rth cycle.

Let us consider the situation during the rth cycle, when we shall be multiplying a_r by b_r and adding the product into location (3). The mathematical formulation of this procedure is

$$S_{r-1} + a_rb_r = S_r \ (r = 1, 2 \ldots n) \text{ where } S_0 = 0.$$

Now a_r and b_r are stored in locations $(200 + r - 1)$ and $(300 + r - 1)$ respectively and so we arrive at the following group of instructions, with the first instruction stored in (100) as usual.

		C(A) during rth cycle	
→100	Copy C($200 + r - 1$) in A	a_r	⎫
101	Multiply C(A) by		Form next
	C($300 + r - 1$)	a_rb_r	product and
102	Add C(3) to C(A)	$S_{r-1} + a_rb_r$	add to C(3)
		$= S_r$	⎭
103	Copy C(A) in (3)		
104	Copy C(4) in A	$r - 1$	⎫ Add 1 to
105	Add C(1) to C(A)	r	⎬ counter
106	Copy C(A) in (4)		⎭
107	Subtract C(2) from C(A)	$r - n$	⎫ Test if further
└108	Jump to (100) if		⎬ cycle needed.
	C(A) is negative		⎭

A scrutiny of these instructions at once reveals a difficulty. The addresses specified in the two first instructions depend on the value of r, and so change from one cycle to the next. Clearly this will not do. Some provision must be made in the program for increasing both of these addresses by unity during each cycle. This can be done quite simply by exploiting the fact that instructions are coded as sets of digits, just as numbers are. Instruction-words, like number-words, can thus be altered by performing arithmetical operations on them. Clearly what is needed in the present case is to arrange matters so that the patterns of digits which represent the two 'awkward' instructions are modified arithmetically each time they are obeyed. To see exactly how this is done we must go farther into the way in which an instruction is coded as a set of digits.

The instructions discussed in this chapter may be regarded as being made up of two parts:

   (i) the specification of the type of operation: addition, jump, etc.,

   (ii) the address of the number to be operated upon.

Since an instruction is coded as a set of digits, the simplest scheme is to code each part of it as a set of digits, and then simply run the two sets together. To fix ideas, let us suppose we have a total of 1,000 storage locations, the addresses of which are numbered from 0 to 999. Three decimal digits are thus needed to specify an address. The obvious method of coding is to represent the address of storage location (n) by the digits of the number n.

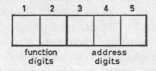

Figure 44. The structure of an instruction-word.

The other part of the instruction-word – that specifying the type of operation – must also be coded as a set of digits. Let us suppose that two decimal places are allocated for this purpose; this allows up to 100 different basic operations – an ample

131

provision. These two digits we shall call the *operation part* of the instruction. An instruction will thus be coded as an ordered set of five decimal digits, as shown in Figure 44.

It will be convenient at this stage to allot digits to each of the instructions that have so far been introduced. This is done in the list below; it must be emphasized that the allocation is quite arbitrary.

<blockquote>
01 Add C(n) to C(A)
02 Subtract C(n) from C(A)
03 Multiply C(A) by C(n)
04 Divide C(A) by C(n)
05 Copy C(n) in A
06 Print C(n)
07 Copy C(A) in (n)
08 Tape to (n)
09 Jump to (n) if C(A) is negative
10 Stop. (Address part irrelevant.)
</blockquote>

Thus the instruction

'Copy C(A) in (125)' is coded as '07, 125'.

We can now return to the problem of how to vary the addresses specified in the first two instructions of our program. We need to alter these instruction-words during each cycle in such a way that each of the specified addresses is increased by unity. Reference to Figure 44 shows that this entails adding a 1 in the fifth digital position of each instruction-word. Now let W denote a word which consists of a 1 in this position and zeros elsewhere – that is $W = 00,001$ – and suppose that this word has been stored in location (5) as part of the setting-up process. To solve our problem there must be incorporated in the loop additional instructions whose effect is to add the word W to the instructions stored in (100) and (101). The group of instructions forming this loop now appears as follows. The set of decimal digits representing the coded form of each instruction (sometimes termed the *detailed coding* of the program) is shown on the right.

Now the effect of obeying the three instructions stored in (104) to (106) is to add the word W to the instruction-word that is stored in (100), thereby increasing by 1 the address that is specified by

		C(A) during rth cycle	Detailed coding	Remarks
→100	[Copy C(200) in A]	a_r	05,200 ⎫	Form next
101	[Mult. C(A) by C(300)]	$a_r b_r$	03,300 ⎪	product and
102	Add C(3) to C(A)	$S_{r-1} + a_r b_r = S_r$	01,003 ⎬	add to C(3)
103	Copy C(A) in (3)		07,003 ⎭	
104	Copy C(100) in A	$05,200 + (r-1)$	05,100 ⎫	Add 1 to
105	Add C(5) to C(A)	$05,200 + r$	01,005 ⎬	address of
106	Copy C(A) in (100)		07,100 ⎭	word in (100)
107	Copy C(101) on A	$03,300 + (r-1)$	05,101 ⎫	Add 1 to
108	Add C(5) to C(A)	$03,300 + r$	01,005 ⎬	address of
109	Copy C(A) in (101)		07,101 ⎭	word in (101)
110	Copy C(4) in A	$r-1$	05,004 ⎫	Add 1 to
111	Add C(1) to C(A)	r	01,001 ⎬	counter
112	Copy C(A) in (4)		07,004 ⎭	
113	Subtract C(2) from C(A)	$r-n$	02,002 ⎫	Test if further
└─114	Jump to (100) if C(A) is negative		09,100 ⎭	cycle needed

that instruction. At the start of the rth cycle, the word W will have been added $(r-1)$ times, and so the instruction stored in (100) will contain the pattern of digits '05, $200 + (r-1)$'.

This word represents the instruction 'Copy C($200 + r - 1$) in A'. It is this instruction that will actually be obeyed during the rth cycle and will cause a_r, stored in ($200 + r - 1$), to be copied into the accumulator. The instructions in (107) to (109) effect a similar modification of the address specified by the instruction in (101). Thus successive pairs of numbers (a_1, b_1), (a_2, b_2), and so on, will be selected in turn during successive cycles of the complete calculation. (The experienced programmer will notice that one instruction could be saved by setting $-n$ initially in location (4).)

It will be noted that the instructions stored in (100) and (101) have been enclosed in square brackets. This is a programming convention to indicate that an instruction is obeyed not in the form in which it is written, but in a modified form which is determined by some other instructions in the program.

The facility of being able to modify instructions during the course of a calculation is of the greatest importance. Most programs contain one or more groups of instructions which are executed a number of times during the course of the calculation, but which operate on different numbers each time. If, as in this case, these numbers are stored sequentially in blocks of consecutive storage locations, the addresses specified in certain loop-instructions must be modified in a regular manner each time such instructions are obeyed. Nowadays most computer designers are prepared to provide extra equipment for the express purpose of making it easy for the programmer to deal with this kind of modification, and the term *modify* and derived terms are used exclusively in connexion with such equipment.

One other matter remains to be discussed – the method of supplying the computer with the numerical data it needs. Although such a simple program as this would, in practice, normally form part of a larger calculation, it is instructive to consider how it could be made self-contained. We have in fact two kinds of initial data: first, the sets of numbers a_1, a_2, . . . a_n and b_1, b_2, . . . b_n; and secondly, the three numbers 1, n, and W. They must all be punched on tape and read into the computer by means of input instructions. The straightforward method used in the squares program clearly suffices for the second group. To read in the first group in this way would need $2n$ successive input instructions. This is not only extravagant in instructions, but is fundamentally unacceptable for the following reason. We want our program to be as general as possible; in particular, we want to be able to carry out the calculation whatever may be the value of n – the quantity which specifies how many numbers there are in each set. Each time the program is used a specific numerical value of n will be supplied to the computer as part of the data of the particular calculation. The number of input instructions cannot be allowed to depend on n, so we must introduce repetitive loops into the input part of the program. We shall again need to modify addresses, but this time those of the two input instructions, one for reading in an a and the other for a b.

As the complete program is somewhat lengthy (forty-two instructions), we shall not write it out in full, but give instead the

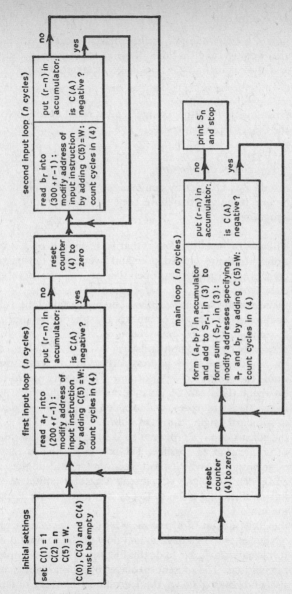

Figure 45. Flow diagram of statistical calculation.

flow diagram (Figure 45). We assume that all storage locations are cleared initially, and that the following sequence of words – the data of the calculation – is punched on a length of tape:

$$1, n, W, a_1, a_2, \ldots a_n, b_1, b_2, \ldots b_n.$$

Note that location (4) (the 'counter') must be set to zero before any of the three loops is entered.

The technique of programming

We conclude this chapter by summarizing the main points of programming technique that have been illustrated in our three simple programs.

(i) The use of repetitive *loops;* that is, of groups of instructions which are obeyed over and over again during the course of a calculation, operating on different numbers each time;

(ii) the use of the *jump instruction* whereby the calculation can be directed to take one or other of two alternative courses, the choice between them being governed by numbers generated by the computer itself;

(iii) the *modification* of the address parts of instructions stored inside the computer by performing arithmetical operations on them. This can be done because both numbers and instructions are represented in coded form by sets of digits of standard length, known as *words;*

(iv) the construction of programs so as to have as wide a range of application as possible. The reason for this is that a large program – which may take several months to prepare and check thoroughly – represents a sizeable capital investment and should be made to pay its way by being used to the utmost;

(v) the construction of a *flow diagram* which gives a picture of the general organization and flow of the computation. It is usually advisable to do this first for all but the simplest calculations. The subsequent stages of programming consist of breaking down the calculation into an ordered sequence of basic operations, each such operation corresponding to a single instruction; allocating storage locations to all the instructions and numbers of the calculation; and coding each instruction as a set of digits. We shall discuss in Chapter 9 how some of these stages may be curtailed, or eliminated altogether, by the use of more sophisticated procedures.

Now that we have some idea of what a sequential digital computer must be able to do, we can discuss (in the next two chapters) how it does it.

7. DIGITAL STORAGE

An automatic sequential digital computer, if it is to be able to deal with large computations, needs a store of large capacity. The von Neumann group in their 1945 report (p. 62) suggested about a thousand words (each of about ten decimal digits) – fifty times as much as in ENIAC. Most modern computers can store at least ten thousand words; with some of them, the figure rises to millions.

Large storage capacity is not enough, however; high speed of operation is also essential. There are many simple and important problems that would take years to solve on a computer of the speed of ENIAC, even though it could get through several thousand arithmetical operations every second. Now because a sequential computer needs only a small number of adders and multipliers, no reasonable expense need to spared in their construction. Nowadays the arithmetical circuits themselves can be made to work a thousand times faster than those of ENIAC. This is pointless, however, unless the store can supply instruction-words, and supply or accept numbers, at comparable speeds.

The speed of operation of a store is measured by the time interval between the control unit (Figure 37) presenting a demand for a particular address to the store, and the completion of the ensuing operation of reading a word from this address, or of writing a word in it. This is called the *access time* of the store. It is feasible nowadays to make a store to hold a few words with an access time of a small fraction of a microsecond. The cost of a store, however, is proportional to its capacity, and the circuits used for this order of speed are too expensive to be used for providing a store of anything like the size that is needed. Thus it is the store, not the arithmetical circuits, which usually limits the computing speed.

The computer designer chooses a type of store that will give him a satisfactory compromise between cheapness and speed, for the necessary capacity. He usually provides, in fact, more than one type; a store of relatively small capacity and short access time (the *high-speed* or *working store*), and a much larger capacity store having a longer access-time (the *auxiliary* or *backing store*). This expedient is called *two-level storage*; one may regard the punched cards or punched tape that are used for input and output as a third level of storage – of still greater access time but of virtually unlimited capacity. Since no existing storage system is both cheaper and faster than all the others, we shall have to describe several systems, based on diverse physical principles, in order to outline current practice.

Any storage system which involves mechanical moving parts, such as the counter wheels in A.S.C.C. or the feed mechanisms in punched-card or punched-tape machines, is too slow for modern requirements. On the other hand, the method used in ENIAC, which needed large numbers of valves, was too expensive, and, more important, would have been unable to provide a much bigger store without intolerably frequent breakdowns.

It is worth pointing out that a valve which goes wrong on one pulse in a hundred will possibly escape notice in a television set, in a radar set, or even in a simultaneous computer. In a sequential computer, on the other hand, it could well mean that less than three numbers could be dealt with without error, an impossible situation where each step necessarily depends on the accuracy of the last. To be useful, a sequential computer must at least be able to perform on the average, say, ten million steps without a fault. A rate of malfunctioning of this magnitude can just about be dealt with by frequent checks, and by re-computing incorrect results, without slowing the computation too drastically. For a computer such as ENIAC, performing 5,000 steps a second, this means no more than one fault every half an hour. Assuming that only the valves were responsible for faults, which is an optimistic view, this means that each valve out of the 18,000 was allowed to misbehave on the average no more than once in 10,000 hours. This was about the length of the life of a valve of superior quality, so clearly the ENIAC was about as big as was reasonable. Its high-speed store held a mere twenty numbers; some fifty times less than what is today thought to be the absolute minimum. Thus the need for a new storage system was clear.

An early system – the delay-line store

A decimal digit in ENIAC had two different representations: as the state of a ten-stage counter in the store itself, and as the number of pulses in a train of pulses when the digit was in transit between one store and another. The first modern storage system to be developed, from a suggestion by the von Neumann group, uses the pulse train representation not only for the transfer of digits, but also in the storage medium itself. The pulse train repeatedly traverses a closed path, the time taken to do this being longer than the duration of the pulse train, so that its head is kept clear of its tail. Now the time taken to traverse any ordinary circuit is far too small for the purpose, so an extra delay is necessary. The component responsible for this is called a *delay line*.

To obtain a long enough delay, it is necessary to use something other than the propagation of electrical energy, which always occurs at a speed comparable with the speed of light. One can use the propagation of mechanical vibrations, of a type similar to sound vibrations, and to do this, the earlier delay lines consisted of a tube about five feet long, filled with mercury, with a crystal of quartz at each end. The function of the quartz at the input end was to convert from electrical pulses to pulses of mechanical vibration, and at the output end to convert back. The delay in passing from one end of the tube to the other was about one thousandth of a second (1,000 microseconds); this time, although brief, is about two hundred thousand times as long as the time an electrical pulse would take to cover the same distance.

In the passage through a delay line the strength of the pulse is very much reduced and its shape is degraded as shown in Figure 46. The amount of loss of steepness of the edges of a pulse determines how wide the input pulses must be to obtain adequate output pulses and also how far apart adjacent input pulses must be to avoid adjacent output pulses running together too much. The mercury delay line mentioned above permits the use of a pulse repetition time of one microsecond (Figure 46), so the train of pulses can contain up to about 1,000 pulses. These are divided into groups, and used to represent more than one digit.

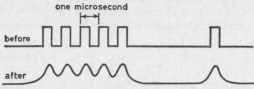

Figure 46. Degradation of pulse shape in passing through a delay line.

A delay-line storage system is shown in Figure 47. The pulses coming out of the delay line are first amplified, and then pass to the pulse reshaping unit. This unit allows a new clean pulse from the oscillator to pass into the delay-line input if, and only if, a pulse arrives at the reshaping unit from the amplifier. This action – known as *pulse regeneration* – removes any possibility of cumulative degradation or change in timing of the pulses; the pulse which feeds the delay-line input is always the same in size, shape, and timing.

All the stored groups of pulses are available in turn at the output of the pulse reshaping unit, for transfer to other units of the computer. In order to put a new group into the delay line in place of an existing one, the switch shown on the left of the diagram is operated at the instant when the first pulse of the group to be superseded is about to enter the delay line, and restored just after the last pulse of the group has passed. Providing the new group has been available at the input terminal during this period, it will have replaced the old. The switch has to work very much faster than an orthodox switch and so an electronic switch is used, the principle of which will be explained in the next chapter.

The delay-line store is still in use in some smaller computers, especially desk-top electronic calculators, because it is quite cheap. Nowadays the delaying medium is usually a solid wire, instead of mercury, with advantages in size and cost, while for very short pulses it is possible to use fused quartz (i.e. non-crystalline quartz). In each case, mechanical vibrations are propagated.

The access time of the delay-line store depends on where the desired group of pulses happens to be in the delay line when a demand is raised. The demand may occur (by luck, or by good judgement on the part of the programmer) just before the group appears at the output terminal (Figure 47). In this case the access

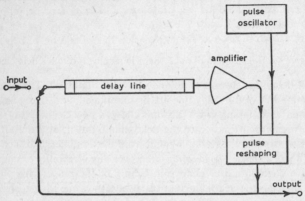

Figure 47. Delay line used for storage.

time is merely the time necessary for all the desired pulses to appear consecutively at the output terminal. On the other hand, the demand may occur just as the group of pulses has been launched into the delay line and is therefore inaccessible. The access time is then the complete circulation time of the store. It frequently happens that the programmer must vary the address he calls for, in the manner of the statistical program of the last chapter or in some less systematic way. In this case, to form an estimate of how long his program will run, he takes the average of the range of access times. For a delay-line store, with 1,000 positions and a pulse repetition time of 1 microsecond, this average would be about 500 microseconds; a long time by today's standards.

Binary notation

One way – perhaps the most obvious – to use a delay line would be to mark off the pulse positions in groups of nine and to let

142

each group represent one decimal digit. The value of the digit would be given by the number of pulses, the rest of the pulse positions in the group being left vacant. This would be wasteful. It turns out that the correct thing is to use one pulse position to represent one digit. Now since there are only two alternative conditions possible for one pulse position – pulse, or no pulse – the digit can be allowed to have only two possible values. We must therefore use the binary notation mentioned on p. 20.

Each binary digit position must have only twice the value or *weight* of the previous position, instead of ten times, as with normal decimal representation. Instead of units, tens, hundreds, etc., digits, we have units, twos, fours, eights, sixteens, etc., digits. The rules for the addition of two binary numbers are therefore very simple: 1 plus 0 is 1, while 1 plus 1 is 0 and 1 to carry. This suffices to build up the table below by starting with zero and successively adding 1 in the units position.

Binary	Decimal	Binary	Decimal
0	0	10000	16
1	1	10001	17
10	2	10010	18
11	3	10011	19
100	4	10100	20
101	5	10101	21
110	6	10110	22
111	7	10111	23
1000	8	11000	24
1001	9	11001	25
1010	10	11010	26
1011	11	11011	27
1100	12	11100	28
1101	13	11101	29
1110	14	11110	30
1111	15	11111	31

Representation of numbers in binary and decimal notations

This table shows that five binary digits can represent 2^5 (i.e. 32) different numbers. Nine pulse positions in a delay-line store can therefore represent 2^9 numbers (0 to 511), instead of a mere ten numbers (0 to 9) as with the 'obvious' system first mentioned.

With this system we would therefore need twenty-seven pulse positions to cater for the numbers 0 to 999, whereas ten would suffice if we use binary notation, because 2^{10} is slightly more than one thousand. The storage space required, and the time to deal with one number, are thus reduced by a factor of 2.7, a worthwhile advantage. Because 2^{10} is approximately 10^3, we may say that three decimal digits are approximately equivalent to ten binary digits. (It is customary, by the way, to contract 'binary digits' to 'bits'.) A numeral of thirty or forty *bits* can therefore express a number with a precision equivalent to nine or twelve significant figures (that is, decimal digits).

We digress to mention a possible everyday application of binary notation. Sticking a postage stamp on a letter or parcel, or not sticking it on, is a binary action. By keeping at hand stamps in denominations of 1p, 2p, 4p and 8p one can make up any amount from 1p to 15p by using at most four stamps.

In digital computers the advantages of binary notation are decisive, and it is universally used, although sometimes in a modified form. The principal reason is that in order to achieve the high reliability needed in a sequential computer, it is desirable to restrict the physical quantity that is used to represent a digit to one of two values only. Thus in the delay-line store we use pulses that are either of full amplitude or of zero amplitude. This gives the biggest possible tolerance for spurious changes in the physical quantity, due to gradual loss of performance, maladjustment, changes in the outside temperature, and so on. With two-valued physical quantities, to use anything other than binary notation results in less than the maximum economy – both in equipment and the time taken to perform a given operation, as is exemplified by the delay-line store. A lesser, but important, advantage is the simplicity of binary arithmetic; in multiplication, for example, we need only the nought times table and the once times table. On the other hand, binary notation suffers from one major disadvantage – human beings do not use it! In fact this is not so serious as it might seem; what it means is that when numbers are supplied to a computer by a man, or vice versa, a conversion between binary and decimal notation is necessary; or even between binary and some queer mixed-radix notation, such as that used for weeks, days, hours, and minutes. Fortunately, it is usually possible to place the burden of this conversion on the computer itself. The input and output conversions can usually be treated as quite a small addition to the main computation, and the computer does not need to have extensive special input and output equipment in order to deal with decimal digits.

A group of four binary digits can be used to represent one decimal digit, as shown below. This is merely the first ten rows of the previous table, with the spaces on the left filled up with *non-significant zeros* to bring each binary number up to four digit-positions.

Binary	Decimal	Binary	Decimal
0000	0	0101	5
0001	1	0110	6
0010	2	0111	7
0011	3	1000	8
0100	4	1001	9

A Binary-Coded Decimal Representation

Other *binary-coded decimal* representations are also used, but there is always some sacrifice in the efficiency with which numbers are represented. The code shown above is not, in fact, very wasteful. To represent three decimal digits it uses twelve binary digits. This compares with the previously mentioned ten binary digits needed in straightforward binary notation; so the wastage in digit-positions amounts to only about twenty per cent.

There is no difficulty in converting between binary-coded decimal and binary representations (we may assume for the moment that the computer can add, multiply, and divide in binary notation). Take as an example the number 873, which would be presented to the computer as 1000; 0111; 0011 for conversion to binary. The first operation specified by the conversion program is to multiply the binary-coded representation of the most significant (hundreds) digit by ten, that is, by 1010. In our example, this yields 1 010 000. To this is added the next (tens) digit, giving 1 010 111. This result is again multiplied by 1010 (ten), giving 1 101 100 110, and the least significant (units) digit is added in, giving 1 101 101 001. This is the binary version of 873, as can be verified by adding up the powers of two corresponding to-the-non-zero digits, name 512, 256, 64, 32, 8, and 1.

For the reverse conversion, from binary to binary-coded decimal, the program causes the binary number to be divided repeatedly by ten. The remainder after each division is one of the required binary-coded decimal digits, starting this time with the least significant. Decimal digits in this coded form are sent to the output printer of the computer, which must print the corresponding decimal digit. The printer, and the keyboard machine used to prepare the input punched tape, are the only portions of the computing system which necessarily cannot work entirely in binary notation. These machines are very similar in principle to the corresponding portions of the teleprinter machines used in the Post Office for sending and receiving telegrams.

In some computers, current in about 1960, binary-coded decimal representation was used exclusively. They were intended primarily for the class of work where there are large quantities of input and output data – typically business data processing (p. 316). In this situation, the increased efficiency of purely binary arithmetic would be outweighed by the time consumed in conversion to and from binary representation.

As we shall see in Chapter 9, however, we cannot tolerate being restricted to only ten different digits in computer input and output data. Four binary digits allow sixteen different combinations (p. 143), and it would be possible to assign further symbols (such as $+$ $-$. , space) arbitrarily to some of the six combinations not used by the digits 0 to 9. This would be too restrictive: we require letters, as well as digits and symbols (collectively called *characters*), and to provide as many different combinations as this six binary digits (giving up to 64 different combinations) are necessary.

To these a seventh bit is often added for technical reasons. The equipment that handles the representations of characters is liable to faults which may cause errors in the character represented. A powerful technique for checking errors in digital representations is to add *redundancy* to each representation, in the form of an extra digit that partially repeats the original representation. By augmenting any binary representation by one extra bit it is possible to allow for the detection of one error anywhere in the augmented representation. The value of the extra bit juxtaposed to the original bits is systematically chosen in each particular case so as to make odd the total number of ones. For example, starting with the four different combinations of two bits, 00, 01, 10 and 11, we obtain 001, 010, 100 and 111, the extra bit being placed on the right. The extra bit is called a *parity bit*, and the odd number of ones in the aggregate is termed *odd parity*.* Clearly any single error in a representation would change the total number of ones from odd to even, so to test the representation for error, one merely counts the number of ones. If this is odd there is most probably no error, and one merely ignores the parity bit to obtain the original representation. If the number of ones is even, a repetition of the transmission or other operation that caused the error is necessary.

Of course, with only one parity bit, two errors, or in general, an even number of errors, are not detected. It is possible to use greater redundancy than just one extra bit – there exists for example a rather elegant encoding of sixteen different characters into seven-bit words. Since four bits are sufficient to specify sixteen different characters, the redundancy is three bits. Each word differs from all the other words in at least three digit places (not necessarily the same three for each pair of words, of course), so three errors in one word are necessary to cause an undetectable error in recognizing which character is intended, by comparison with a list of the sixteen correct words. If it is decided on the basis of statistics of observed error that more than one error is sufficiently improbable, then there are two design choices:

(a) to use seven-bit words, and when an incorrect word is received, replace it with that correct word that differs from it in only one digit place: of course, if two errors have in fact occurred, this correction is itself erroneous;

(b) to use five-bit words, i.e., the minimum of four bits plus a parity bit, so that errors are merely detected, and repetition of the operation is necessary for correction.

Alternative (b) needs in general only about five sevenths of the

*The alternative system that makes the total even is also possible (*even parity*).

time, or five sevenths of the cost, of alternative (a), and is much more common in practice.

Six bits plus a parity bit are therefore the normal way of representing a character, unless both upper and lower case letters are required, when seven plus parity are used. Internationally standardized codes are available for these cases, amongst others.

Stores based on magnetic recording

The successful development of magnetic sound-recording naturally led computer engineers to seek to apply the same techniques to their digital storage problems. The use of a moving magnetic medium – which may be a rotating drum or disc, or a length of tape – has, indeed, proved a most convenient means of storing large quantities of digital data at a reasonable cost. Nearly every contemporary computer has some kind of magnetic store – usually in the role of a backing store (p. 139).

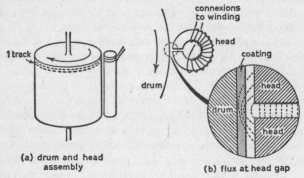

Figure 48. Magnetic drum.

Such a store consists basically of a thin layer (typically a half of one thousandth of an inch thick) of magnetizable material (called the *medium*), usually iron oxide, which is moved past a recording head (the *write head*). This latter is an electromagnet, and leaves a magnetized *track* in the medium. The direction of magnetization changes along the track in accordance with the changes in direction of the current in the write head, which correspond to the binary digits to be recorded. (Thus north-south magnetization might correspond to a 1 and south-north to a 0.) When the medium subsequently moves past a reproducing, or playback, head (the *read head*), a voltage is induced in the windings of this head by the changes in magnetization of the track, and from this voltage, after amplification, the original binary digits can be recovered.

For a magnetic drum (Figure 48), invented in 1947, the medium is coated on to the curved surface of a cylinder, typically nine inches in diameter and twelve inches long, which is spun at a steady speed (at 2,000 revolutions per minute, for example) by an electric motor. Numerous write and read heads are provided, the track associated with each pair of heads being a ring-shaped portion of the surface of the drum. One track on the drum is similar in some ways to a delay-line store and the time taken by the drum for one revolution corresponds to the circulation time of the delay-line store. During this time, all the stored digits are presented in sequence to the read head. It is easier with the drum than with the delay line to understand how the identity of a particular storage location is preserved, for on the drum a given storage location consists of a definite portion of the surface. One common arrangement is for the locations on one track to have consecutive addresses, differing in the less significant places, while the more significant digits of the address denote which track. For example, each track might consist of one hundred locations, the addresses on (say) track 17 running from 1700 to 1799. In this case, to serve all tracks, the numbers 0 to 99 can be marked round the periphery of the drum. Some means must be provided to read the marks in order to determine when a particular location is passing under the reading head. No new technique is needed for this purpose – the marks can be magnetic marks on one particular track set aside for storing addresses (the *address track*). An alternative arrangement is to mark a single bit with the value 1 on this track at the start of each storage location, and to count these marks electronically as they pass the read head. In this case, a special mark would be needed at location 0, to ensure that the counter started in synchronism with the addresses when the store was switched on.

In principle, the delay-line store does not need something which corresponds to an address track. Provided the delay is stable to within, say, one tenth of a digit period, and providing an equally stable oscillator is available, it is only necessary to count pulses from the oscillator in an electronic counter, and to use the state of the counter as an indication of which storage location is currently available for access. That is to say, the division of the total circulation time into digit and word periods is imposed on the store from an external source. This is satisfactory because the delay-line store is a *volatile store* – its content is lost when the computer is switched off – and the allocation of addresses can legitimately be done afresh when it is next switched on.

For a magnetic disc store, the magnetic material is coated on to the upper and lower surfaces of a disc about the shape and size of an L.P. gramophone record; over 100 tracks are arranged as concentric circles on each surface. Ten discs are assembled one above the other on a central driving pillar with a gap between each one and the next to allow space for the head assemblies. To reduce the number of heads, each with its individual electronic circuits, the heads can be arranged to move radially, so that each head has access to several different tracks on the same surface. It is a simple extension of this idea to make the heads capable of being completely retracted, allowing the set of discs to be easily removed and replaced by an operator. An advantage of both drum and disc store is that they are *nonvolatile*; this means that no time need be spent in loading standard data into the store when the computer is switched on; the data is still there from yesterday. The removable set of discs can further be used to change rapidly a large volume of the data available to the computer, by replacing one set of discs with another.

The write head on a track of a magnetic disc or drum is only used when it is necessary to store fresh data, another consequence of the non-volatile nature of the store. Since the recording is a binary process, the medium is always magnetized to saturation in one direction or the other, so, in contrast with tape recorders for speech and music, a separate erase head is unnecessary. To ensure that the timing of access to a storage location is the same whether for writing or for reading, it is convenient for the same head to be used for both purposes, with electronic switching to connect it either to the input of a reading amplifier or to the output of a writing amplifier.

The main advantage of the magnetic disc or drum store is its low cost; its main disadvantage is that it is comparatively slow. The average access time, which for a drum is just over half the period of rotation, is usually much greater than that of a delay line. Thus a drum rotating at 2,000 revolutions per minute would have an average access time of about fifteen milliseconds, as compared with about half a millisecond for a typical delay-line store. The average access time for a disc is similar to that for a drum, providing the head assembly does not have to be moved to pick up the new address. If this is not the case, the time increases to about 200 milliseconds. On the other hand, each track on the disc or drum can store more than one delay line (e.g. 2,000 bits or fifty words of forty bits), and the drum can have several hundred tracks, while the disc store can have several thousand. This is why the magnetic disc or drum is often used as a backing store in conjunction with a more expensive, faster, working store of much smaller capacity. The programmer tries to arrange matters so that access to the disc store is deferred until substantially a whole track-full of data is needed and can be transferred to the working store in one revolution. This reduces the effective access time to only one word period, and the performance of the computer approximates to that of a computer with a store of the speed of the working store, and the capacity of the disc store. Needless to say, the programmer does not always achieve this in practice.

Although magnetic recording on tape had been done for many years, it was not applied to early computers, despite the enormous storage capacity that it offered. (For example, about a million numbers on one reel of tape.) Two reasons for this delay may be suggested. The first is that magnetic tape stores, having long access times (e.g. two minutes), are mainly useful for the class of work in which one has a large volume of data and only a modest amount of computation on each item of data; wages calculations, for example. In the early days, however, interest in sequential computers was concentrated on their ability to carry out prodigiously laborious calculations on relatively small amounts of

151

data. The second reason is that the difficulties of making the magnetic tape recording process good enough for sequential computers were seriously underestimated. For example, tape which is satisfactory for recording speech and music is found to have large numbers of small flaws, each one enough to prevent several digits being recorded correctly.

Figure 49 illustrates a typical magnetic tape unit. The tape transport has two reels, each 10½ inches in diameter, carrying 2,400 feet of tape. One reel is permanently mounted in the unit, the other is changed by the operator as required after the tape has been rewound on to it. The new tape is then led into the permanent reel, threading the head and tape drive assembly. In operation, each of the reservoirs holds a length of tape to act as a buffer between the reel drive and the tape drive. A constant-speed capstan drives the tape between the reservoirs and a pinch roller forces the tape into contact with the capstan when necessary. Disengagement of the pinch roller and subsequent application of the tape brake stops the tape, and a complementary drive and brake assembly (not shown in the Figure) provides for reverse motion. The reservoir levels are maintained by the independent

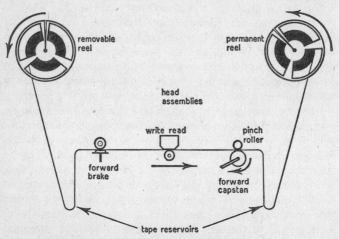

Figure 49. Schematic Diagram of Magnetic Tape Transport. (Arrangements for backward motion not shown).

servo systems which drive the corresponding reels; the devices that sense how much tape is in the reservoir can take various forms, and are not indicated in the diagram.

The tape runs in contact with the heads in contrast with discs and drums, the heads of which are spaced about half a thousandth of an inch away from the surface. The tape passes the write head before the read head in forward motion, so that data written on the tape can be read shortly afterwards, while writing continues. The construction of the write head does not permit it to be used during reverse motion, but there is no such restriction on reading. The head assembly includes a number of write heads, across the width of the tape, and an equal number of read heads. This provides for a number of channels, each with a write head and a read head, on one track out of several across the width of the tape. Digital tape units usually store data in groups of seven, eight, or sometimes nine bits since this number is adequate to represent a character as noted above. The bits in a group are written on all tracks simultaneously, on one 'row' across the tape. Shortly afterwards, a parity check takes place on the read head outputs, and if this fails, the tape is backspaced and the data rewritten.

A number of characters written consecutively along the tape forms a *block* of data, and is separated from adjacent blocks by an unused gap. The minimum length of this *inter-block gap* is the sum of the tape stop and start distances plus the distance between the read and write heads. This allows the forward tape motion to be stopped after the last character of a block has been read, and then restarted so as to reach nominal speed before writing the first character of the next block. The gap therefore enables the unit to operate intermittently, and to provide access to consecutive blocks on demand; one block is the unit for data transfer. To keep this gap small, rapid starting and stopping is essential, and the tape acceleration can amount to 500 g. The tape reservoir is necessary to isolate the rather heavy reels from violent manoeuvres.

In spite of the precautions against error that are built into magnetic tape units, dust must be rigorously excluded from the room where they are installed as otherwise it would get between the tape and the heads. This is one reason why computer operators benefit from an air-conditioned working environment. Tape units are complex and elaborate precision machines, and the cost of the ten or twenty units in a large computer installation is a large fraction of the total.

Coordinate stores

At the same time as the mercury delay line was being incorporated in some of the early computers, a completely new storage system was under development in the Electro-Technical Laboratory at Manchester University. This was one of several projects for the use of a cathode-ray tube as a store and is known as the *Williams-tube store*, after Professor F.C. Williams who led the work. It is a volatile store since the bits are represented by the electric charges on small areas of the screen of the cathode-ray tube, and in the absence of regular regeneration these would gradually leak away. The bits of one word are stored on one row, out of numerous rows, arranged in a rectangular array of small storage areas. The beam of electrons in the cathode-ray tube is used for both reading and writing, and can be caused to scan one row just as readily as another, so the access time of the store does not depend on which address is selected. This is a great help to the programmer, since it enables him to specify his addresses in either a systematic or a random manner, whichever is the more convenient in the particular case. This type of store is therefore called a *random-access store*.

The Williams-tube store was used in several models of computers – British, American, Swedish, and Russian. However it was superseded after a few years, about 1955, by a cheaper random access store, known as the *core store*. This is now used in nearly every sequential digital computer, and so we shall describe how it works in some detail.

By comparison with the stores so far described, the core store is very simple in concept. Each bit is stored in its individual magnetic core, a small ring-shaped piece of ferro-magnetic material, typically about 0.03 inch in diameter with a 0.02 inch hole in the middle – that is about half the size of a letter o in this typeface. When a large enough current is passed along a wire through the hole, the core is magnetized to saturation; when the current is switched off, the core remains magnetized. Current in the opposite direction would leave the core magnetized to saturation in the opposite direction (Figure 50(a)). The two states of remanent magnetization represent a stored zero or a stored one. Note that the value zero need not be represented by zero magnetization; it is only necessary to have two different magnetic states. Positive and negative states are twice as different as positive and zero states, which is so much the better.

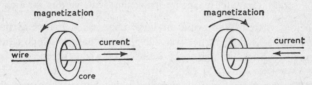

Figure 50(a). Alternative directions of current and magnetization in a core.

To find out whether a 0 or a 1 has been stored, a second wire is threaded through the hole in the core. This is called a *sense wire* because it senses, or reads, the value of the stored bit, the first wire being the *write wire*. To read the state of the core, a current is passed along the write wire in such a direction as to write 0. If this causes little change in magnetization because the core was already storing 0, then only a small voltage is induced between the ends of the sense wire. If on the other hand, it causes a large change in magnetization, because the core was storing 1, then a much bigger voltage (typically 50 millivolts) is induced. This is illustrated by Figure 50(b).

There are two branches to this graph, one representing the behaviour when the current is growing more positive, and the other when it is growing more negative, as indicated by the arrows. The point *A* represents the magnetization after negative current has recorded a 0, and the point *C* that after positive current has recorded a 1, in each case when the write wire current has again become zero. Point *D* represents the condition when 0

155

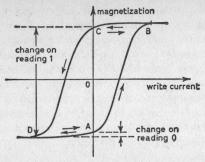

Figure 50(b). Graph of magnetization against write-current for a core.

is being written, with small or large changes of magnetization from points *A* or *C* respectively. It is these changes which cause a small or large voltage to be induced between the ends of the sense wire.

When the current in the write wire is switched off, however, the magnetization is represented by point *A*, irrespective of what it was before. This means that the stored digit has been lost from the core during reading, which for this reason is called *destructive reading*.* Arrangements must therefore be made to store the digit temporarily in some other way, preparatory to re-writing it in the core immediately after it has been read. What this means is that if, on reading, the stored value turns out to be 1, then the current in the write wire, which is switched off at the end of the reading process, must be switched on and off again in the opposite direction, so as to regain point *C* via point *B*.

The remarks made so far apply to one core; however, reading and writing arrangements must, in practice, be shared by a large number of cores, in order to reduce the cost of the complete store. When we shortly come to this topic, the relevance of the following artifice will be seen. The write wire is replaced by two write wires, each of which carries half the necessary current, called a *half write-current*, the total of the two being the *full write-*

---

*The concept is applicable principally to non-volatile storage (p. 150); a magnetic disc store is an example of *non-destructive reading*. The names 'destructive' and 'non-destructive read-out' are sometimes used ('*DRO*' and '*NDRO*').

current. The crucial thing is what happens when only one half write-current flows – virtually nothing. To achieve such a desired state of inactivity required years of development effort!

Thus, in Figure 51, switching either half write-current, by itself, on and off again in the positive direction causes a transition from A to E and back to A, or from C to F and back to C. Only if both half write-currents are present together does a transition to B occur, whether from C or A, with reversion always to C on switching off. This is an example of what is generally called a *threshold* effect.

The material of which the core is made is similar in physical properties to a ceramic, although it is black in colour; in particular it is a good insulator, unlike most magnetic materials which are metallic and hence good conductors. It is called a *square-loop* material, because its graph (Figure 51) can be approximated by a shape with square corners. This is the property which was sought so patiently by American research workers, and which makes writing possible by a threshold operation.

The cores are made on an automatic machine and are then tested individually on another automatic machine.

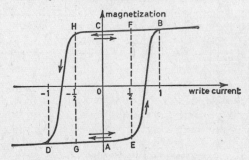

Figure 51. Graph of magnetization against write-current for a square-loop core.

The next step towards the complete store is to consider a set of, say, 4,096 cores, arranged in a square 64 by 64, each core being threaded by two write wires, designated x and y. (A similar 4 by 4 arrangement is shown in Figure 52(a)). This is called a *storage plane* or a *matrix plane.* When a half write-current passes

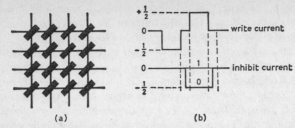

Figure 52 (a). Matrix of storage cores, showing write wires only.
(*b*) Write and inhibit currents.

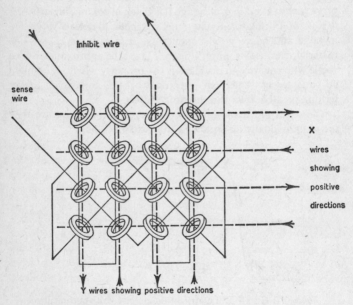

Figure 52 (c). Practical Method of wiring a core plane.

along one only of the sixty-four *x* wires and another half write-current along one only of the sixty-four *y* wires, writing will take place only in the single core threaded by both these wires, the remaining cores being unaffected. As long as the wire threads the hole, the angle at which it goes through makes no difference, so

158

two wires at right angles can each have the same effect. Thus, to obtain access to one core, two selection operations, in two co-ordinates, are necessary, giving rise to the name *co-ordinate store*. The advantage of this method of selecting one core out of 4,096 is that instead of 4,096 sources of write current, we need only 128; sixty-four for the x wires and sixty-four for the y wires. Since such sources are much more expensive than the cores themselves, a big economy results.

For a similar reason, it would be intolerable to have 4,096 read amplifiers, each connected to a sense wire through one core only. In fact, it turns out that it is sufficient to use a single read amplifier connected to a single sense wire, which threads all the 4,096 cores in turn. As stated before, the reading process includes writing, and since the desired core is selected in the writing process it is unnecessary to have further selection in the reading process.

We now describe the complete cycle of reading a selected core, and re-writing in it the binary digit that is removed in the reading. This is called the *read-write cycle*. First each of the two selected write wires carries a pulse of half write-current (called a *half write-pulse*) in the negative direction. The purpose of this is to drive the selected core to point D in Figure 51, while observing at the same time the voltage generated in the sense wire, to find out whether the transition to D is from C or from A, i.e., whether the core was storing 1 or 0. In principal, the unselected cores generate a negligible voltage in the sense wire. During the second part of the cycle, each of the two selected write wires carries a half write-pulse in the positive direction (Figure 52(b)). If, in fact, the selected core was storing a 1, the effect of the two successive pairs of half write-pulses is to drive it from C to A via D, and then from A back to C via B, leaving it in the original condition as required, and at the same time determining that this was the 1 condition.

If, on the other hand, the selected core was storing a 0, which is revealed during the first, negative, half write-pulses, something must be done to prevent the second, positive, half write-pulses from converting this to a 1. It is sufficient to make one of the two positive half write-pulses ineffective, so that in the complete read-write cycle, the core is driven from A to D and back to A, and then from A to E and back to A (Figure 51). For a reason which

159

will appear shortly, we use an extra wire (the fourth) to make the positive half write-pulses ineffective. This wire is called the *inhibit wire*, and it carries a negative half write-pulse if the core was found to be storing a 0, and no current if it was found to be storing a 1 (Figure 52(b)). The inhibit wire threads all the cores in the plane in the same direction as, say, the positive direction of the x write wires. Since it contributes a possible negative half write-pulse at a time when only positive half write-pulses are otherwise being generated, it cannot affect any of the unselected cores.

The sense wire cannot thread all the cores in the plane in the positive direction. The reason is that the loop in Figure 51 is not quite square, that is the lines HCF and GAE are not quite horizontal. This means that a half write-pulse producing a transition from A to G or C to H in Figure 51 induces a small voltage in the sense wire. This happens during reading in sixty-three cores on the selected x write wire, and another sixty-three on the selected y write wire. If the sense wire threaded all cores in the positive direction, as the inhibit wire must, 126 such small voltages would add up in it, and would swamp the genuine read voltage from the selected core. The sense wire is therefore threaded so that these small voltages oppose one another (see Figure 52(c)). This means that the comparatively large voltage pulse from a selected core storing a 1 may be of either polarity, depending on which core is selected. The read amplifier therefore incorporates a rectifier, so that it produces output pulses always of the same polarity.

Where the word length of the data to be stored is forty bits, the complete core store consists of forty planes, and with a plane of size 64 by 64 would hold 4,096 words. The planes are mounted one above the other, and each x write wire is connected in series with the other thirty-nine x write wires in similar positions in the other planes. The same applies to the y write wires, and each composite write wire follows a zigzag path through the planes. Thus all the forty bits of a particular word are selected simultaneously by the same two half write-pulses. The forty sense wires are kept separate and each one is connected to a voltage amplifier. Apart from contributing to the output from the store, each of these read amplifier outputs feeds a a circuit which controls the negative half write-pulse (Figure 52 (b)) to the inhibit wire of the same plane. It is now clear why the inhibit wire is necessary; if only one plane were served by the write wires, the positive half write-pulse on one of the two active write wires could be deleted when the core had to be left in the 0 state. When, however, the write wire serves several planes, the selected cores in different planes will not have the same requirements (unless all the digits in one word happen to have the same value, which is not the usual thing), so the write wire currents must not be altered. A separate device is therefore required for each plane, hence the inhibit wire.

The four wires threading each core are the classical way of meeting the requirements; however, assembly of core planes has not been completely automatized, and it represents a substantial fraction of their cost. A method of distinctly lower assembly cost, but comparable overall cost taking into account the greater amount of electronics it needs, requires only three wires – two write wires, and a combined sense and inhibit wire. Since the read and inhibit operations take place at different times in the read-write cycle, the circuits for these operations can be switched electronically to use a single wire in turn. There is a centre tap to this wire, which threads the cores in a rather elaborate way, and the two halves of the wire are used in parallel for inhibiting, and in series for sensing. Cores of 0.018 inch diameter are used today in the U.S.A. (i.e., not much bigger than a well-inked fullstop on this page) in order to decrease store cycle time, and even 0.012 inch cores are being considered, so clearly fewer wires is a big advantage.

The store arrangement just described, a square stack of core planes, is called a three-dimensional (3D) store. All the bits in one word, each bit in its own plane, are positioned vertically above one another, and the different words are arranged in a square shape in plan, like a bundle of straight sticks standing on end. A much simpler, much faster, and much more expensive arrangement is in concept a two-dimensional (2D) one, in which the words are arranged in one core plane, like sticks lying side by side. In this case the *y* wires are called the *word wires* (each threading all the cores of one word), and the *x* wires are called the *bit wires* (each threading all bits in the same position in all words). A full current pulse on one selected word wire performs the reading operation, the bit wires being used as sense wires; and then a half current pulse on the word wire, and a possible half current pulse on the bit wire (no separate inhibit wire is needed) complete the read-write cycle as in the 3D store.

An arrangement intermediate between the 2D and 3D stores is usually called a $2\frac{1}{2}$D store, although it is really just a double 2D store. The words are arranged conceptually in two layers, side by side in each layer. Each word wire in the bottom layer doubles back through the word above in the top layer, and similarly, each bit wire in the bottom layer doubles back through corresponding bits in the top layer, like the x and y wires in a rudimentary 3D array having only two core planes. The bit wires thread the cores in the two layers in opposite directions through the holes in the cores, compared with the word wires. Reading is performed by a negative half current pulse on the selected word wire, and simultaneous half current pulses on all bit wires, which are negative to select a word in the bottom layer, and positive for the top layer. A separate sense wire may be provided for highest speed, or the bit wire may be used, in which case the sensing operation is effectively a measurement of its impedance to the half current pulse. Writing, in the second half of the read-write cycle, is performed by a positive half-current pulse on the selected word wire, and, for the bottom layer, a simultaneous positive half current pulse on each bit wire where a 1 is to be rewritten, or no pulse for a 0. For the top layer, either a negative half current pulse, or no pulse, similarly.

This so-called $2\frac{1}{2}$D arrangement is not only rather faster than the 3D arrangement, it is also becoming competitive in cost because of developments in the fabrication of the word wire selection circuits.

In all these core stores, the digits of the selected word are all available from the store at the same time, from the forty read amplifier output terminals. This is called *parallel representation* of the word. It contrasts with the representation available from the delay line store, where the digits of a word are available one after the other at the same terminal. This is called *serial representation* of the word. Both have their uses, and methods exist for converting from one to the other. Obviously parallel representation is faster, but needs more equipment.*

To write a different word in one location in a core store, the same read-write cycle occurs, but in this case the output of the read amplifiers is ignored. Instead, the new word, which must be available in parallel form, controls the inhibit or bit wires.

The access time of a core store can be made very small (less than one fifth of a microsecond), since access is complete in the first part of the read-write cycle. Before a further word can be read, however, time must be allowed for the remainder of the cycle, and the interval between reading two words (the *cycle time* of the core store) varies from one half to six microseconds, depending on the size of the cores, the method of wiring, the quality of the components used and on the degree of elaboration of the circuits. In one computer, announced in late 1968, the cycle time of a small size core has apparently even been reduced to 0.275 microseconds, by a technique known as 'partial switching' of the cores. Sufficient time is allowed in the read-write cycle for only the inner portion of the core, surrounding the holes, to have its magnetization reversed (Figure 50(a)). Naturally this causes severe problems for the store designer.

Some computers use a newer technique for magnetic coordinate stores in which a layer of nickel-iron alloy of thickness from 4 to 30 millionths of an inch is deposited on a highly polished glass or metal substrate. In spite of the microscopic thickness of this layer, the terminology shows great restraint – the device is called merely a *thin-film* store. The film is usually *anisotropic* – that is it requires a higher current to magnetize it in one direction (the 'hard' direction) than in the perpendicular direction (the 'easy' direction). The easy direction has a square loop characteristic, but the hard direction characteristic shows only a very narrow loop.

The advantages of thin films, compared with cores, are four-fold: the switching time is ten to thirty times less, automatic fabrication is easier, reading is non-destructive, and the power consumption is lower.

*The Williams-tube store was also used as a coordinate store, with parallel representation of words. One cathode-ray tube corresponded to one plane of cores, and a similar read-write cycle took place.

In one embodiment, which results in a 2D store using destructive reading, of capacity of about 850,000 bits and a cycle time of half a microsecond (i.e. 500 *nanoseconds*), the thin film consists of two arrays of rectangular spots, sandwiching word, bit and sense wires in the form of thin tapes.

In other embodiments, the thin magnetic film is electroplated on to a wire, typically five-thousandths of an inch in diameter. These wires can be used as the combined bit/sense wires in an arrangement similar to the two-wire $2\frac{1}{2}$D core store; the word wires define some twenty-bit storage sites per inch of the plated wire. The word currents, acting in the hard direction, can produce adequate sense signals from remanent magnetization in the easy direction without destroying it, so that a cycle of only half the duration of a read-write cycle is possible when the stored word does not have to be altered. A cycle time of 500 nanoseconds has been achieved, and the non-destructive reading can effectively reduce this, say to 300 nanoseconds depending on the balance between reading and writing in the store that the programmer needs. One Japanese manufacturer has successfully woven together the bit and word wires on a loom, and an American firm has made read-only stores on a Jacquard loom, using punched cards to specify the data to be wired into the store. So, once again this ingenious device has assisted the development of computer technology.

This completes the description of the principal types of large-capacity store in current use. We should notice that it is not merely the physical process used for the actual storage which characterizes a store; even more important are the speed and cheapness of the means used to obtain access to a nominated address, out of a large number of addresses. The access methods we have noted, in order of increasing speed, are: (i) mechanical movement on demand (the magnetic tape and disc stores); (ii) regular circulation of the stored data (the delay-line, magnetic drum and disc stores); (iii) deflection of a beam of electrons to the location of the desired word (the Williams-tube store); (iv) selection of the desired word by electronic switching (the core and thin film stores).

8. THE DESIGN OF DIGITAL COMPUTERS

Once they had developed a large-capacity digital store – delay line, Williams-tube, or magnetic drum – the pioneer computer designers were able to go ahead with the development of the rest of the computer. For the store, the circuit techniques and physical principles are of first importance, but for the rest of the computer they are a minor matter. What is important is the concept of how the programmer is to specify the details of the computation – the subject of Chapter 6 – which must be worked out before the design of equipment can proceed. This demands close cooperation between two different specialists – the designer and the programmer. In the early days, such collaboration provided (and on occasions still does) an entertaining study in human behaviour, marked sometimes by disbelief and arrogance on the part of the electronic engineer, and by condescension and lack of appreciation on the part of the mathematician. In spite of some early difficulties, their liaison has proved most fruitful, and there is now a substantial body of theory of computer design.

In this chapter we shall describe first the properties and behaviour of some computer component parts which are universally used, paying hardly any attention to the circuit details. We shall then describe some standard sub-assemblies and techniques, and finally give an idea of how a complete computer works by taking a very simple one as an example.

The building bricks – logic elements

The control and arithmetic units of the digital computer (Figure 37) are constructed from the same basic circuits, some of which we shall now describe. One way to keep down the cost of a computer is to use only a few different types of component unit, but many specimens of each type. Fortunately, the digital computer lends itself to this treatment, as is shown by the numbers of similar units in the core store; for example, the read amplifiers. Although the number of one type of unit is not often large enough to justify the term 'mass production', substantial savings are achieved, if only because design and development costs can be spread more thinly. Other advantages are that spare units of each type can reasonably be held on the spot at the computer installation, and that the maintenance engineer can become more proficient in the rapid diagnosis of faults, since he has fewer different unit circuits to remember.

The way in which these numerous units are interconnected, and connected also to the store and the input and output equipment, is called the *logic* of the computer, and largely determines its properties and features. 'Logic' is not a very good word here, but it is in universal use, and apparently nobody can think of a better one. The units themselves are called *logic elements*, and a diagram which shows, in symbolic form, the logic of a computer or a part of one is called a *logic diagram*.

Some simple types of logic element have two binary digits at a time as inputs, from which they produce a single binary digit as output. For one type of element, the output is 1 only when both inputs are 1 and is 0 otherwise; this is called an *and-element*, or an *and-gate*. For a somewhat similar type, the output is 1 when either input, or both, is 1, and is 0 only when both inputs are 0; this is called an *or-element*. These inelegant names come from the terminology of formal logic, which deals with the truth or falsity of a proposition as a binary quantity. One can explain them as follows: if the inputs are designated x and y, then the output of an and-element is 1 when x *and* y are 1, and of an or-element when either x *or* y (or both) is 1.

Another simple element has one input bit only, the output bit being 0 when the input is 1, and vice-versa. Since this corresponds to the interchange of true and false in formal logic, it will not surprise the reader to learn that the element is called a *negater* or *not-element*.

In the circuits which are the physical embodiment of these elements, a certain voltage level usually represents the value 1 of a binary digit, and a different level represents the value 0. Two different values of current, or even two distinctive shapes of pulse, are sometimes used, but the normal thing is to take some value of a voltage, for example +5 volts with respect to earth, to represent 1; and 0 volts to represent 0.* The pulse or no pulse representation used in the delay-line store is of this nature. The voltage level

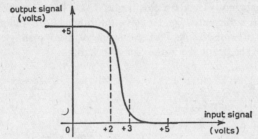

Figure 53. Graph of output signal versus input signal for a negater.

in the middle portion of the digit period (see, for example, Figure 57 (b) and (c), on p. 172) is what characterizes the value of the digit; what happens in the rest of the digit period is irrelevant. Figure 57(d) shows a reference signal consisting of a regular train of steep-sided pulses. This defines for the computing circuits the portion of the digit period when the train of digit pulses can be relied on to have attained, more or less, one of the two significant voltage levels. It is termed the *clock signal*.

A negater can be made from a single transistor circuit, arranged as an amplifier. What is basically required is a sign reversal (p. 91), so that as the input signal increases from, say, 0 to +5 volts, the output signal decreases from +5 volts to 0. The elaborate amplifier circuits used in analog computers are quite unnecessary here, because the two voltage levels representing 1 and 0 need not be defined with great accuracy, so long as they are sufficiently different. Direct coupling (p. 88) is often advantageous, however; so also is limiting of the output voltage (p. 93). By making the limiting output voltages 0 and +5, it is possible to arrange that the negater output signal is +5 volts for any input voltage less than, say, +2, and is 0 for any input voltage greater than, say, +3

*The logic element designer chooses the voltage levels and polarities to suit the type of semiconductor components he proposes to use.

(Figure 53). By this trick, signal levels can be restandardized; that is to say, if a signal has deviated by even as much as two volts from the proper level, on being passed through a negater, the deviation will be corrected. The negater circuit provides another example of *threshold* operation (p. 157), the threshold being +2.5 volts. All signals sufficiently less than the threshold have the same effect, and all signals sufficiently greater have the other effect. Indeed, the circuit is often used solely for this property, as for example at the output of the delay line in the delay-line store.

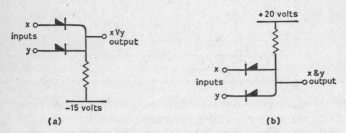

Figure 54. (*a*) Or-element. (*b*) And-element.

Figure 54(a) shows a common circuit of an or-element with voltages of +5 and 0 representing 1 and 0. It consists of a resistor and two diodes, and uses a negative supply of fifteen volts with respect to earth. The reader who knows something about electronics will understand that this supply tends to make the potential of the output terminal negative, and that current from the more positive input terminal through its diode successfully resists this tendency. The potential of the output terminal is then equal to that of the more positive of the two input terminals or to the potential of both if they are the same.

Thus, if both input terminals are at 0, the output terminal is also at 0, while if either or both are at +5 volts, representing 1, the output terminal is at +5 volts. The output signal then represents the result of performing the or-operation on the bits (*x* and *y*) represented by the input signals. This is often written as *x* ∨ *y*, as in Figure 54(a), the ∨ symbol standing for *vel*, a Latin word for 'or'.

The usual circuit for an and-element (Figure 54(b)), is arranged oppositely, and the voltage of the output terminal is the less positive of the two input voltages. This correctly performs the and-operation, the result being written $x \& y$.

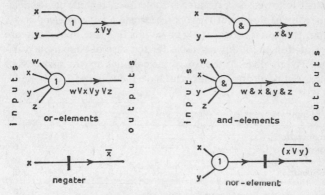

Figure 55. Symbols for logic elements.

It is possible to have more than two inputs to and-elements and or-elements. One diode is required for each input terminal, and each diode is connected between its own input terminal and the output terminal as in Figure 54. The output of the and-element is then 1 only if all the inputs are 1, and the output of the or-element is 1 when any one or more of the inputs is 1.

The output of a logic element must, in practice, be able to supply several inputs to other logic elements. The negater circuit can do this, but the circuits of Figure 54 usually require a simple buffer amplifier, which does not affect the value of the output bit of the element, being necessary merely for electrical reasons. The and-element and the or-element, including their buffer amplifiers, are used so frequently that shorthand symbols are needed for them, for use in logic diagrams. These are shown in Figure 55, with the symbol for a negater. Note that a bar over a letter symbol represents the operation of negation. The negater circuit is sometimes used as a buffer amplifier for and-elements and-or elements; after all, it consists of only one transistor and not much else, and in some circumstances is the cheapest suitable circuit. This negation must, of course, be allowed for in the logic, and is similar to the inherent sign-reversal in some analog computing circuits (p. 91). An or-element followed by a negater is called a *nor-element* (Figure 55) since the output is 1 when neither x nor y is 1. An and-element followed by a negater is sometimes, regrettably, a *nand-element* by analogy, but is properly termed a *not-and-element*. Its output is 1 when either x or y or both is 0. These operations are illustrated in the following table for the case of four input variables. The numbers at the top of the columns are the numbers of inputs, out of a total of four, that have the value of 1.

No. of inputs of value 1 :	0	1	2	3	4
And operation	0	0	0	0	1
Or operation	0	1	1	1	1
Not-and operation	1	1	1	1	0
Nor operation	1	0	0	0	0

Results of various operations on four input bits

If all the inputs to an element were negated, these numbers would be reversed, and would read 4, 3, 2, 1, 0 from left to right. This shows, for example, that the nor-operation performed on negated inputs gives the same result as the and-operation performed on normal inputs. In symbols,

$$\overline{(w \vee x \vee y \vee z)} = w \,\&\, x \,\&\, y \,\&\, z,$$

where the bar denotes negation; a result which could have been predicted by comparing the two circuits in Figure 54. In fact, there is no difficulty, by this and similar methods, in using negaters, nor-elements and not-and-elements exclusively, and avoiding the need for plain and-elements and or-elements. This technique is called *nor logic*, and can result in an economy of buffer amplifiers.

More complicated logic elements can be built up from those described so far; as an example, we take an element which has two inputs, the output being 1 when they differ, and 0 otherwise. It is therefore called a *non-equivalence element*. One way of synthesizing this element (there are many others) is shown in Figure

56(a). The output of the upper and-element in the figure is 1 only when x is 0 (because of the negater) and y is 1. Similarly, the output of the lower and-element is 1 only when x is 1 and y is 0. The or-element on the right of the figure makes the output of the complete element 1 when either of these conditions occurs. When, however, x and y are both 0, or both 1, the or-element receives 0

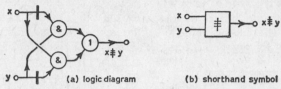

(a) logic diagram   (b) shorthand symbol

Figure 56. Non-equivalence element.

at both inputs, and the output is therefore 0. Using the notation shown in Figure 56, the non-equivalence operation is described by $(x \neq y) = (x \,\&\, \bar{y}) \lor (\bar{x} \,\&\, y)$. There are many other logic elements made up of standard arrangements of simpler elements, but we will describe some of these only when we need them.

Storage for one bit

All the logic elements so far mentioned have a common feature: the output signal depends only on the present values of the input signals, and not on their previous values. Strictly speaking, this statement is not literally true, because after an input signal changes there is a slight delay before the output signal changes to correspond. This is because nothing can happen at infinite speed, in electronics no less than in mechanics. The slight delay is always of practical importance, usually because it sets a limit to the speed with which the circuit can deal with different consecutive inputs. Furthermore, the delay is different in different circuits, even in different specimens of the same circuit, so signals which are nominally simultaneous are never exactly so in practice. However, with some logic elements, the output signal depends intentionally on previous values of the input signals. Such elements are basically small stores, which hold only one bit, and which are used individually, or at least associated only in small groups.

The simplest such element is one which delays the input signal by one digit-period (Figure 57). At the same time the element conveniently re-standardizes the voltage levels and timing of the signal pulses, in the same way as the pulse re-shaping unit used with a delay-line store (Figure 47).

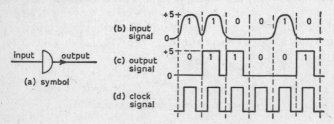

Figure 57. Digit-period delay element.

This element is often used simply to delay a signal, but it can alternatively work as a rudimentary delay-line store if the output is connected to the input. It holds one bit; if this has the value 1, the output (and input) of the element is a continuous sequence of pulses; while if it is zero, the output is a steady voltage of zero. The arrangements for altering the stored bit are slightly simpler than those for the longer delay-line store, since there is no need to bother about the timing of the alteration; it can be done in any digit period. Two input signals are used for this purpose: one for altering the stored digit from 0 to 1 (the *set* input), and the other for the opposite alteration (the *reset* input) (Figure 58(a)). The connexion from the output of the delay element back to its input passes through an and-element and an or-element. When both set and reset inputs represent 0, there is no interference with the functioning of this connexion. The signal from the delay element output passes directly to the and-element output, since the other input signal to the and-element represents 1, by the action of the negater. The output signal from the and-element passes directly to the output of the or-element, since the other input to this element represents 0. In this condition, therefore, the input and output signals of the delay element are the same, and the output of the circuit could be taken from either point.

172

When, however, the upper input to the circuit takes the value 1, the input to the delay element becomes 1 irrespective of what signal is carried by the connexion from its output. Thus the input signal can set the content of the store to 1 (hence the name, 'setting' or 'set' input) by transiently taking the value 1 for one digit period. Similarly, the lower input to the circuit can reset the content of the store to 0 by transiently taking the value 1. When the circuit has been set, subsequent setting inputs have no effect, and similarly with resetting inputs.

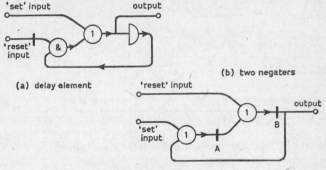

Figure 58. Single-bit stores.

The circuit of Figure 58(b) works in a somewhat similar way. When the set and reset inputs are at 0, the lower input of each of the or-elements is in effect connected directly to the or-element output, so the negaters are connected in a loop. If each has the characteristic shown in Figure 53 then Figure 59 is appropriate for studying the circuit. This consists of the characteristic of negater *B*, with the axes of the graph interchanged, superimposed on the characteristic of negater *A*. The axes of this composite graph then correctly represent the two voltage levels in the loop, each of which has two designations.

The pairs of voltages represented by points where the two characteristics intersect correspond to equilibrium conditions in the circuit; in fact, the intersections on the axes correspond to stable equilibrium, and the middle intersection to unstable equilibrium which is of no practical importance. In practice,

173

therefore, the outputs of the negaters are steady voltages, one of +5 volts, representing 1, and the other of 0 volts, representing 0, as long as both set and reset inputs remain at 0. If the appropriate one of these momentarily takes the value 1, for long enough to allow the elements to respond to the change, the levels of the negater outputs are interchanged by an inherent 'triggering' action.

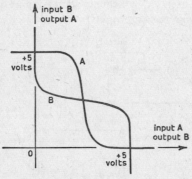

Figure 59. Operation of bistable trigger circuit.

The prototype of this circuit is due to W. H. Eccles and F. W. Jordan, who used two triode valves working as negaters. They described the circuit in an article which appeared in 1919, and used the word 'trigger' in their title. This is recalled by the modern name for this type of device – a *bistable trigger circuit.**

Groups of logic elements

A group of bistable trigger circuits, sufficient to hold all the bits of one word, forms a *parallel register* – 'parallel' because the word is stored by the register in parallel representation. A difference now appears between the set and reset inputs to the individual circuits; the set inputs remain separate but all the reset inputs are connected together. This means that a single pulse on the common

---

*Alternatively, a *bistable*, *trigger*, or *flip-flop*, although the last term means, strictly, a rather different circuit which has only one state that is stable for an indefinite time.

reset terminal suffices to cause all the digits of the stored word to become zero; that is, to clear the register, the previous contents being lost. A new word, connected in parallel representation to the set inputs, can now enter the register. That is, the digits of the new word that have the value 0 have no effect, while those of value 1 set their individual circuits to 1.

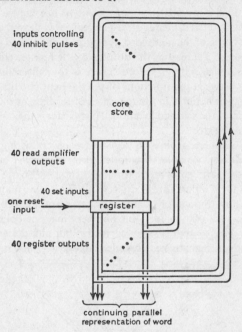

Figure 60. Reading and rewriting a word in a core store.

A register is used in this way in the reading process in a core store. It is first cleared, and then receives the parallel representation of a word from the read amplifier output terminals. Thereafter, the outputs of the register control the inhibit pulses (Figure 52(b)). The reader will remember that these are the means by which the word that has been read (destructively) is rewritten in the selected cores; at the same time it is available for other purposes as well at the register outputs. Figure 60 shows the circuits

175

symbolically; as soon as the first half-write pulse occurs, and indefinitely thereafter until a reset pulse occurs, a parallel representation of the word that has been read is available.

The process of reading the content of a selected location thus involves a writing operation as well. If, on the other hand, we want to write a different word in the selected location, and not to read its content, it is nevertheless convenient to use the same read-write cycle, and the same register. The register is cleared and is set from the source of the new word, the outputs of the read amplifier being ignored. Thereafter, the outputs of the register control the inhibit pulses, exactly as before. There is thus the minimum of difference between the functions of the different circuits, and the timing of their actions, in the two cases of reading, or of altering, the content of the selected location. The register is the only way in and out of the store.

If two numbers, from two registers, each consisting of, say, forty bits, are available in parallel form, a *parallel adder* can generate the parallel representation of their sum (Figure 61). The adder has forty inputs for the digits, u_{39} to u_0, of one number, and a further forty inputs for the digits, s_{39} to s_0, of the second number.* The sum of two forty-bit numbers may, of course, need forty-one bits to represent it correctly, but the design of the parallel adder treats this as an undesirable case. There is a special

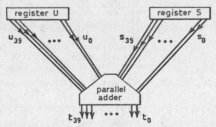

Figure 61. Addition of two numbers in parallel representation.

overflow output signal when it happens, so that corrective action can be initiated. The normal output may be taken, therefore, as a forty-bit total, or *sum*, t_{39} to t_0.

*The letters u and s will later serve to recall the sources of these numbers, the accumulator and the store.

The parallel adder consist of forty similar units (Figure 62), each of which adds together a pair of digits, u_n and s_n, to generate a digit t_n, taking account also of a carried input x_n from the next lower place, and generating a carry output, y_n, for the next higher place. (That is, $y_n = x_{n+1}$, for $n = 0$ to 38.) Each unit is called a *three-input adder*. The weight (in the sense explained on p. 19) of the digits dealt with by any three-input adder is twice as great as that of the digits dealt with by the adder on its right, the least significant digits being on the right of the diagrams.

What goes on inside the three-input adders, the boxes of Figure 62? When three bits have to be added in one adder, the rules of addition become a little more elaborate than those quoted

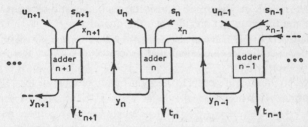

Figure 62. Interconnexion of typical three-input adders in a parallel adder.

on p. 143, since there are four different cases that may arise: either none, one, two, or all three of the inputs may have the value 1. The corresponding values of t and y are:*

No. of inputs of value	1:	0	1	2	3
Sum digit	t:	0	1	0	1
Digit to be carried	y:	0	0	1	1

This table is obtained by finding values of y and t (either 0 or 1) to satisfy the equation $2y + t = u + s + x$ for the four cases.

*We drop the suffix n in this description, since it is the same for all the symbols u, s, x, t, and y.

Now when the sum of u and s is 1, the middle columns of the table apply:

	$u+s+x$:	1	2
Table for $u+s=1$	therefore x:	0	1
	t:	1	0
	y:	0	1

so in this case $y=x$. (This is exactly analogous to the case $u + s=9$ in decimal arithmetic; 1 is to be carried, and the sum digit set to 0, only if a carry has been brought forward from the previous place. This is Babbage's 'anticipatory carry' of p. 46). That is why the x input signal in Figure 63 passes through the and-element to become the y output signal when the quantity $u \not\equiv s$ is 1. This quantity is 1 only when $u + s = 1$, and is 0 when $u + s = 0$ or 2. The non-equivalence element that generates $u \not\equiv s$ has been described on p. 171.

When u and s are both 1, the right-hand columns of the table apply:

	$u+s+x$:	2	3
Table for $u=s=1$	therefore x:	0	1
	t:	0	1
	y:	1	1

so y is 1 irrespective of the value of x, and the left-hand and-element in Figure 63 feeds a 1 to the y output. Finally when u and s are both 0, the left-hand columns of the table apply:

	$u+s+x$:	0	1
Table for $u=s=0$	therefore x:	0	1
	t:	0	1
	y:	0	0

so y is 0 irrespective of the value of x, and in this case neither and-element in the Figure can have 1 as output.

The generation of t splits up in a similar way. The tables for $u = s = 0$ and $u = s = 1$ can be combined:

	$u+s+x$:	0 or 2	1 or 3
Table for $u=s$	x:	0	1
	t:	0	1

The case when $u = s$ can alternatively be designated $(u \not\equiv s) = 0$; the result is that $t = x$. The case when $u + s = 1$ can, as we have seen, be designated $(u \not\equiv s) = 1$, and here $t = \bar{x}$. So $t = x$ or $\bar{x}$ according as $u \not\equiv s = 0$ or 1, which is the same as $t = (u \not\equiv s) \not\equiv x$, as shown in Figure 63. There are three binary inputs, eight cases

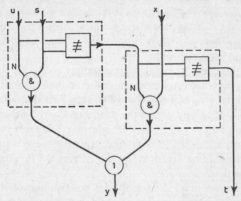

Figure 63. Logic diagram of a three-input adder.

arise, and the signals at each point in the circuit for each case appear in the following table:

u :	0	1	0	1	0	1	0	1
s :	0	0	1	1	0	0	1	1
x :	0	0	0	0	1	1	1	1
$u+s+x$:	0	1	1	2	1	2	2	3
$u \not\equiv s$:	0	1	1	0	0	1	1	0
$(u \not\equiv s)$ & x :	0	0	0	0	0	1	1	0
u & s :	0	0	0	1	0	0	0	1
y :	0	0	0	1	0	1	1	1
t :	0	1	1	0	1	0	0	1

The three-input adder just described is especially suited for incorporation in a parallel adder, because it permits the use of types of and-element and or-element in the path from x to y which delay the x-signal hardly at all. In the electronic parallel adder, however, unlike the mechanical adder described on p. 46, this very slight delay is the factor which governs the maximum speed at which addition can be performed. It is in fact possible that a carry signal will have to propagate from adder 0 to adder 39 (see Figure 62) before the addition is complete, so this point is most important for the highest possible speed.

The three-input adder can be made up from two similar portions, shown enclosed by broken lines in Figure 63, plus an or-element. Each of these portions is termed a *two-input adder*, since it adds only two bits together, while a three-input adder adds three bits. There are many other ways of making a three-input adder from logic elements.

If two numbers in serial representation are to be added, the addition in each digital place can be completed before the next pair of digits arrives, provided, of course, that the start is made at the least significant end of the numbers. Carrying then consists of delaying y by one digit period to form x. Only one three-input adder is necessary (Figure 64), and it generates the sum in serial representation. Some people say that it zips the two input pulse trains together.

Consider now the subtraction of a positive number (s_{39} to s_0) from a larger positive number (u_{39} to u_0). A three-input subtracter has three input bits, u, s, and a carried (or borrowed) digit x; it must generate two output bits, t (the result) and y to be carried to (or borrowed from) the next higher place. The equation which now gives a tabulation of required values is $-2y+t=u-s-x$; and from this one can obtain:

u :	0	1	0	1	0	1	0	1
s :	0	0	1	1	0	0	1	1
x :	0	0	0	0	1	1	1	1
$u-s-x$:	0	1	-1	0	-1	0	-2	-1
y :	0	0	1	0	1	0	1	1
t :	0	1	1	0	1	0	0	1

Now, strangely enough, these values of t turn out to be the same as those required for addition (c.f. the previous table), but the values for y differ. They can be obtained, to quote one method, by inserting a negater in the two connexions marked N in Figure 63, which changes this figure into a diagram of a three-input subtracter. By one method or another it is possible to convert a three-input adder into a three-input subtracter at the dictate of an external addition/subtraction signal. A parallel adder/subtracter

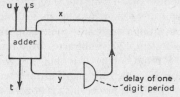

Figure 64. Three-input adder used as a serial adder.

can be made, arranged like Figures 61 and 62 or a serial adder/ subtracter arranged like Figure 64.

Representation of negative numbers

The foregoing reference to subtraction raises the question of how negative numbers are to be represented. The obvious method is to use one special bit to denote $+$ or $-$ instead of 0 or 1 (a *sign digit*); this is called the *modulus and sign* system, and is the system people are used to. It has the disadvantage that some quite complicated preliminary manoeuvring is necessary to deal correctly with any combination of signs of the two numbers, u and s, when the instruction calls for $u + s$ or $u - s$.* First, if the signs of u and s differ, then subtraction must be performed if addition is specified, and vice versa. Secondly, if u is less than s in absolute magnitude, the roles of u and s in the operation are to be interchanged. Thirdly, the sign of the answer is the sign of the larger of u and s in absolute magnitude, except when s is larger and subtraction is specified, when it is the opposite. All this we learn at school, and

---

*In this section we are using u and s to stand for a number and not for a typical digit in the representation of the number.

later on imagine nothing could be simpler. In fact, however, there is a much simpler system if we accept that all numbers are to be represented by the same number of digits, as they are in a computer. That is to say, small numbers must be brought up to standard length by prefixing non-significant zeros, as in the table on p. 145.

The *complement* of a number, in some specified system for representing numbers, is what must be added to the number to get a suitably large power of the radix of the representation. Thus 870 is the complement of 130 in a system where three decimal digits are used to represent numbers, since these numbers add up to ten cubed. If, in this system, 130 is subtracted from zero (that is, from 000), the result '870 and borrow 1' is obtained. We now decide to ignore the 'borrow 1', which we ought to take account of in the next digit place. This is the place which is not present, because we are using three decimal digits only. By this trick, subtracting a positive number from zero generates the complement of the number, and we therefore decide to use the complement of a positive number to represent minus that number. This is equivalent to writing, say, -130 as $(-1,000 + 870)$, but since we are only using three decimal digits, it is neither necessary nor possible to represent the $-1,000$. Both addition and subtraction sums come out right, provided we ignore carries generated in the most significant place. For example, 273 add 870 gives the answer 143, which equals $+273$ add (-130). We must notice, however, that we cannot represent numbers bigger in magnitude (or modulus) than 499; numbers from 501 to 999 must be taken as complements, representing negative numbers from -499 to -1. The table gives some further examples which illustrate the different cases mentioned in the last paragraph.

Notice that the operation (add or subtract) that is specified is the one that is actually performed; that u and s are never interchanged; and that the sign of the answer is automatically correct, that is, when the first digit of the answer is from 5 to 9, the answer is really negative.

Complements work equally well in binary notation. If Figures 61 and 62 represent a parallel adder/subtracter for forty-bit numbers, the carry generated in the highest place (y_{39}) can readily be

Modulus and sign representation		Complement representation		
u	s	u	s	answer
+273	A +130	273	A	130 = 403
+273	S −130	273	S	870 = *403
+273	A −130	273	A	870 = *143
+273	S +130	273	S	130 = 143
−130	S −273	870	S	727 = 143
−273	S +130	727	S	130 = 597, meaning −403
−273	A −130	727	A	870 = *597, meaning −403
−273	S −130	727	S	870 = *857, meaning −143
−273	A +130	727	A	130 = 857, meaning −143
+130	S +273	130	S	273 = *857, meaning −143

(A means add, S means subtract; *indicates that the carry from the highest place has been ignored.)

disregarded. The division, at the midpoint of the range of representations, between what are taken to be positive numbers and what are taken to be complements, occurs at the binary number $1000 \ldots 000$ (i.e. 2^{39}). Positive numbers extend from $0000 \ldots 001$ to $0111 \ldots 111*$ (i.e. from 1 to $2^{39} - 1$) and complements from $1000 \ldots 001$ to $1111 \ldots 111$ (i.e. from $2^{39} + 1$ to $2^{40} - 1$) representing the negative numbers from $- 0111 \ldots 111$ to $- 0000 \ldots 001$ (i.e. from $- 2^{39} + 1$ to $- 1$). The characteristic of a complement is that its most significant (first) digit is 1, corresponding to the range 5 to 9 in the previous example. This is a most important and valuable feature of complement representation with binary numbers; the first digit is, in fact, a sign digit.

Two representations have not been classified: $0000 \ldots 000$ and $1000 \ldots 000$ (0 and 2^{39}). By reference to the first digits, it is convenient to say that $0000 \ldots 000$ represents a positive number ($+0$), and $1000 \ldots 000$ (2^{39}) is a complement, and therefore represents a negative number, which turns out to be $-1000 \ldots 000$ (-2^{39}). Similarly, in the previous example, the three digits '500' represent the number minus five hundred.

The reader may think that complements are all very well, but

* Note that a binary number consisting of a row of ones, n in number, represents $2^{n-1} + \ldots + 4 + 2 + 1$. By the formula for the sum to n terms of a geometric progression, this equals $2^n - 1$.

their use prevents the most significant carry (y_{39}) acting as an overflow signal. This is true, but an overflow signal can be generated, from the three input signals to the most significant three-input adder/subtracter, by means of a few extra logic elements, so this is a very slight disadvantage. In fact, complements are used to represent negative numbers in most computers.

A simple computer

By combining Figures 60 and 61, and making some additions, we obtain the nucleus of a rudimentary computer, Figure 65. The register in Figure 60 becomes register S in Figures 61 and 65, and is called the store register. Register U in Figure 61 becomes the accumulator register of Figure 65; a further register (T), some logic elements, and the punched-tape reader and the printer are added. Furthermore, in Figure 65, one connecting line is used to represent a set of up to forty such lines, to make the diagram easier to follow. Similarly, each and-element or or-element shown represents a set of such elements. For example, each of the forty outputs of register T goes to one input of an and-element, the output of which goes to one input of register U. The second inputs of all forty and-elements are connected together, and supplied with a signal designated E. The method of selecting an address in the core store is not shown in the diagram, nor is the control unit of Figure 37. The accumulator register, adder/subtracter, temporary storage register (T), and their interconnexions, together make up the arithmetic unit of that figure; except that the equipment shown in Figure 65 is restricted to the operations of addition and subtraction for simplicity. A detailed explanation of the extra equipment for performing multiplication and division would be straightforward, but lengthy, and will not be given. The store register (S) corresponds to the store of Figure 37. The core store block and the and-elements controlled by the signal F, in Figure 65, are from this point of view minor adjuncts of the store register.

The apparatus represented in Figure 65 can perform the following operations, assuming that each signal E, F, G, etc. correctly actuates its associated set of and-elements (that is, opens its gate) so as to allow the passage of parallel signals representing the binary word in question:

1	Add	$C(n)$ to $C(U)$		6	Print	$C(n)$
2	Subtract	$C(n)$ from $C(U)$		7	Copy	$C(U)$ in (n)
5	Copy	$C(n)$ in U		8	Tape to (n)

The notation above is that of page 132 of Chapter 6, except that the accumulator is now denoted by U, instead of A. However, whereas the computer of Chapter 6 works in decimal notation, the present one works in binary. Further, operations 6 and 8 now deal with only a part of a binary word instead of the whole word – that is, with sufficient binary digits to represent one decimal digit, or, more generally, one character (page 146).

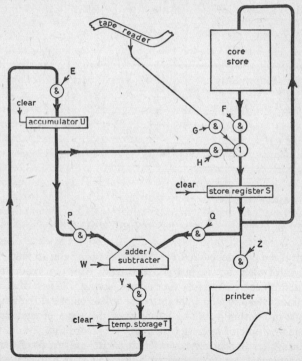

Figure 65. Store, input, output, and arithmetic unit of a rudimentary computer.

Figure 66 sets out the detailed processes by which these six operations may be carried out. At the top is a copy of Figure 52(b) (p. 158), to give the timing of the read-write cycle of the core store; there follows the allocation of ten Roman numerals to consecutive periods of time in a cyclic manner. The remainder of the Figure shows what happens during these periods; first, things that happen irrespective of which operation is executed, and under-

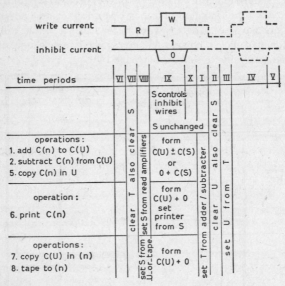

Figure 66. Timing of the performance of operations 1, 2, 5, 6, 7, and 8.

neath those that depend on the particular operation. In fact, the process of obeying one instruction extends over two read-write cycles in the core store (say four microseconds), the first of which is spent in determining what instruction is to be obeyed, and the second in obeying it. We wish to explain this latter process first, so the first time of interest is period VII. Before this period, by means which we shall explain later on, there has been determined the particular operation required, and the address n in the core store, concerned in the operation. This address is selected in period

VI and remains selected during periods VII, VIII, and IX. Obeying the instruction overlaps the first part of the process of determining what the next instruction is, which starts in the next period I.

In period VII the store register, S, is cleared, preparatory to being set in period VIII, either from the store read amplifiers for operations 1, 2, 5, and 6, or from U for operation 7, or from the tape reader for operation 8. During period IX the word contained in S is written in location (n); this word is the previous $C(n)$ for operations 1, 2, 5, and 6, In fact. for these operations, $C(n)$ is available in S during periods IX, X, and I.

For operation 7 and 8, the operation is complete when $C(S)$ has been written in (n), and the other things which take place are, strictly speaking, unnecessary. It is convenient, however, not to make special arrangements to stop them.

The adder/subtracter is always in use during periods IX, X, and I. For operations 1 and 2, one input is $C(U)$ and the other $C(S)$; either $C(U) + C(S)$ or $C(U) - C(S)$ is formed, and is available during period I, after the propagation of any carries during periods IX and X. For operation 2, signal W selects subtraction, while for all other operations, it selects addition. For operation 5, signal P cuts off the input from U, so $C(S)$ has zero added to it, and passes through the adder unchanged. Similarly, for operation 6, 7, and 8, signal Q cuts off the input from S, so $C(U)$ passes through the adder. For all operations, the adder/subtracter output sets register T during period I, and $C(T)$ sets U during period III. This makes $C(U)$ the same as before for operations 6, 7, and 8, or the required new value for operations 1, 2, and 5.

From Figure 66, the correct behaviour of signals E, F, G, etc., can now be specified:

E: 1 during period III always, 0 otherwise;

F: 1 during period VIII when operation 1, 2, 5, or 6 is specified, 0 otherwise in period VIII and 0 in periods VII, IX, X, I, and II;

G: 1 during period VIII when operation 8 is specified, 0 otherwise;

H: 1 during period VIII when operation 7 is specified, 0 otherwise;

187

P: 0 at all times when operation 5 is to be or is being performed, 1 otherwise;

Q: 1 during periods IX, X, and I, when operation 1 or 2 or 5 is specified, 0 otherwise;

W: subtraction at all times when operation 2 is to be or is being performed, addition otherwise;

Y: 1 during period I always, 0 otherwise;

Z: 1 during periods IX, X, and I when operation 6 is specified, 0 otherwise;

Clear S: 1 during period II and 1 during period VII, 0 otherwise;

Clear T: 1 during period VII, 0 otherwise;

Clear U: 1 during period II, 0 otherwise.

To generate these control signals, and others to be mentioned later, we shall use two sets of signals, called *timing signals* and *operation signals*. The first timing signal, designated aI, takes the value 1 during period I, and 0 during other periods; the second (aII) takes the value 1 during period II, and 0 during other periods; and so on. These signals can be generated by the same techniques as the timing signals used in the core store, since they do not depend on what operation is being performed (except for operation 10, stop). They are repetitive, since the time periods follow one another in sequence, and I follows X. The first operation signal ($b1$) takes the value 1 only when operation 1 is specified, the second ($b2$) only when operation 2 is specified, and so on. As will appear, all these signals take the value 0 during periods V and VI, the appropriate one of them taking the value 1 for the duration of periods VII to X and the following I to IV. It is now a straightforward matter to generate signals E, F, G, etc., from signals aI, aII, etc. and $b1$, $b2$, etc., as required by the table above. Here are two examples, shown as (a) and (b) in Figure 67:

$$P = \overline{b5}$$
$$Q = (a\text{IX} \lor a\text{X} \lor a\text{I}) \ \& \ (b1 \lor b2 \lor b5).$$

Apart from these examples, we shall not explain further the apparatus needed to generate these signals.

We come now to the remainder of the rudimentary computer, the control unit. This is shown in Figure 68, the same core store as

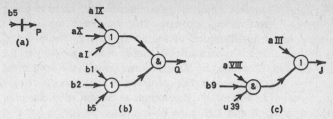

Figure 67. Examples of generation of controlling signals.

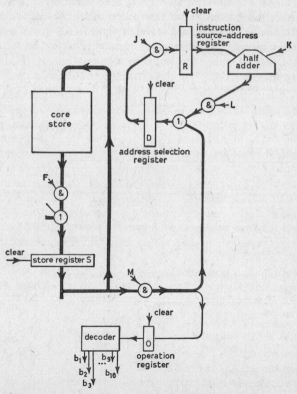

Figure 68. Store and control of a rudimentary computer.

in Figure 65 appearing once again. These two figures together comprise the outline logic diagram of the complete computer, and are a more detailed version of Figure 37, p. 111. The two-way switch supplying the store input in that figure corresponds to the and-elements controlled by G and H, together with the or-element that they are connected to. The three-way switch connected to the store output in Figure 37 corresponds to the and-elements controlled by M, Q, and Z (Figures 65 and 68).

The previous description started with the assumption that, prior to period VII, the particular operation required, and the associated address n in the core store, had been determined. Both of these are determined by the instruction to be obeyed, which is itself stored in the core store. It will be remembered from Chapter 6 that an instruction comprises an operation part and an address part, each part being represented by a group of binary digits. If we say that the instruction which has just been obeyed came from address r, then the instruction to be obeyed next comes from the

	Store and Arithmetic Unit	Control Unit	If a jump operation is specified, and if $C(U) < 0$, then:
IX		⎱ Form	
X		Clear D ⎰ $C(R) + 1$	
I		Set D from $\frac{1}{2}$ adder	
II	Clear S	Clear R ⎱ D controls	
III	Set S from read amplifiers	Set R from D ⎰ address selection	
IV	S controls inhibit wires		
V		Clear D and O	
VI	$C(S)$ still available ——→	Set D and O from S	
VII	Clear S	⎱ D controls address selection	Clear R
VIII	Set S from appropriate source		Set R from D
IX	S controls inhib. wires ⎱ S unchanged	⎱ Form $C(R) + 1$	⎱ Inhibit K
X	⎰ while adder/ subtracter	Clear D	
I	⎰ works	Set D from $\frac{1}{2}$ adder	
II	Clear S ⎱ Answer		
III	⎰ transferred to U.		

next address, that is $r + 1$. During periods IX, X, and I, r is stored in the Instruction Source-Address register, R, Figure 68. The foregoing table is analogous to Figure 66. In addition to summarizing that figure, it shows how the new instruction is extracted from address $r + 1$ and then obeyed.

In order to add 1 to r, a parallel adder is provided. Since this adder is never required to add anything other than 1 (or perhaps 0), it can be simplified. In the notation of Figure 62 (p. 177), each s_n is 0, except for s_o, which is 1 (or perhaps 0); also x_o is always 0. Each adder in Figure 62 therefore has one input permanently 0, and a two-input adder (p. 180) is all that is necessary. A digital adder (whether parallel or serial) that is made from two- instead of three-input adders is called a *half adder*. This is because two half adders can be combined to make the complete adder of Figure 62 or 64; these are therefore called *full adders*. Further, the half adder of Figure 68 need not have as many as forty digit places. Since r is an address in the core store, it will never be larger than the total number of addresses. A core store with a maximum size of 32,768 (i.e. 2^{15}) words is quite common, in which case fifteen bits are sufficient to enable r to specify any address in the store. The parallel adder need therefore have only fifteen digit places, and the same applies to the instruction source-address register, R, and the address selection register, D.

During period IX and X, then, the signal K, representing 1, and the fifteen bits of $C(R)$ in parallel, representing r, are presented to the inputs of the half adder, and any carries propagate through. During the following period I, signal L allows the sum, $r+1$, to set register D, which has been cleared in period X. Register D is the address selection register for the core store, and selects, during periods II, III, and IV, one write wire from each of the two sets of write wires (see the wave forms in Figure 66 again). The quantity $r + 1$ is now safely stored in D, so in period II, R can be cleared. In period III, signal J causes $r + 1$ to set R, where it is stored until it is required again in period IX.

Also in period II, the store register S is cleared, and receives, in period III, the binary-coded representation of the instruction to be obeyed. In period IV, the instruction word is re-written from S in location $(r + 1)$ since it may well be required again later; the action of the core store in periods II, III, and IV is the same as already described for periods VII, VIII, and XI when operations 1, 2, 5, or 6 are specified. During these six periods, the content of D must not be changed, as it is selecting the core store address. It is changed in periods X and I as mentioned, and again in V and VI. (Now refer again to the table on p. 190, and to Figure 68.) During V, D is cleared, and during VI, signal M causes fifteen of the bits of the coded instruction, from S, to set D. These bits are, in fact, the address part of the instruction. The operation register, O, is also cleared in period V, and in VI receives the bits of the instruction which represent the operation part, from S. The content of register O is only changed in periods V and VI, that is, half as often as that of register D.

The output signals from register O, the parallel binary version of the operation part, go to a decoder. This consists of one and-element for each of the output operation signals, $b1$ to $b10$, with inputs from the outputs of register O, either directly, or via negaters, as appropriate for the particular operation signal. In this way the operation signals are generated, and persist, as stated, all the time that the content of register O is undisturbed, that is from period VI when it is set to the following period V.

We notice that the action of the control unit in periods VI to X has similarities to its action in periods I to V, differing in the source of the word set in register D. In I to V this word is the serial number of the instruction to be obeyed. The control unit extracts this instruction from the store, while the arithmetic unit is tidying up after the previous operation, directed by the operation register, which does not participate at this time in the activity of the control unit. In VI to X, registers D and O are set to the instruction word from S, and the instruction is obeyed. This needs a further read-write cycle in the store to obtain from a different address the number specified in the instruction. During VIII, IX, and X different things happen in the arithmetic unit and S according to the particular instruction. At other times, and elsewhere in the computer at all times, the action is the same whatever instruction is being obeyed.

There are two exceptions to this, in the cases of the stop and jump operations. When the operation signal for the stop opera-

Plate 1. The differential analyser formerly in the Mathematical Laboratory, Cambridge. In the foreground are the integrator cabinets, behind them the interconnecting shafts, and in the background, the input and output tables

Plate 2. The world's first stored-program digital computer in the Electro-Technical Laboratories of Manchester University early in 1949.

A Power supply distribution rack
B Master oscillator (100 kHz)
C Horizontal deflection circuits for CRT stores
D Read/write selection circuits
E Vertical deflection circuits
F Monitor CRT displaying contents of stores
G Operating consoles
H High voltage power supply for CRT's
I Pulse separator rack (generating pulses in each of the 40 different digit positions)
J Operation and timing signal generating circuits
K Movable oscilloscope of advanced design
L 6 storage CRT's in double-screening boxes
M Store regeneration circuits
N Subtractor
P Selecting circuits and gates
Q Adder
R Multiplier

(The photograph exaggerates the size of the room, since it is a composite of numerous individual shots taken from just inside the doorway. The magnetic drum store was installed in another room upstairs.)

Plate 3. A hybrid computer installation.

A Input/output typewriter
B Digital controls and indicators
C Paper tape reader and punch
D Digital-analog interface
E Readout and display console
F Logic controls and indicators
G Analog controls and indicators

H Detachable patch board
I Operating console
J Multi-channel chart recorder
K Second operating console—allows the computer to be
 split and used on two jobs at once
L Second chart recorder
M Independent small digital computer

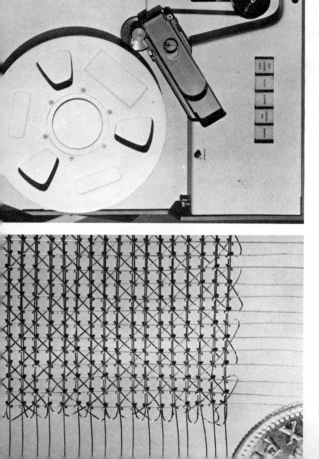
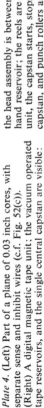

Plate 4. (Left) Part of a plane of 0.03 inch cores, with separate sense and inhibit wires (c.f. Fig. 52(c)). (Right) A digital magnetic tape unit; the vacuum operated tape reservoirs, and the single central capstan are visible: the head assembly is between the capstan and the right-hand reservoir; the reels are $10\frac{1}{2}$ inches in diameter. In this unit, the capstan starts, stops, and reverses, so a second capstan, and punch rollers and brakes, are not necessary.

Plate 5. A medium-large computing installation of the 1960s. The cabinets housing the central processor can be seen at the far end of the room to the left; the magnetic tape units along the back wall to the right; some peripheral units and the operator's console in the foreground.

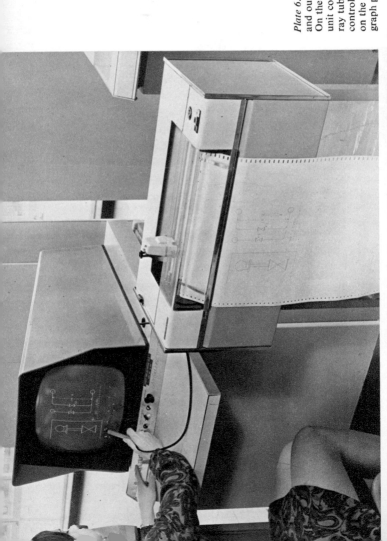

Plate 6. Graphical input and output equipment. On the left a visual display unit comprising a cathode ray tube, push button controls and a light pen; on the right an automatic graph plotter.

Plate 7. Alphanumeric Visual Display Unit or Terminal.

Input to the computer is composed on the keyboard and appears on the screen as it is typed. It can be checked and edited before being passed into the computer store. Output from the computer can be displayed on the screen under operator control.

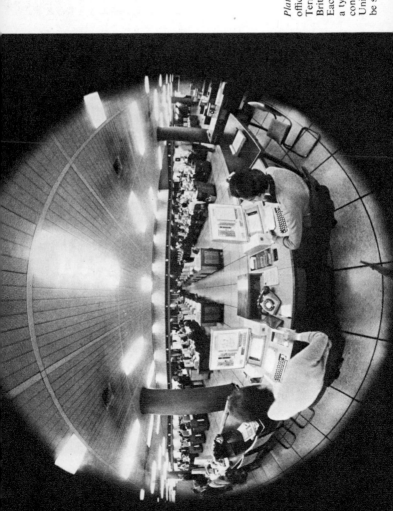

Plate 8. The main booking office at the West London Terminal Building of British European Airways. Each reservation clerk uses a typewriter-push button control instrument called a Uniset, two of which can be seen in the foreground.

tion is generated, in period VI, it inhibits the generation of any
further timing signals, including in particular aV, which would be
used to reset register O. The stop operation signal therefore per-
sists indefinitely, and the human attendant must intervene before
the computer can restart.

When a jump instruction is obeyed the number, r, in the instruction source address register must be replaced by the number, n,
the address part of the jump instruction, if the content of U represents a negative number. In this case, the extra actions shown in
the right-hand column of the table on p. 190 take place, to produce the desired result. At the same time, the content of location
(n) in the core store is read, and re-written, although it is completely irrelevant. It is cheaper not to stop this waste motion.

From the table on p. 190 the correct behaviour of signals J, K,
L, etc., can be specified, to complete the list on p. 187–8:

J: 1 during period III, and 1 during period VIII when a
jump is specified and $C(U) < 0$, 0 otherwise;

K: 0 during periods IX, X, and I when a jump is specified and $C(U) < 0$, 1 otherwise;

L: 1 during period I always, 0 otherwise;

M: 1 during period VI always, 0 otherwise;

Clear R: 1 during period II, and 1 during period VII when a
jump is specified and $C(U) < 0$, 0 otherwise;

Clear D: 1 during periods V and X, 0 otherwise;

Clear O: 1 during period V, 0 otherwise.

In addition the specification for signal F, which was left incomplete before, can be dealt with:

F: 1 during period III, and 1 during period VIII, when
operating 1, 2, 5, or 6 is specified, 0 otherwise.

The sign of the content of the Accumulator is relevant to the
generation of some of these signals; Figure 66 shows that it does
not change in the time periods (VII to X and I) when this is so.
The most significant bit of $C(U)$ (u_{39}, see p. 176) is 1 when $C(U)$ is
less than 0, and is used in the following way, for example to
generate signal J:

$J = a\text{III} \lor (a\text{VIII} \& u_{39} \& b9)$. (See also Figure 67(c).)

The reader has probably found this explanation heavy going, but after working through it he will have a good insight into the design and working of the general-purpose digital computer. Further facilities for the programmer are added by more of the same sort of thing; that is, by means of large quantities of simple elements each performing a simple but vital part of the whole operation, to a rigidly defined schedule. We shall not give detailed explanations of any further facilities, not even of multiplication and division, because such explanations, though not difficult, are tedious and too long for this book. We will, however, mention the existence of some less obvious facilities.

Computer hardware facilities

With pencil and paper computation it is easy to ensure that no significant digits are lost – for example when multiplying 0.0201 by itself to an accuracy of three significant digits, one automatically adds two extra digit places in writing 0.000404. If these extra places were not available, the last two digits would be lost and the accuracy considerably reduced. Furthermore, results of arithmetical operations can cause an overflow (pp. 176 and 184). Early programmers had quite directly the responsibility of avoiding both loss of significant digits and overflow, but nowadays they scarcely need to worry about these points, because a method known as *floating-point representation* of numbers is used. Two words are used to represent a number, z, one representing the *fixed-point part*, x, and the other, the *exponent*, y, which is an integer. We have

$$z = x \, 2^y$$

where, broadly speaking, x gives the significant digits and y states where the binary point (c.f. decimal point) is located. It is quite usual to use an eight-bit word to represent y, and a forty-bit word for x; this means that the number z can have the equivalent of about twelve significant decimal digits, of which the most significant is located anywhere in a range of thirty-eight decimal places either side of the decimal point. Floating point representation is usually built into the computer hardware directly, and there is automatically generated the correct floating-point representation of the result of an arithmetical operation on two numbers represented in floating-point form.

Another important facility is provided in connexion with the transfer of data between the core store and magnetic tape units, disc stores, punched tape or card equipment, and other 'peripheral' equipment. There is a big discrepancy between the speed of operation of modern core stores and arithmetic and control circuits (collectively called the *central processor*) and the peripheral equipment, and with only the simple type of transfer instructions so far described (instructions 6 and 8 on pp. 132 and 185) the central processor would waste a great deal of time waiting for the peripheral equipment to be ready for the transfer of the next character or word. The solution is to allow the programmer to specify the transfer of a whole block of data (p. 153) in the expectation that he can find, or the supervisory program (p. 259) can find, a useful alternative job for the central processor while the block transfer is taking place. This transfer must therefore occur in what is called an *autonomous* manner; sufficient extra hardware (an extra control unit in the sense of Figure 37) must be provided to organize access to consecutive store addresses, within the set originally allocated by the programmer, as soon as the peripheral unit is ready to transmit or receive each consecutive word. Of course, the actual access to the core store must be allowed the possibility of delaying the central processor's performance of its alternative job, but this delay need only be small. As an example, consider transfer between a store with forty-bit words, of cycle time 1 microsecond, and a magnetic tape unit working at 100,000 characters per second, each character having eight bits. Then the tape unit takes 50 microseconds to accept or produce forty bits and the store only 1 microsecond, so for ninety-eight per cent of the time the store is free for other purposes. Even small computers are nowadays usually equipped for such autonomous transfers, and are said to have 'channels' (each with a channel control unit) to which peripheral equipment can be connected. Several peripheral units can be connected to each channel, to work alternatively, and the different channels all engage in what is called 'cycle stealing' from the core store. Some computers have 'multiplex' channels; these are able to deal with several block transfers, from different peripheral units, at the same time.

There are three main different indications for the choice of word length in a computer:

1. a word of correct length to represent a character;
2. a word of correct length to represent an instruction;
3. a word to contain both the fixed-point part and the exponent of a floating-point representation.

A character needs seven bits, and this length of word or slightly longer is also adequate to represent an integer, for use in counting the number of times a loop in a program has been executed (p. 119). An instruction must contain a store address, and for this fifteen bits is normally sufficient (p. 191), and also an operation part and other oddments, say ten bits, giving a total of twenty-five bits. A floating point number needs forty to fifty bits.

Many ways of reconciling these rather incompatible requirements exist, but they all have as their objective to avoid wasting storage space, for example by storing only one character in a forty-bit word. The store could be arranged with a word-length of seven bits, so that a complete read-write cycle was required for each such word, but this would mean that most operations would require several read-write cycles, and would be slow. At the other extreme, a word-length of forty to fifty bits could be chosen, but this would increase the cost per bit of a 3D core store, compared with a shorter word. A suitable compromise is to choose a word length of twenty to thirty bits, which is adequate for an instruction. The designer then accepts that operations in floating-point arithmetic need two store access cycles, and that he must make special arrangements to pack three or four characters into one word in the store.

Some computers have a word of eight bits as a basic unit, which can be called a *syllable*,* since it is normally part of a storage word. They use one such unit to represent a character, two, three, or four for an instruction, and six for a floating-point number –

*The name 'byte' is common in the U.S.A.

five for the fixed-point part and one for the exponent (p. 194). The address part of an instruction is made adequate to specify one eight-bit word out of the complete core store, and so would need to be at least eighteen bits long, rather than fifteen, for the store size we have been considering as typical. The programmer then has a very wide choice of the word-length with which he wishes to work.

9. COMPUTER PROGRAMMING TODAY

The early computer programmers, most of whom were trained as mathematicians, started by writing programs that resembled the simple ones in Chapter 6. They quickly concluded that programming was an excessively tiresome and laborious business. They found that while they could conceive and outline a method of solving a problem in an hour or two, it often took them many days to write a computer program to implement this. As so often happens, impatience, or even laziness, stimulated invention, and since those days great advances have been made in techniques for quicker and easier programming. We shall give a general idea of these in this chapter.

To illustrate the point, consider the program for the last of the examples of Chapter 6 – the statistical calculation on p. 129 – which contains no less than forty-two instructions. (That is why it was not set out in full.) Five instructions suffice to deal with the calculation itself and four more with input and output. All the rest are concerned with the organization of the computation; counting the number of cycles round a loop, modifying the address-digits of certain loop-instructions to ensure that the correct numbers are selected in successive cycles, resetting the counters to zero, and so forth. If so many 'housekeeping' instructions are necessary for such a trivial calculation, what is the situation likely to be with a full-sized job?

In a computing organization, writing new programs is a continuing task, and the early programmers soon realized that to exploit fully the speed and versatility of the new 'von Neumann' type computers, it was essential to reduce the labour of programming. How was this to be done? The group at the Cambridge University Mathematical Laboratory led the attack on the problem; their approach may be explained by an analogy. Constructing a complicated program is like building a house; the labour needed 'on the site' can be greatly reduced by using pre-fabricated units made up beforehand. Now what the programmer needs in the way of prefabricated units are groups of instructions, each doing some specific job, such as evaluating a square root, or establishing a particular layout of results on the printed page, or sorting and filing a mass of information in a prescribed order. Such a self-contained group of instructions is called a *subroutine* or *subprogram*. Many subroutines – the one just mentioned for evaluating square roots, for example – deal with common numerical processes that are often required in the course of larger calculations. In effect, such routines extend the instruction set – the repertoire of basic operations – of the computer. In some small computers, indeed, even such a common operation as division is not included in the basic set, but is dealt with by means of a short subroutine.

It is clearly a great boon for the programmer to have at his disposal a collection of standard subroutines which have been thoroughly tested in advance and are known to work correctly. It is common practice for the various users of a particular computer to pool their efforts and contribute to a common program-library. Such a library would contain a collection of subroutines and also a number of complete programs of general utility.

Besides augmenting the computer's basic instruction set, subroutines play an important role in a more general way. When programming a lengthy calculation, it is usually convenient – and indeed prudent, in view of the risk of human or machine error – to break the job down into a number of separate parts. The complete program is then built up from a number of subroutines – some taken from the library and some made specially for the particular job – together with the necessary linking instructions.

The results of the early Cambridge work were published in 1951 in a book with the self-explanatory title *The Preparation of Programs for an Electronic Digital Computer with special reference to the EDSAC* and the use of a library of subroutines*. Progress since then has been rapid and continuous. Indeed it is probably true to say that during the last twenty years as much effort has

---

*The first Cambridge-built computer.

199

been devoted to the task of making life easier for the programmer as to the design of the computers themselves. A typical medium-sized computer of today (1969) is about 1,000 times as fast and has about 1,000 times the storage capacity of a vintage computer of 1952; it is also about 1,000 times as easy to program. The big breakthrough came in the mid-1950s, with the development of what are called *high level* programming languages.

What, then, does a computer program written in the idiom of the late 1960s look like?

Let us start with an extremely simple example – the first of those discussed in Chapter 6; namely, the evaluation and tabulation of the squares of the integer numbers 1, 2, 3 . . . up to some specified number, N. Now the essential instructions that must be given to a computer (either a machine or a human being) to enable it (or him or her) to carry out this calculation are three in number: (i) use this particular value of N, (ii) calculate i^2 for successive values of i from 1 to N, in steps of 1, (iii) after each such calculation, print out (or write down) the current values of i and i^2 on a fresh line.

This is how the programmer naturally thinks of the calculation and he would like to be able to write his computer program in the same way – something like this perhaps:

> *read N*;
> *for i* $=1$ *in steps of* 1 *until N*
> *start new line*; *print* (i); *print* $(i \times i)$.

Acceptable computer programs can indeed be written in this way – in a language that is very different from the basic computer language of Chapter 6.* A number of such high level languages have been constructed and used during the last fifteen years, and the process goes merrily on. Most of them bear a strong resemblance to the language of mathematics, supplemented by a kind of pidgin English. How is it that such languages can be made intelligible to a computer, which is, after all, no more than a collection of bits of hardware animated by jostling electrons?

---

*Languages of this type are variously referred to as machine languages, low level languages, or assembly languages.

Compiling schemes

The crux of the matter is that a computer can be programmed to alter its operating instructions before they are obeyed. (We have explained on p. 132 how this can be done.) It follows from this that a program need not be presented to the input unit in the form in which it will eventually be executed. The computer itself can be made to 'translate' the program from one form to the other – from what is called the *source language*, in which it is written by the programmer, into the *object language*, the language of the computer. Since the computer is extremely good at this kind of job, the question arises: why not allow the programmer to write his program in a language that is convenient to himself, and place on the computer the whole burden of translating the material into a set of computer instructions which it can then execute? Current programming techniques enable us, in fact, to do just this. To put the matter in simple terms, there is no need to address the computer in *its* language; we can teach it to understand *our* language.

How do we so teach it? Since the computer can do only what 'we order it to perform', it must be provided with a translation program which must be placed in the store before the source language for any particular calculation is read in. The preparation of the translation program is the difficult part. Indeed, the development of translation schemes (often referred to, somewhat optimistically, as 'automatic programming') has become, and is likely to remain, a major preoccupation of the *corps d'élite* of programmers all over the world. The cost of developing and making the computer itself (the *hardware*) is matched by the cost of making programming schemes to use it effectively (termed, regrettably perhaps, the *software*).

Why, it may be asked, is software activity on this scale worth while? Perhaps the best answer to this question is to summarize the main things than an efficient and comprehensive programming scheme can do for the programmer.

(i) It can relieve him of most of the organizational chores such as allocating specific addresses to instructions or numbers, counting cycles, and modifying address-digits.

(ii) He need not bother with the design peculiarities of the particular computer he is using, such as its storage arrangements, its basic instruction set, or the form of its instruction-word.

(iii) Programs can be written with many fewer instructions, since one instruction in the source language may be equivalent to many computer instructions. This also means that the main plan of an intricate computation is not overshadowed by a mass of detail.

(iv) Programming becomes so easy that it can be learnt in a few days, instead of a few weeks or even months. This means that large numbers of occasional users can be taught the art; they can then program their own calculations as and when the occasion arises. (We shall have more to say on this matter in the next chapter.)

(v) Since programs are so much easier to write, mistakes are less likely, and so less time is spent in testing and correcting programs.

(vi) Programs can be amended much more easily, either by the original programmer or by someone else.

Programming schemes which involve translating from one language to another make use of three different kinds of program, and it is important to distinguish between them. First, there is the written program or *source program*, in which the calculation is specified, or described, in a language that is convenient to the programmer. Secondly, there is the computer program, or *object program*, in which the same calculation is described by a set of instructions which can be executed whenever the computer gets the signal to do so. Thirdly, there must be a *translation program* that operates on a version of the source program coded as binary digits, and generates from it a different sequence of binary digits that represents the object program. For the translation program, the source program is merely the input data and the object program is the output. The translation program is like a foreman, who interprets and amplifies the manager's instructions for a workman. This program is often called the *compiling program*, or simply the *compiler*. It is prepared once and for all and must be stored in the computer before any source program is read in.

The process of carrying out a particular computation thus consists of two stages. First, the source program is translated, or compiled, into the equivalent object program; and secondly, the object program is executed. The two stages are kept separate. Compilation is completed before any actual computation begins, and in fact the whole of the object program is stored away before any part of it is executed. This arrangement has a number of technical advantages, and may be contrasted with an alternative procedure in which each separate source program instruction is *interpreted* (i.e., translated into a set of computer instructions) and executed immediately.

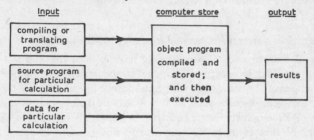

(a) object program compiled and executed in a single pass through the computer

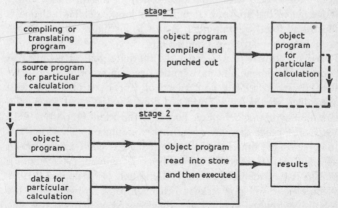

(b) object program compiled in first pass and executed in second pass

Figure 69. Compiling schemes; two alternative procedures.

At the completion of the first stage (compilation), one of two things may happen. The object program may be obeyed straight away, or it may be recorded, for use later, on some suitable medium, such as paper tape, punched cards, or magnetic tape. In the latter case, the object program must be read back into the computer before the second stage (the actual computation) can occur. This may be necessary when the program is fairly large and is to be used many times over a period of time, or, as is perfectly possible although not very frequent, when a program is compiled by one computer and executed by another. The alternative procedures are illustrated in Figure 69(a) and (b).

Towards a universal computer language: ALGOL

One of the purposes of a compiling scheme is to free the programmer from the constraints imposed by the particular computer he happens to be using; to enable him to write his programs in the way that is most convenient to him. The logical end point of this line of development is to construct a universal programming language that contains no reference to any specific computer. A compiler program would have to be written for each type of computer to deal with the translation from the universal source language to the appropriate computer language. The scheme is illustrated for two computers, A and B, in Figure 70, which has an obvious similarity to Figure 69.

We are still some way from the ultimate goal of a universal computer language, but have made a certain amount of progress towards it. In 1958 a conference of European and American specialists was held in Zurich to consider the ideal form of a common symbolic computer language for scientific purposes. In 1960, after much discussion, another conference was held in Paris to agree on the final form of the language, which became known as ALGOL 60 (short for *Algo*rithmic *L*anguage, 1960 version), and to issue a definitive report. Some two years later a further conference was held in Rome to clear up some ambiguities in the report. A revised report was then issued which became the defining document of ALGOL 60.

Although this language has attracted considerable international support, it has remained controversial and is clearly capable of further development. Under the auspices of the International Federation for Information Processing a group of experts has been labouring for some years to produce a more comprehensive and powerful programming language of the Algol type. This language has come to be known as ALGOL 68; its future at the time of writing (early 1969) seems uncertain. In January 1968 some leading members of the group circulated a 'Draft Report on the Algorithmic Language ALGOL 68'. The group now seems to be seriously split between those who support the proposals in the draft report (some of which is almost unreadable!) and those who believe them to be too complicated and obscure to be acceptable to the programming community.

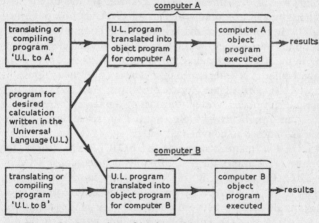

Figure 70. Operation of 'universal language' programs on two computers.

The name ALGOL needs some explanation. An *algorithm* is simply the mathematician's term for a computing procedure – for a method of reaching the desired goal in a finite number of steps.* (Infinite processes are excluded.) The iterative procedure discussed in Chapter 6 for evaluating a square root is an example

* 'Algorithm' should be distinguished from 'algorism', the meaning of which has been explained on p. 24. The two words clearly have a common origin.

of an algorithm. The objectives of ALGOL, in the words of the report of the Zurich Conference, are:

1. The new language should be as close as possible to standard mathematical notation and be readable with little further explanation.
2. It should be possible to use it for the description of computing processes in publications.
3. The new language should be mechanically translatable into machine programs.

We shall shortly give some examples of programs written in the ALGOL 60 language, so the reader will be able to make his own assessment of how far the first objective has been met. The second objective is already being realized to the extent that computational procedures written in ALGOL are now published regularly in a number of mathematical and computing journals in Europe and America. A series of international reference volumes in the ALGOL language covering the whole field of numerical mathematics is being issued by a German publishing house.

As to the third of the Zurich objectives, ALGOL compiler programs have been written for most of the larger computers in current use, particularly those engaged on scientific and technical, as opposed to commercial, tasks.

ALGOL's main competitor is FORTRAN (short for *For*mula *Tran*slation), the first form of which was constructed by the IBM Corporation in 1955. A greatly improved version, known as FORTRAN II, was published a few years later, following discussions between IBM and their major customers. In 1964 IBM issued an extended version, known as FORTRAN IV, which incorporated a number of the features of ALGOL. For the last ten years or so FORTRAN, in its various versions, has been the most widely used high level language for scientific and technical work. The vast amount of programming capital and experience invested in FORTRAN ensures that it will remain at the front of the stage for several years longer.

It must, however, be superseded eventually, and it is significant that in 1964 its creator, the IBM Corporation, when announcing a new range of computers (the 360 Series), took the opportunity to announce a new programming language, known as PL/1. It was released to IBM's customers in 1966. Its creators have sought to combine the advantages of FORTRAN and ALGOL, to exploit recent advances in programming technique, and to produce a 'universal' language suitable for both scientific and commercial work. PL/1 is certainly a powerful and comprehensive language; whether it is too difficult for the ordinary programmer is still a subject of debate. It is too early to assess the extent of its eventual success, but with the powerful sponsorship of IBM, PL/1, possibly in some restricted version, may well prove to be the dominant language of the 1970s.

Descriptions of FORTRAN, ALGOL and the other main high level languages can be found in the literature. A comparison between them would take us into technicalities beyond the scope of this book. In this Chapter we shall concentrate on ALGOL because of its role as the main language for the publication of computer programs.

In the specification of ALGOL 60 nothing is said about how data and programs are to be supplied to the computer, nor about how the results of its labours are to be presented to the person who wants to make use of them. The official language thus needs some extension before it can be used to produce working programs. In fact, each writer of an ALGOL compiler has to establish his own conventions for dealing with any input and output processes he may wish to use.

To fix ideas, let us assume that the text of an ALGOL source program is typed on a special typewriter, like a teleprinter with a larger character set, so designed that everything which is typed is simultaneously punched on paper tape. When the time comes to execute the program, the tape is loaded into the tape reader of the computer. Then, when the operator presses a button on her desk, the contents of the tape will be read into the store of the computer. At this stage the ALGOL compiler itself will already be in the store, the tape containing it having been read in previously in a similar way. The source program is then translated, or compiled, as already explained, into an object program which the computer can execute. The source program will contain instructions for reading in any necessary data and for recording the computed results, as and when required. These input and output instructions will be compiled, just like all the others, into corresponding instructions in the object program. We shall assume, again to fix ideas, that the results of the computation are to be printed on a sheet of paper, the layout of the various symbols (numbers, letters, punctuation marks, and so forth) being controlled by instructions contained in the source program itself.

Two short ALGOL programs

As our first example, we give an ALGOL program for computing the value of π (the ratio of the circumference of a circle to its diameter) from a formula which is usually attributed to François Vieta (1540–1603). A lawyer by profession, Vieta was an amature mathematician of outstanding ability. After practising for some years at the Paris Bar, he devoted the rest of his life to the public service, where his mathematical reputation soon brought him to the notice of the King, Henri IV. At that time France and Spain were at war and the Spaniards were using an elaborate cipher containing nearly 600 characters, which was periodically changed. They naturally believed it was impossible to decipher – at any rate by merely human agencies. Henri gave Vieta an intercepted dispatch and asked him to see what he could do. He succeeded in finding the key, and the French used it, to their great profit, for the remainder of the war. When Philip II found that his plans were known to the enemy he complained to the Pope that the French were using sorcery against him, 'contrary to the practice of the Christian Faith'.

Vieta's formula for π is:

$$\frac{2}{\pi} = \frac{\sqrt{2}}{2} \times \frac{\sqrt{2+\sqrt{2}}}{2} \times \frac{\sqrt{2+\sqrt{2+\sqrt{2}}}}{2} \times$$

$$\frac{\sqrt{2+\sqrt{2+\sqrt{2+\sqrt{2}}}}}{2} \times \dots \textit{ad infinitum} \tag{1}$$

Now π, and hence $2/\pi$, is what mathematicians call a transcendental number; it cannot be expressed exactly by a string of decimal digits of finite length. We can get as close an approximation as we like; we can never get quite there. That is why Vieta's formula goes on *ad infinitum*. In practice, we must always stop eventually, and so can never arrive at an exact value for π itself. The formula gives $2/\pi$ – from which, of course, π can easily be computed – as the product of an infinite number of factors, which we shall denote by $f_1/2, f_2/2, f_3/2$, etc. Successive factors get steadily larger and approach nearer and nearer to 1 without ever quite reaching it. The values of the first four are approximately 0.7071, 0.9239, 0.9808, and 0.9952. We can calculate $2/\pi$ as accurately as we like by taking a sufficient number of factors. A factor may be ignored only if it is so nearly equal to 1 that the error made by not multiplying it in is too small to matter. As in the square root program on p. 125, we shall specify the accuracy we require in terms of a small quantity, e, and shall stop the multiplication process when we first reach a factor which falls short of 1 by less than $e/2$.

The factors in the formula (1) clearly form a regular pattern and in fact the relationship between any two consecutive f's is

$$f_{n+1} = \sqrt{2 + f_n} \tag{2}$$

This result is true for all values of n greater than or equal to 1. If we set $f_0 = 0$, it will be true for $n = 0$ as well. The procedure is to compute successive approximations $(g_1, g_2 \ldots g_n)$ to the value of $2/\pi$ by multiplying in one more factor each time. Thus we have $g_1 = f_1/2$; $g_2 = g_1 \, f_2/2$; $g_3 = g_2 \, f_3/2$ and so on. If we put $g_0 = 1$, we have the general formula

$$g_{n+1} = g_n \, f_{n+1}/2 \text{ for } n = 0, 1, 2 \ldots \text{etc.} \tag{3}$$

We shall apply this formula repeatedly until we find we are multiplying by a factor that is greater than $(1 - e/2)$; we shall then stop the calculation and print out the resulting approximation to the value of π.

It is also of interest to know how many factors are needed to achieve the specified accuracy. We shall arrange to discover this in our program by counting the number of times we apply the formula (3).

209

Here, then, is the text of an ALGOL program for this calculation.

```
begin        comment Evaluate pi from Vieta's formula;
             real e, f, product; integer count;
             e := read tape;
             f := 0; product := 1; count := 0;
             for   count := count + 1 while f < 2 — e do
                   begin   f := sqrt(2 + f);
                           product := product × f/2
                   end;
             newline; print (2/product); print (count)
end
```

The output of this program consists of two numbers: the value of π to the specified accuracy, and the number of factors that must be multiplied together in order to achieve this accuracy. It turns out that fourteen factors are needed to compute the value of π correct to seven places of decimals (3.141 592 7), and twenty-five factors to get it correct to fifteen places (3.141 592 653 589 793).

The program certainly looks a little odd. Part of the reason is that ALGOL is a highly formalized, symbolic language which uses names rather like algebra uses letters. Indeed, the programmer is at liberty to invent his own names for the items he needs. Our program makes use of four variable quantities (or 'variables', as they are usually called). We have given them the names e, f, *product* and *count*; we could equally well have chosen to call them Matthew, Mark, Luke, and John. As Humpty-Dumpty remarked to Alice: 'When I use a word, it means just whatever I choose it to mean – neither more nor less.' Usually, however, a programmer would choose a name which gives some kind of clue to the role played by the corresponding variable, as we have done here. ALGOL is, in fact, a language with almost no fixed vocabulary, but with a rigid and elaborate grammatical structure – a very curious language indeed.

During the course of a computation (that is, when the equivalent object program is being executed), each of the variables is given a numerical value – or more usually, a succession of different numerical values (hence the use of the term 'variable'). To fix ideas, let us focus attention on a single variable; the one we have called *product*, for example. We may think of this variable (and hence of the word it is known by) as being associated with a particular storage location. The number stored in this location at any stage of the computation is called the 'current value' of the variable called *product*.

The word *product* may be used in an ALGOL instruction, or 'statement' as it is more usually called, in two grammatically different senses. It is important to distinguish between them. An ALGOL statement may call for the current value of *product* to be used in evaluating some algebraic expression. An example of this would be

$$result := 1 + 2/product.$$

If the current value of *product* were 5, this statement would cause the computer to work out $1 + 2/5 = 1.4$. The word *product* is used in the other sense when a statement calls for its current value to be put equal to the result of a piece of calculation. This is referred to as 'assigning a value to the variable', and such a statement is called an 'assignment statement'. The variable concerned must be written on the left. Thus we might have

$$product := a \times b$$
or
$$product := 1.$$

The word for a variable may be used in both senses in a single statement, as in

$$product := product \times f/2$$

which occurs in our program. This statement means that the new value of *product* is to be the old value multiplied by half the current value of the variable f.

Assignment statements, which constitute the arithmetical 'body' of an ALGOL program, must be written in the form

$$x := E$$

where E denotes some algebraic expression made up of variables and numerical constants connected by the usual symbols for add, subtract, multiply, and divide. What this statement says is: 'works out the value of the expression E (which is, of course, a number)

211

and make it the current value of the variable x.' The programmer need not concern himself with where this – or any other – number is actually stored. (Anyone who has done some old-fashioned programming will appreciate the value of this.)

Although assignment statements look rather like equations, they are nothing of the sort. The special symbol ':=' is used to emphasize the lack of symmetry between the two sides ($x := y$ is quite different from $y := x$) and to enable us to write such statements as $x := x + 1$ without violating the programmer's sense of algebraic seemliness.

The symbols which constitute the alphabet of the ALGOL language are called 'basic symbols'. They include:

the 26 small and the 26 capital letters of the English alphabet
the ten digits 0 to 9
a number of mathematical symbols, such as $+ \times > =$
various separator symbols such as $:= ; ( )$

Now in fact ALGOL requires a lot more basic symbols and so the founding fathers of the language introduced a mechanism for creating new ones. The rule is very simple: an English word, if written in bold type, represent a single basic symbol. Thus **begin** has nothing to do with the five letters b, e, g, i, n. (In hand- or typewritten programs, where bold type is not available, under-lining is used instead.) About twenty-five new basic symbols have been introduced in this way; we shall refer to them as 'additional basic symbols'. The program on p. 210 contains eight different ones; two of them (**begin** and **end**) are used twice.

We have said that the expression, E, in the assignment statement $x := E$ must consist of variables and constants, connected by arithmetical signs ($+$, $-$, $\times$, etc.). This statement as it stands is too restrictive since ALGOL also allows functions to be used in such expressions. Nine of the commoner mathematical functions, such as square root, sine, cosine, and logarithm, are treated as 'standard functions'. What this means is that the ALGOL language allocates a name to each of these functions (for example, *sqrt*, *sin*, *cos*, or *ln*) by which the programmer may refer to it without more ado. Thus, if we limit ourselves to the standard function *sqrt* by way of illustration, we can have assignment statements such as

$$x := sqrt(A)$$

or $\qquad stress := (B + sqrt(C))/(B + sqrt(D))$

where *A*, *B*, *C*, and *D* are algebraic expression of the same kind as *E*.

After these preliminary explanations, we are in a position to dissect our ALGOL program in more detail. Let us start in the middle – at the computational heart of the program – with the pair of assignment statements

$$f := sqrt(2 + f);$$
$$product := product \times f/2.$$

Their action will be clear if we compare them with equations (2) and (3) on p. 209. These two statements are contained between the words **begin** and **end**. The purpose of these two basic symbols is to bracket together a piece of program (in this case no more than two statements) which is to be treated as one whole.

The preceding line, namely

for *count* := *count* + 1 **while** $f < 2$ — e **do**

if an example of what is known as a 'for-statement'. (Note the three words in bold type; they are basic symbols. **do** means 'do repeatedly'.) Its purpose is to cause the statement which immediately follows the symbol **do** – or a group of statements if they are enclosed between **begin** and **end** brackets – to be executed a number of times. This provides for repeated cycling round loops in a program, as discussed on p. 118. After each repetition, the decision whether or not to repeat once more is taken in accordance with some criterion which must be stated within the body of the for-statement itself. In this case, the program calls for another repeat so long as the current value of *f* is less than a specified number denoted by $(2 - e)$. Note that the for-statement contains within itself an assignment statement, namely

$$count := count + 1.$$

This increases the current value of *count* by 1 during each passage round the loop and so maintains a running record of how many factors have been taken account of at any stage.

Immediately above the for-statement we find three assignment statements, which set the correct initial values of the variables *f*, *product*, and *count*. Immediately above is another assignment statement

$$e := read\ tape.$$

This is an input statement which corresponds to the instruction 'tape to (*n*)' of Chapter 6. It reads the *next* number on the punched tape, and makes it the current value of the variable (in this case, a constant) named on the left-hand side.

Passing now to the end of the program, we have three output statements which deal with the printing of the final answers. Their action should be clear from what has already been said. Since the final value of *product* is the approximation to $2/\pi$, the number we want to print out is given by $2/product$.

Immediately above the *read* statement we find two rather odd phrases, namely

real *e*, *f*, *product*

and 　　　　　　　　　　**integer** *count*.

These are not statements, but what are called 'declarations'. Their purpose is not to initiate action, but to convey information: in fact to tell the ALGOL compiler what it needs to know about the meaning of the various names that will be used in the program that follows. The first declaration says that the current values of the variables named *e*, *f*, and *product* are to be treated as ordinary numbers, that is to say, as 'real numbers' in the mathematician's jargon. The second declaration says that the variable called *count* may take integral values (that is, whole numbers) only. The obligation to declare his intentions is the price that the programmer must pay for the liberty of being able to chose his own names for the variables, functions, subroutines, etc., that he needs.

Another convenient feature of ALGOL is that the programmer is able to insert explanatory remarks at salient points in his program. Such remarks are intended to inform the human reader; they are of no interest to the computer. An interpolation of this kind may be introduced by the special symbol **comment**, the rule being that everything that comes after his symbol, up to and including the first semicolon, is ignored by the ALGOL compiler and so has no effect on the object program that is eventually executed. This completes our discussion of the program for evaluating π, except to remark that statements and declarations must be separated either by semicolons or by some other separator symbols such as **begin** or **end**.

Here, as our second exhibit, is an ALGOL program for the squares calculation of Chapter 6. The skeleton text of this program has already appeared on p. 200.

```
begin    comment   Tabulate the squares of the natural numbers
                   from 1 to N;
         integer   i, N;
         N :=      read tape;
         for i :=  1 step 1 until N do
         begin     newline;
                   print (i);
                   print (i ↑ 2)
         end;
end
```

This program needs little comment. The for-statement has a different form from the previous one. This one means that a series of values (in this case 1, 2, 3, up to N) is given in succession to the integer variable i, and that for each such value the statement which follows (or, as in this case, the group of statements enclosed between **begin** and **end** symbols) is executed once. The triad of symbols '$i ↑ 2$' is simply the ALGOL way of writing i^2 (or $i \times i$). In this case the specification of the actual computation is so simple that it only needs to appear as part of the final *print* statement.

Use of procedures in ALGOL

We have already commented on the convenience of being able to build up a complex program from a number of constituent parts, or subroutines, each of which can be written and tested separately before the complete program is put together. Subroutines should be written in as general a form as possible so that they may be used in a number of places in the same program – or even in different programs – without having to be written afresh each time.

Suppose, for example, that we wish to write a subroutine for doing the calculation on p. 129; that is, to compute the value of $(a_1b_1 + a_2b_2 \ldots + a_nb_n)$, where n is the number of products to be added together. We want to arrange matters so that the subroutine can be used on different occasions, not only with different numbers each time, but also with different values of n. We must make n what is called a 'parameter' of the subroutine; a particular numerical value must be assigned to this parameter each time the subroutine is called into use. In ALGOL subroutines are called 'procedures'. We can best illustrate how they work by a few examples. Let us start with a very simple one – a program for adding a set of numbers together. The first thing to do is to give our procedure a name; let us simply call it *sum*. We want to arrange matters so that whenever we wish to add a string of numbers together in the course of a calculation, all we have to do is to write the word *sum* in the appropriate place in the program. Clearly, we can do this only if the action of the *sum* procedure has previously been notified to the computer. This is done by what is called a 'procedure declaration', which first defines the name of the procedure and then gives the piece of program that the name stands for.

The procedure declaration for *sum* might be as follows:

procedure   *sum* (*w*, *i*, *m*, *R*);
           value *m*;
           integer *m*, *i*; **real** *w*, *R*;
begin   **real** *s*; *s* := 0;
           for *i* := 1 **step** 1 **until** *m* **do** *s* := *s* + *w*;
             R := *s*
end;

This looks simple enough, but a great deal can be done with it, as we shall see shortly. Indeed, the ease with which highly generalized and flexible procedures can be handled is one of the most potent features of ALGOL.

The four symbols (w, i, m, and R), which are enclosed within brackets immediately after the name of the procedure, specify what are known as the 'formal parameters' of the procedure. (The significance of the word 'formal' will be explained shortly.) The symbol m denotes the number of items to be added together; the symbol w represents any such item; the function of i is the same as in the squares program of p. 122; the result of the calculation is put in R (that is to say, the current value of the variable R is made equal to the required answer).

Now to enable a fresh number to be added on during each cycle round the loop (with i taking first the value of 1, then 2, then 3, and so on), the value of w must be made to depend in some way on the value of i. How can this be done? This brings us to another important feature of ALGOL; the facility of being able to allocate a single name to a whole group of numbers (called an 'array'), and to distinguish between individual items by means of subscripts. Suppose, for example, we denote a set of ten numbers – or more precisely, a set of ten variables, each of which can be given a numerical value – by H_1, H_2 . . . up to H_{10}. Now in order to be able to refer to these numbers in the course of an ALGOL program, we must first tell the compiler what notation we propose to use. We do this by means of an array declaration thus:

array H [1:10].

Having made this declaration, we can specify individual items in the array by means of subscripts; thus the third term in the set would be referred to as $H[3]$. (In ALGOL numbers in square brackets are used instead of subscripts, for convenience in typing and printing paper tapes.)

The elements of an array need not form a single sequence; they can be arranged in a two-dimensional rectangular pattern (in which case the array itself is called a 'matrix') or even in more complicated ways. Suppose, for example, an ALGOL program contains the declaration:

array *Cost* [1:3, 1:4].

This declares a rectangular array called *Cost*, having three rows and four columns. Set out in full it would look like this:

$$Cost\ [1, 1]\ Cost\ [1, 2]\ Cost\ [1, 3]\ Cost\ [1, 4]$$
$$Cost\ [2, 1]\ Cost\ [2, 2]\ Cost\ [2, 3]\ Cost\ [2, 4]$$
$$Cost\ [3, 1]\ Cost\ [3, 2]\ Cost\ [3, 3]\ Cost\ [3, 4]$$

An array which has only a single row, or a single column, is called a 'vector'. All the elements of a vector form a single sequence.

We can now return to the question of how to use our *sum* procedure to add together the ten elements of the vector array *H*. What this procedure does – as we can see by looking at its declaration – is to add up consecutive current values of the variable denoted by *w*, as the variable denoted by *i* runs from 1 up to *m* in steps of 1. Thus to get the answer we want, we must set $m = 10$ and arrange for *w* to take the values $H[1]$, $H[2]$, $H[3]$ and so on, up to $H[10]$ in turn; or in general terms, *w* must be put equal to $H[j]$ when *i* reaches the value *j*. How do we convey these requirements to the computer?

When a programmer wishes to use a procedure in the course of a computation, he inserts into his program a special type of ALGOL statement, known as a 'procedure call'. An example of such a statement is

$$sum\ (H[j], j, 10, t);$$

This statement is an instruction to the computer to put the current value of the variable *t* equal to the sum of the ten elements of the array *H* – which is what we set out to do.

The way it works is roughly as follows. When this statement is reached by the ALGOL compiler during the process of compilation, it is deleted and replaced by that part of the corresponding procedure declaration (i.e., the one called *sum*) which lies between the **begin** and **end** brackets. At the same time – and this is the important point – the parameter *w* is replaced by $H[j]$, *i* is replaced by *j* and *m* is replaced by 10. The 'formal parameters' of the declaration are replaced by the 'actual parameters' that are specified by the procedure call in this particular instance. We see that the parameter *m* has been given a numerical value – in this case 10 – while the other three parameters – w, i, and R – have been replaced by 'names' whose meanings must be explained somewhere in the program.

These two ways of dealing with the formal parameters of a procedure are known as 'calling by value' and 'calling by name'. Parameters in the first category are specified by means of a 'value declaration' – as in the phrase **value** m' in the procedure declaration on p. 216. Value declarations must be placed immediately after the name of the procedure. At the point of call the actual parameters corresponding to those called by value are either specific numbers (as in this case) or expressions which at that stage of the computation have definite numerical values (as in our next example on p. 221). Parameters called by name, on the other hand, are really dummies in that no values are assigned to them. At the point of call these formal parameters are replaced, in the sense of copying, by the corresponding actual parameters of the call. The operations specified in the procedure body are carried out on these actual parameters. Thus the piece of program that replaces the procedure call statement above is

```
begin      real s; s := 0;
           for  j := 1 step 1 until 10 do s := s + H[j];
           t := s
end
```

It is impossible to explain so abstract and formal a language as ALGOL without introducing a certain amount of mathematical symbolism. An analogy – admittedly very imperfect – may be helpful to those who have found the last few pages heavy going.

An ALGOL program is like a town which consists of houses and other buildings connected by roads and paths. The inhabitants of the town conduct their affairs in accordance with the law of the land and they also observe certain codes of conduct (the grammar and conventions of the ALGOL language). A procedure is like a house which is occupied over a period of time by a succession of different tenants. The procedure declaration is the estate agent's description of the empty house; it gives the address (the name of the procedure) and the layout of the rooms and services (the steps in the calculation in terms of formal parameters). Before a particular tenant can occupy the house, he must sign the appropriate documents (make a procedure call) and furnish the house for his own use (specify a set of actual parameters). After a while he moves out and takes his furniture with him. Later on another tenant comes along, informs the estate agent and signs the papers (makes a new procedure call), and furnishes the house afresh in accordance with his own taste (specifies a new set of actual parameters). In the course of time, the agent deals with many different houses (procedures), some of which are occupied by a succession of different tenants (procedure calls). Each new tenant brings his own furniture (actual parameters) with him.

The kind of procedure we have been discussing up to now is used as a complete statement in itself – the procedure call statement. ALGOL also allows for a somewhat different form of procedure, namely one which can be used within an expression, E, on the right hand side of an assignment statement such as

$$x := E.$$

A procedure of this kind is called a 'function-designator'. We have already encountered some examples of it in the standard functions, such as *sqrt* (p. 212). These functions occupy a special position in that they may be used without explicit declaration and are available whenever required. This is because the procedure declarations for all the standard functions form part of the ALGOL compiler itself.

The programmer can go much further than this – he may create and name his own functions to suit his needs; another striking illustration of the power and flexibility of the ALGOL language. All such 'personal' functions must be declared and defined in advance, just as procedures of the other kind must be. An example will clarify how this is done.

Let us suppose we are writing a program for a fairly complicated computation, in the course of which we frequently want to add the squares of four numbers together; that is to say, to evaluate expression of the form $(a^2 + b^2 + c^2 + d^2)$. Faced with this situation we may decide to create a function-designator to take care of this little calculation whenever it crops up. We are completely free in our choice of name for the function, so let us call it, say, *penguin*, and define it by the following procedure declaration.

> **real procedure** *penguin* (a, b, c, d);
> **value** a, b, c, d; **real** a, b, c, d;
> *penguin* := $a \uparrow 2 + b \uparrow 2 + c \uparrow 2 + d \uparrow 2$;

Let us see what happens when this function is encountered later in the program, as it might be in the statement

$$x := penguin \ (p+q, \ p-q, \ 10, \ n+3).$$

The computer first returns to the declaration of the *penguin* function and find that, in this case, all the formal parameters are called by value. It therefore returns to the main program, works out the current values of $(p + q)$, $(p - q)$, and $(n + 3)$ and assigns the numbers so obtained to a, b, and d respectively. The number 10 (already a value) is assigned to c. It then carries out the calculation specified in the procedure declaration, and finally assigns the computed value of *penguin* to x.

Let us see how this would work out in a particular case. If, when the above assignment statement came to be executed, the current values of p, q, and n were 5, 2, and 6 respectively, the variable x would be given the value

$$(5+2)^2 + (5-2)^2 + 10^2 + (6+3)^2 = 7^2 + 3^2 + 10^2 + 9^2$$
$$= 49 + 9 + 100 + 81$$
$$= 239.$$

This particular calculation could in part be handled equally well by means of a procedure statement. The real usefulness of function-designators is that they allow self-created functions to form part of algebraic expressions on the right-hand side of assignment statements. Thus a program might contain the statement

$$y := L \times M + penguin \ (P-D, \ Q-D, \ R-D, \ S-D)/n.$$

When this statement comes to be executed, the effect is the same as if *penguin* were a single variable. Its value would be found, as before, by obeying the procedure declaration, after replacing the formal by the actual parameters. The expression $(LM + penguin/n)$ would then be worked out and its value assigned to y. We shall shortly give some further examples of the use of functions within expressions.

We have explained how to use a procedure statement to add a set of numbers together. We can do the job equally well by means of a function-designator; we have only to declare a function – let us call it *SUM* – whose value is equal to the sum of the values of a set of variables. (In the ALGOL language the words *SUM* and *sum* are entirely unrelated.) We can do this by means of the following procedure declaration:

real procedure   *SUM* (*w, i, m*);
    value *m*;
    integer *m, i*;   **real** *w*;
    begin   **real** *s*; *s* := 0;
        for *i* := 1 **step** 1 **until** *m* **do** *s* := *s+w*;
        SUM := *s*
end

Comparing this with the non-functional declaration for *sum* given on p. 216, we find three differences: (i) the basic symbol **real** is added at the start to indicate that a computed value of this function is to be treated as an ordinary number, (ii) the number of parameters is reduced to three by eliminating the one used for the answer, (iii) the final statement (namely, *SUM* := *s*) assigns the result of the calculation as the 'current value' of the variable called *SUM*.

If we wish, as before, to compute the sum of the ten elements of the array *H* and to set the result as the current value of the variable *t*, we would write the following assignment statement:

$$t := SUM (H(j), j, 10).$$

In this case it so happens that the expression on the right of the assignment statement is the function itself. This need not be so; the function-word *SUM* may be used quite freely within such expression, as we explained when discussing our *penguin* function.

A further ALGOL facility is that the actual parameters may themselves be defined by algebraic expressions, instead of by simple variables. Consider, once again, the calculation discussed on p. 216; namely, the evaluation of $S = a_1b_1 + a_2b_2 \ldots + a_nb_n$. If we regard $a_1, a_2, \ldots$ up to a_n as being the elements of a vector array, a, and b_1, b_2, ... b_n as elements of a vector array, b, all we need is the single assignment statement:

$$S := SUM\ (a[j] \times b[j],\ j,\ n).$$

We are assuming, of course, that the ground has been properly prepared earlier in the program – by declaring the SUM function itself and also the two arrays a and b. These must be declared in the form

array a, b [1:n].

It is perhaps worth while emphasizing once again that the programmer is at liberty to use whatever names he likes for his variables, arrays, functions, and procedures. If, for instance, he were eccentric enough to want to call the two arrays GOG and $MAGOG$, he would express the calculation of S by a statement such as

$$S := SUM\ (GOG\ [k] \times MAGOG\ [k],\ k,\ p)$$

having previously declared the two arrays by

array GOG, $MAGOG$ [1:p].

An ALGOL program for a statistical calculation

We have now described most of the salient features of ALGOL. In order to convey to the reader something of the distinctive flavour of ALGOL as a programming language, we conclude this part of the chapter by discussing a more realistic – and hence a rather more complicated – example. The calculation itself will be familiar to anyone who has made use of statistical methods.

We have already commented on the convenience of being able to use names to stand for self-contained pieces of calculation. Indeed, the greater part of the text of an ALGOL program may well consist of procedure declarations, with the program proper compressed into a relatively small number of statements. By the 'program proper' we mean the instructions that are actually translated (with appropriate replacements, as already explained) by the ALGOL compiler into the object program that is eventually executed.

Most people have a general idea of what is meant by the degree of association, or correlation, between two variable quantities. Tall fathers are more likely than not to have tall daughters, for example. There is no certainty about it; many tall girls have short fathers. The effect is a statistical one, true on the average but not in each individual case. We say that there is a positive correlation between the heights of girls and the heights of their fathers. If we plot the measured heights of a group of men and their daughters,

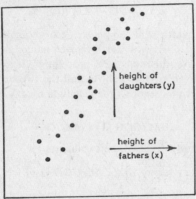

Figure 71. A scatter diagram.

as in Figure 71, we get what is called a 'scatter diagram' – in this case with the points concentrated in the top-right and bottom-left parts of the picture.

Now the statistician wants to express the notion of correlation in precise terms – to put a number on it. He does this by defining a quantity called a 'correlation coefficient', usually denoted by r, which he can use as a measure of the degree of correlation between two variables; x and y, say. The value of r always lies between $+1$ and -1. A positive value of r means that an increase in x tends to be associated with an increase in y; the larger the value of r, the higher the degree of correlation. Similarly, a negative value of r means that an increase in x tends to be associated with a decrease in y. In between we have $r=0$, which indicates complete dis-association – as we might expect between intelligence and eye-colour, for example. A typical value of r for the 'height of father

224

/height of daughter' association is about +0.73, indicating a fairly high, but far from complete, degree of correlation between the two variables.

An example of rather greater interest is discussed by M.J. Moroney, in his admirable book *Facts from Figures*.* The data is tabulated overleaf and is shown graphically in Figure 72.

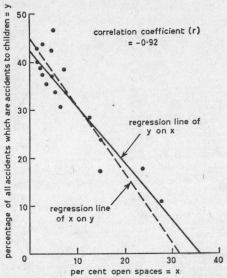

Figure 72. Scatter diagram with regression lines.

In this case the value of r comes out to be —0.92; a very high degree of negative correlation.

Having calculated the correlation coefficient, we may ask the question: for any given value of x (the percentage of open space), how do we estimate the corresponding value of y (the children's accident percentage)? To answer this we must calculate what is called the 'regression line of y on x'.† This line is drawn in Figure 72; we can use it to read off the best estimate of the value of y corresponding to any desired value of x. We can also turn the

* Pelican Books.

† A fuller discussion of the significance of the correlation coefficient and regression lines will be found in Moroney (op. cit. Chapter 16).

District	Proportion of open spaces %=x	Proportion of accidents to children as percentage of all accidents =y
Bermondsey	5.0	46.3
Deptford	2.2	43.4
Islington	1.3	42.9
Fulham	4.2	42.2
Shoreditch	1.4	40.0
Finsbury	2.0	38.8
Woolwich	7.0	38.2
Stepney	2.5	37.4
Poplar	4.5	37.0
Southwark	3.1	35.3
Camberwell	5.2	33.6
Paddington	7.2	33.6
Stoke Newington	6.3	30.8
Hammersmith	12.2	28.3
Wandsworth	14.6	23.8
Marylebone	23.6	17.8
Hampstead	14.8	17.1
Westminster	27.5	10.8

question round and ask for an estimate of the percentage of open space (x) that would be necessary to give an expectation of some specified accident percentage (y). This leads to another line – the 'regression line of x on y', which is shown dotted on Figure 72.

The fact that these two lines are not the same may seem somewhat surprising, but there is really no reason why the process of estimating y from x should be the exact reverse of that of estimating x from y. Our problem, then, is to calculate the correlation coefficient and the equations of the two regression lines; that is to say, the values of $r, a_1, b_1, a_2,$ and b_2 from the following formulae.*

$$\left.\begin{array}{l}\text{Equation of regression line of } y \text{ on } x : y = a_1 + b_1 x \\ \text{Equation of regression line of } x \text{ on } y : x = a_2 + b_2 y\end{array}\right\} \quad (4)$$

*These formulae are equivalent to those given by Moroney (op. cit.).

$$\text{Correlation coefficient: } r = \pm \sqrt{b_1 b_2} \qquad (5)$$

where

$$a_1 = \frac{(\Sigma y) - b_1(\Sigma x)}{n}, \qquad a_2 = \frac{(\Sigma x) - b_2(\Sigma y)}{n},$$
$$b_1 = \frac{n(\Sigma xy) - (\Sigma x)(\Sigma y)}{n(\Sigma x^2) - (\Sigma x)^2}, \qquad b_2 = \frac{n(\Sigma xy) - (\Sigma x)(\Sigma y)}{n(\Sigma y^2) - (\Sigma y)^2} \qquad (6)$$

and n is the number of different observations; that is, the number of points on a scatter diagram. (We shall assume in what follows that n is not more than 1,000.) We can denote these observations by their coordinates, using the subscript notation, thus:

$$(x_1, y_1)\ (x_2, y_2) \ldots (x_n, y_n).$$

The symbol 'Σ' stands for 'the sum of'; thus we have

$$(\Sigma x) = x_1 + x_2 \ldots + x_n$$
$$(\Sigma x^2) = x_1^2 + x_2^2 \ldots + x_n^2$$
$$(\Sigma xy) = x_1 y_1 + x_2 y_2 \ldots + x_n y_n$$

and so on.

Some readers may be puzzled by the notion of the 'equation' of a regression line (formulae 4). If two quantities x and y are related by a straight line (or linear) law, the relationship between them may be expressed by an equation of the form

$$y = mx + c.$$

The meaning of the two parameters, m and c, is explained in Figure 73.

We shall speak of b_1 as the 'slope' and a_1 as the 'intercept' of the regression of y on x; similarly for the regression of x on y.

In formula (5) we have written $r = \pm \sqrt{b_1 b_2}$. How do we decide which sign to take? Now the denominators of b_1 and b_2 are always positive, while the two numerators are the same. This means that b_1 and b_2 are either both positive or both negative. In either case the product $b_1 b_2$ is positive, so we are quite safe in asking the computer to evaluate the square root of this quantity. The rule is that r is positive when b_1 and b_2 are positive and is negative when they are negative. We may express this formally as

$$r = sign\ (b_1)\ \sqrt{b_1 b_2} \qquad (7)$$

where *sign* (b_1) takes the value $+1$ when b_1 is positive, 0 when b_1 is zero, and -1 when b_1 is negative. This rather curious function is, fortunately, one of the standard ALGOL functions.

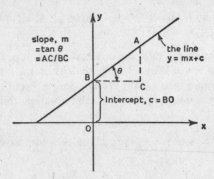

Figure 73. Illustrating the equation of a straight line.

Here, then, is the text of an ALGOL program for this calculation.

```
begin
    comment To evaluate the slopes and intercepts of the regres-
            sion lines, and the correlation coefficient, of a set
            of points;
        real b1, b2;   integer n;   array x, y[1:1000];
    procedure   READ NUMBERS (w, m);
        value m;
        integer m;   array w;
        begin integer i;
            for i := 1 step 1 until m do w [i] := read tape
        end;
    real procedure   SUM (w, i, m);
        value m;
        integer m, i;   real w;
        begin   real s;   s := 0;
            for i := 1 step 1 until m do s := s+w;
            SUM :=s
        end;
```

```
real procedure SLOPE (u, v, m);
    value m;
    integer m;   array u, v;
    begin   integer p;
            SLOPE := (m × SUM (u[p] × v[p], p,m) −
            SUM (u[p], p, m) × SUM (v[p],
            p, m) )/(m × SUM (u[p] ↑ 2, p, m)
            − SUM (u[p], p, m) ↑ 2)
    end;
real procedure   INTERCEPT (u, v, m, c);
    value m, c;
    integer m;   array u, v;   real c;
    begin integer p;
            INTERCEPT := (SUM (v[p], p, m) −
            c × SUM (u[p], p, m))/m
    end;
procedure REGRESSION WITH PRINT OUT (a, b, q, z);
    value q;
    integer q;   real z;   array a, b;
    begin   newline;
            write text ('Slope=');
            z := SLOPE (a, b, q);
            print (z);
            write text ('Intercept=');
            print (INTERCEPT (a, b, q, z));
            newline
    end;
start :      n := read tape;
            READ NUMBERS (x, n);
            READ NUMBERS (y, n);
            write text ('y on x');
            REGRESSION WITH PRINT OUT(x, y, n, b1);
            write text ('x on y');
            REGRESSION WITH PRINT OUT (y, x, n, b2);
            write text ('Correlation coefficient=');
            print (sign (b1) × sqrt(b1 × b2));
            newline;
            go to start
end
```

The meaning of most of the individual statements and declarations should be clear from what has already been said, but the overall structure may be confusing. We start with a commentary to help the reader; we then declare the variables we shall be using, namely, b_1, b_2, n, and the arrays x and y. Next follow five procedure declarations, and finally we come to what we have called the 'program proper'. It will be seen that the text of this part begins with the word *start*. We have chosen this word to label one of the instructions – in this case, the first statement of the program proper.

The purpose of a label is to enable the programmer to deal with jumps out of the normal sequence, as discussed on p. 119. Thus the statement 'go to L' where L stands for any label, causes an unconditional jump to the statement which is prefixed by the label L. (A label must be separated from the associated statement by a colon (:).) Labels can also be used to deal with conditional jumps in such statements as

> **if** $x < 0$ **then go to** *Repeat*

or V: **if** $u > v$ **then** $q := q + 1$ **else go to** *Town*

where *Repeat*, V and *Town* are the names of labels.

The reason for the **go to** statement at the end of our program is to tell the computer, after it has completed the calculation, to go back and 'see' if any more numbers are punched on the tape. If there are, the computer will assume that the calculation is to be done again with the new set of data, and will proceed accordingly.

The names we have given to the five procedures, in the order in which they are declared, are:
READ NUMBERS, *SUM*, *SLOPE*, *INTERCEPT*, and *REGRESSION WITH PRINT OUT*. (We have used capital letters solely for convenience in exposition.) The first and last are non-functional procedures which are called into use by procedure call statements. The other three are function-designators, one of them (*SUM*) being used in each of the other two.

The purpose of the *REGRESSION WITH PRINT OUT* procedure is to arrange for the computation and printing of the two coefficients which specify a regression line. In this program these coefficients appear as the 'values' of the function-designators, *SLOPE* and *INTERCEPT*. We have made this part of the calculation into a procedure because it must be carried out twice; once for computing the regression of *y* on *x*, and again for computing the regression of *x* on *y*.

The computation of the correlation coefficient, on the other hand, is entrusted to the 'program proper', which indeed does little else than call in the appropriate procedures and control the printing of the results. If this program were executed with the input data of the Table on p. 226, the answers would be displayed on the printed page like this:

> *y on x*
> Slope = − 1.21   Intercept = 42.7
> *x on y*
> Slope = − 0.70   Intercept = 31.1
> Correlation coefficient = − 0.92

With this layout as a guide, the action of the three kinds of output statement (*print*, *write text* and *newline*) should be clear.

It is worth noting that the values of each of the functions *SLOPE* and *INTERCEPT* are computed by means of a single assignment statement. Indeed, the evaluation of the expressions on the right hand sides of these two statements constitutes the entire computation, apart from the final calculation of the correlation coefficient. A comparison between these two expressions and the corresponding formulae (6 on p. 227) provides a good illustration of the convenience, flexibility, and conciseness of ALGOL.

This concludes our discussion of ALGOL. To sum up, we may say that ALGOL, like any other language, has an alphabet (a set of basic symbols), a syntax (a set of rules specifying what are meaningful combinations of basic symbols), and semantics (a set of rules specifying the 'meanings' of these combinations; that is to say, the action to be taken by the computer when an ALGOL statement is executed). It differs from most other languages in being highly formalized, completely logical, compact, and absolutely precise – as it must be to do its job. This means that a program witten in ALGOL is bound to appear more than a little forbidding to someone who is not familiar with the use of symbolic languages in mathematics and logic. Most of us, indeed, are in this position; certainly most commercial people are, and they need to use computers just as much as scientists and technologists, who may be presumed to have an adequate mathematical background. ALGOL, with its esoteric symbolism, does not really qualify for the role of a universal language; it certainly would not find a congenial home in the average business office. Something else is needed to meet the needs of the commercial community. Although many business programs are indeed still written in 'low level' languages which are specific to the particular computer being used, a number of 'high level' programming languages have been developed for commercial and administrative purposes. We conclude this chapter with a brief discussion of the most widely used of them.

COBOL: A common computer language for commercial data-processing

ALGOL, as we have seen, is a symbolic language designed for the specific purpose of expressing scientific numerical procedures in a form suitable for communication between professionals and for presenting such procedures to a computer for translation into a useable program. The counterpart of ALGOL for the commercial user is known as COBOL (short for Common Business Oriented Language). The two languages seek to meet almost exactly the same requirements, each in their own field of application; the final products look very different.

The first version of COBOL was developed in 1959 in the U.S.A. by a Committee representing a number of government users and computer manufacturers. It was clear that a number of improvements and additions would need to be made from time to time and the founding organizations very wisely set up an Executive Committee to examine new proposals and introduce changes in an orderly fashion. Support for COBOL has steadily increased over the years; it is now used by large numbers of programmers all over the world.

A program written in COBOL consists of three parts.

(i) A 'Procedure Division' in which the programmer specifies the operations to be performed on the information read in to the computer.

(ii) A 'Data Division' which specifies the various blocks of information that are read in and put out, and the inter-relationships between the blocks, together with any other numerical data that is needed.

(iii) An 'Environment Division' which specifies the equipment on which the program is to be executed.

Let us consider the Data Division first. The typical large business calculation requires information to be fed into the computer from a number of different sources, and entails the production of several different sets of results. Thus, to take a familiar example, the input might consist of (a) all the data relating to customers' accounts that has resulted from previous transactions (this would probably be stored on a reel of magnetic tape) and (b) customers' new orders and payments (probably on punched cards); and the output of (c) updated customer accounts (on magnetic tape, with perhaps an optional print out) and (d) statements for customers (in printed form).

In most business computing (or data processing as it is usually called) we have the situation in which several streams of input data operate on one another to produce several streams of output data. In COBOL, each such stream of data is called a 'file', and a major subdivision within a file is called a 'record'. Thus the set of printed statements (d) is a file; a statement for a particular customer would be a record. Records can be further subdivided into 'fields', and so on down successive levels in the hierarchy. The programmer has a good deal of freedom as to how he subdivides his input and output material; the deciding factor is that a record must either be read in from an input file or written on to an output file as a single block.

Each file, record, field, etc., is given a name (known as a 'data-name') and a classification. Thus in our example, the input file (b) which contains customers' orders and payments might be described thus:

FD	Movements
01	Order
02	Type-of-record
02	Order-number
02	Customer-number
02	Date
02	Product-number
02	Quantity
01	Payment
02	Type-of-record
02	Customer-number
02	Date
02	Amount.

The complete file (designated *FD*) is called *Movements*. It contains two types of record, one called *Order* and the other *Payment* (Records have the level-number 01). Within the *Order* record we have six fields (each with level-number 02). These specify the type of record (i.e., either an *Order* or a *Payment*), the order number, the customer's reference number, the date of the order, the reference number of the product, and the quantity. Similarly, the *Payment* record contains four fields specifying the type of record, the customer's reference number, the date of payment and the amount. If any field needs to be further subdivided, its constituent sub-fields would be given the level number 03. For instance, the field called *Product-number* might be divided into *Warehouse-number* and *Item-number*.

The Procedure Division specifies how the output files are to be derived from the input files; it effectively describes the actual computation. The text of the Procedure Division is divided into a sequence of paragraphs, each consisting of a series of 'sentences'. Each sentence specifies an operation to be performed; it corresponds to the statement in ALGOL. The COBOL programmer constructs his sentences from a repertoire of standard 'keywords' (these are English-language verbs, adverbs, prepositions, etc.) and 'symbols' (such as $+$, $-$, $=$) which operate on the data-names defined in the Data Division.

Sentences can specify that a certain operation is to be performed either unconditionally or only if certain stated conditions are satisfied. A simple example of the former is

Compute *Net Pay* $=$ *Gross Pay* $-$ *Deductions*.

If, however, there is a stipulation that an employee's gross pay must not fall below £10, then we might have, as an example of a conditional type of sentence:

If *Gross Pay* **is greater than** *Minimum*
compute *Net Pay = Gross Pay — Deductions* **otherwise**
compute *Net Pay = Minimum — Deductions.*

The fields labelled *Net Pay*, *Gross Pay*, and *Deductions* will have been defined in the Data Division of the program, as also will the amount of the *Minimum* wage. The other words in these sentences must be selected from the list of allowed keywords and symbols. The full COBOL language contains several hundred of these.

Four of the most important keywords, other than those already mentioned, are:

read (to make a record from an input file available in the computer store)

write (to transfer a block of information, specified as a record, to an output file)

go to (to enable the program to specify a jump out of sequence – the familiar jump instruction)

move (to copy information from one field to another).

The business man's preference for plain English is not forgotten! The words **add, subtract, multiply,** and **giving** can be used as arithmetic verbs as an alternative to the corresponding mathematical symbols. Thus these two COBOL sentences are synonymous:

(a) **Multiply** *Rate* **by** *Hours* **giving** *Gross Pay*
(b) **Compute** *Gross Pay = Rate × Hours.*

Finally we have the Environment Division which specifies the equipment on which the program is to be run. This Division is written in English phrases selected from a set of standard forms. It is divided into two sections:

(i) a 'Configuration Section' which specifies the type of computer to be used and the amount of working storage and auxiliary storage that is needed for the particular job; for instance, 800 words of core store and 15,000 words of magnetic drum storage, and

(ii) an 'Input-Output Section' which states which files are to be assigned to which input and output units. Thus, in our invoicing example, this Section might contain statements such as:

> **assign** *Customer-account* **file to magnetic tape 3;**
> **assign** *Movements* **file to card reader;**
> **assign** *Updated-account* **file to magnetic tape 4;**
> **assign** *Statement* **file to printer.**

The distinguishing feature of the Environment Division is that the information in it relates to a specific installation. The point we have already made in connexion with ALGOL thus arises again here. COBOL, as a common language, needs some further specification in order to produce working programs that can be run on a particular computer. That is why it is convenient to segregate the 'computer oriented' information. The rules for writing the Procedure and Data Divisions can be embodied in the specification of the common language; the specification of the Environment Division must be tailored to suit each installation.

10. COMPUTERS AT WORK

During recent years the computer industry has been expanding (in terms of sales income) at a rate of about twenty per cent per annum. This growth rate is substantialy higher than that of any other important industry; for motor cars, for example, the rate is about ten per cent per annun.

By 1960 the electronic computer had established itself as an essential tool of the scientist, the engineer, and the accountant. During the last decade it has moved into new fields – medicine, the law, the marriage bureau and management planning, to mention only a few. Nowadays computers are to be found almost everywhere, doing almost everything: calculating, checking and controlling the movement of space vehicles, unravelling the structure of the living cell, predicting tomorrow's weather, controlling a chemical plant, playing war games, analysing literary texts, working out railway timetables or oil tanker schedules, keeping 20 million social security records up to date, and so on, and so on. In the next chapter we shall look at a few of the jobs that computers are doing; in this chapter we deal with the working environment of the computer itself.

How many computers are there altogether? This question is not quite so simple as it looks: apart from the difficulty of getting the complete story, census-takers differ among themselves as to what should properly be included. The smaller 'electronic calculators', for instance, are sometimes admitted and sometimes not. Here is a rough estimate of the global distribution of computers in the middle of 1968:

North America	46,000
United Kingdom	3,000
Western and Central Europe	11,000
U.S.S.R., Eastern Europe and China	5,000
Other areas	5,000
Total	70,000

About two-thirds of the world's stock of computers is to be found in the United States; a still higher proportion – more than seventy per cent – are of American manufacture. Even more striking is the dominance of a single firm, the International Business Machines Corporation, which enjoys about seventy per cent of the computer market in America, Asia and Western Europe. (The position in the U.K. is rather different.)

British Computers since 1946

British computer activity began in the winter of 1946–7 in the Universities of Manchester, Cambridge and London, and the National Physical Laboratory. Manchester was first in the field with a small laboratory model designed by Professor F.C. Williams, Dr (now Professor) T. Kilburn and one of the present authors. This computer, which had only the minimum of facilities, first operated successfully in June 1948 – the first electronic digital computer in the world to hold its program and data in the same store. (Plate 2 shows this historic computer as it was in the early months of 1949.) Work was immediately started on larger machines and two more were completed in 1949. Indeed, the University of Manchester has largely set the pace for the British computer industry ever since. Four full size computers have been designed there up to the present time. Each could claim to be the most advanced British design of its day, and each has served as a prototype for commercial manufacture.

Cambridge followed hard on the heels of Manchester. The EDSAC (Electronic Delay Storage Automatic Calculator), which was designed and built in the Cambridge University Mathematical Laboratory under the direction of Dr (now Professor) M. V. Wilkes, performed its first fully automatic calculation in May 1949. The important Cambridge contributions to the art of programming have been mentioned in the last chapter.

The National Physical Laboratory completed its first experimental computer, known as the ACE Pilot model, in 1950. Parts of this machine, the fastest of the early computers, are now at the London Science Museum. The high speed storage of both the EDSAC and the ACE Pilot model consisted of mercury delay lines (p. 140). As might be expected, the early Manchester machines used the locally invented Williams-tube store. The other type of storage to be introduced at this time, the magnetic drum, was developed in Britain by Professor A.D.Booth of Birkbeck College, London, and at Manchester.

These early computers served as prototypes for the commercially built machines that began to appear in 1951. The Ferranti Mark I computer, based on a 1949 Manchester University design, was the first general purpose computer to be put on sale. The first computer intended primarily for business work, as opposed to scientific or technical calculations, was also completed in 1951. It was known as LEO (short for Lyons Electronic Office) and was based on the Cambridge EDSAC.

Two other early British computers were the small HEC machine built by the British Tabulating Machine Co., and the English Electric DEUCE. The former used a magnetic drum store and was derived from an experimental machine at Birkbeck College; the latter was based on the N.P.L. ACE Pilot Model. The other important British computers of the first decade (1946–56) were the Elliott 401–405 series and the Ferranti Pegasus, each of which used nickel delay lines in their high speed stores. Up to the end of 1954 only eight British commercially built computers had been delivered (six Ferranti Mark Is, one LEO 1 and one Elliott 401). Thereafter the trickle began to turn into a steady flow; the DEUCE appeared early in 1955, the HEC and the Pegasus soon after. Since then the story has been one of rapid technological progress and industrial growth, with each new model in turn becoming technically obsolescent almost as soon as it appears. The main British landmarks of the first computer decade are charted in Figure 74.

Throughout its first twenty years of life, the British computer industry, like the goods it produces, has been in a continual state of change – some would say of upheaval. In no less than nine of the last fifteen years (1954–1968) there have been mergers or changes of one kind or another. Two types of firm entered the field during the 1950s. On the one hand there were manufacturers of electrical equipment, such as English Electric, Ferranti, Elliott and E.M.I. On the other hand there were the manufacturers of office machinery such as punched-card equipment. These included The British Tabulating Machine Company, Powers Samas, and IBM (U.K.). There was also LEO Computers, in a class by itself. When the catering firm of J. Lyons &

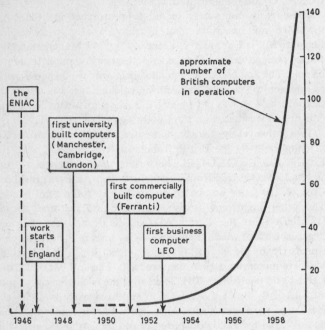

Figure 74. Time chart of the first decade of British computer development.

Co., decided as early as 1947 to install an electronic computer in their head office, they decided to build it themselves since no commercial machine was available at that time. The success of their first computer – the LEO machine already referred to – led to the formation of a company to make computers for the general market.

By the end of the 1950s the manufacture of digital computers had come of age as a substantial British industry. Total sales averaged about £10 million per annum, exports accounting for

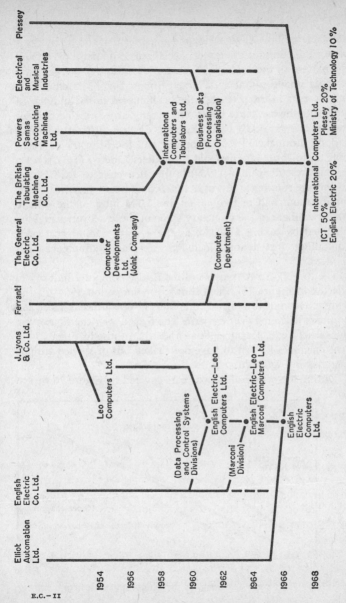

Figure 75. The British Computer Industry (1954–1968).

about £2 million. It soon became apparent that too many firms were competing for the rather specialized computer market, and the pattern of the 1960s has been one of successive mergers into an ever smaller number of larger groups. Figure 75 charts the main events in the process, which culminated in the summer of 1968 with the merger of the two remaining large British computer manufacturers, I.C.T. and English Electric, with substantial support from the Plessey Company and the Ministry of Technology, to form International Computers Limited (ICL).

The present position (1969) is that deliveries to British customers are running at just over 1,000 computers a year, with I CL taking about half of the market and IBM most of the rest. A rough estimate of the monetary value of these deliveries may be obtained by taking £100,000 as the average capital cost of a computing installation, including ancillary equipment and services.

The overall growth pattern of the British computer industry is charted in Figure 76, which shows, for the period 1954–68, the cumulative annual totals of computers in operation and also the numbers delivered year by year. The reason why the figures for the earlier years are substantially less than those in Figure 74 is that machines known to have been taken out of service are not included in Figure 76.

During the period of fifteen years covered by Figure 76 we are

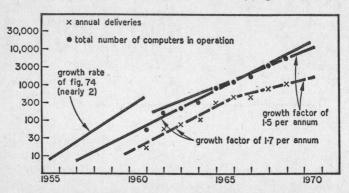

Figure 76. Twenty-five years of British computer development.

concerned with factors of increase of several hundredfold. The most satisfactory way to present numerical information spanning so wide a range is to use what is called a 'logarithmic scale', and we have done this for the vertical scale. This means that moving upwards a given distance does not increase the quantity by a given *amount*, but by a given *factor*. The scales are marked for successive factors of 10, and since a factor of 3 corresponds to a distance very nearly half that for a factor of 10, it is convenient to mark these as well. One important feature of the logarithmic scale is that a straight line corresponds to a constant *rate* of growth (as in accumulation by compound interest) rather than a constant increment (simple interest). Figure 76 shows that the rate of growth has remained fairly steady at about 1.7 per annum (a seventy per cent increase every year) during most of the 1960s, although there are signs of a slight falling off at the end to about 1.5 per annum. With such a high growth rate some further reductions are inevitable, otherwise by the end of the century there would be one computer for every man, woman and child in the country.

The computer of the fifties

A typical computer of the 1948–58 decade consisted of a main cabinet, full of thermionic valves, capacitors, resistors, wires, and soldered joints; an operator's desk; a smaller cabinet containing the necessary power supplies; an input unit (usually either a card or paper tape reader); and an output unit (a card or paper tape punch). The main cabinet housed the electronic circuits, most of which were concerned with arithmetical, control, or storage functions. The store itself – either delay lines, Williams-tubes and/or magnetic drums – might also be housed either inside the main cabinet or in a separate unit.

We need say no more about the parts of the computer that perform the arithmetical, control or storage functions; they have been sufficiently discussed in Chapters 7 and 8. It will be convenient at this point, however, to make a few remarks about the other two of the five basic constituents of Figure 37 (p. 111) – the input and output units. The medium of communication between our early computer and the outside world would almost certainly have been either 'Hollerith' punched cards, as shown in Figure 11 (p. 51), or five-track punched paper tape of the kind used to operate teleprinters. In either case, the function of the input unit is to convert space-patterns of holes on pieces of paper or card into time-patterns of electrical pulses. These pulses then pass into the main cabinet and actuate the appropriate electronic circuits. The function of the output unit is exactly the reverse; to convert electrical pulses into patterns of holes.

With punched cards, the mode of operation of the input and output units will be clear from what has been said in Chapter 3. In an early computer like DEUCE, for example, the input cards were read at about 200 cards per minute, while the computed answers were punched out on another set of cards at about 100 cards per minute.

With five-track tape there are five positions across the tape in which holes may be punched, so one row represents five binary digits. This gives thirty-two possible 'hole' or 'no-hole' combinations. We have pointed out on p. 146 that sixty-four different combinations are needed to represent in this way all the required input and output symbols (or characters) – the letters of the alphabet, the numerals (0, 1, . . . 9), and some other essential symbols. With five-hole tape we have only thirty-two combinations. To overcome this limitation matters are arranged so that the same pattern of holes can be interpreted in one or other of two ways; roughly speaking, as a letter of the alphabet if the computer is instructed to interpret the tape in what we may call 'letter mode', and as a numeral or special symbol if in 'figure mode'. The shift key on an ordinary typewriter performs a similar function, but in this case the two modes distinguish between upper and lower case letters, instead of between numbers and letters.

Both the tape reader and tape punch of our early computer would have stood on the operator's desk; they are much smaller than the corresponding card equipment. Until about 1956 the holes in paper tape, like those in cards, were usually 'sensed' electro-mechanically, at a speed of not more than thirty characters per second. Since that time, with the advent of photoelectric means of sensing, it has been possible to read tapes very much faster – at speeds of up to 1,000 characters per second. Tape punching is a much slower process. The devices available in the mid 1950s could punch between ten and twenty-five characters in a second.

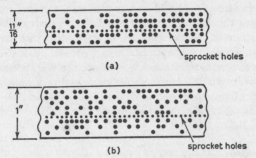

Figure 77. (*a*) Five-track paper tape. (*b*) Eight-track paper tape.

The immediate output of our computer would consist of a pack of punched cards or a length of punched paper tape. These may be intelligible to the expert, but the ordinary person wants his answers in a more easily readable form. The information on the cards or tape had therefore to be converted into a printed record –

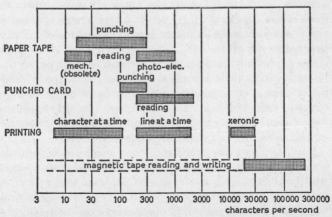

Figure 78. Speeds of various input and output devices.

or in special cases, into a set of graphs or charts. This was usually done as a separate operation, away from the computer itself. With cards, the usual procedure was to load the pack of output cards by hand into the card-feed of a line-at-a-time printing device – probably a rudimentary tabulator of the kind described in p. 54. With paper tape the procedure was similar, the output tape being loaded into the reading unit of a teleprinter. In this case, however, the data would be printed out character by character, thus limiting the speed to six to ten characters per second. In some early computers several teleprinters were needed to keep pace with the output of results. Figure 78 shows the speed of a representative selection of input and output devices. The left-hand portions of the bands relate to the situation up to about 1956.

The computer of the sixties

If we transfer our attention from a computer designed in, say, 1954 to one of the larger ones designed in 1964, we see a very different picture. Instead of a main cabinet with a few append-ages, we see a number of separate cabinets – perhaps fifteen or twenty altogether – spaced well apart in an air-conditioned, sound-proofed room. One person is sitting at a desk with a type-writer in front of him; two or three others are moving about the room carrying packs of cards, reels of magnetic tape or sheets of paper. A maintenance technician is working on one of the units temporarily out of use.

The reason why there are so many pieces of equipment is that nowadays most designers adopt a unit-assembly approach, so that a computing installation can be made to measure. Every customer starts with a central computer unit, now usually called a *central processor* (p. 195), which can be selected and inter-connected to suit his individual requirements. The central pro-cessor deals with the arithmetical and control functions and contains a certain amount of high speed storage, some of which will probably be reserved for special purposes such as holding supervisory programs or commonly used subroutines. The operator's desk and the power supplies may also be regarded as part of the central processor.

The central unit is provided with a number of input and output terminals to which can be connected any desired combination of storage, input and output units.

A large installation would include most of the following:

(i) A group of high speed storage units consisting of ferro-magnetic cores. Each unit would have a capacity of between 4,000 and 16,000 words, a word being between thirty-two and sixty binary digits; there would be between two and sixteen such units altogether. '

(ii) A number of magnetic storage devices to supplement the core store. These, as we have seen in Chapter 7 (pp. 148–154), can take a variety of physical forms: drums; discs, which may be either fixed or removeable (these are often called exchangeable discs or disc packs); or tapes.* Most installations contain at least two of these three kinds of magnetic store; many of the larger ones have all three. Here again, in choosing between them, we must compromise between the conflicting requirements of high speed, large storage capacity and low cost. Typical characteristics of the various types of magnetic storage are shown in the table below; there is of course a wide spread within each type.

Type of storage	Magnetic Drum	Exchangeable Disc	Fixed Disc	Magnetic Tape	Ferrite Core
Average access time in millisecs.	10	100	100	10,000	0.001
Capacity per unit in millions of characters	5	10	500	100	0.01
Transfer rate of thousands of characters per second	1,000	200	200	200	N.A.

The figures for capacity refer to a single physical unit of the type of store concerned; a large installation might have half-a-dozen magnetic drums or discs of various kinds and

---

*It is convenient to refer to magnetic tapes, drums and discs collectively as 'magnetic stores', although of course cores are also magnetic in their mode of operation.

up to twenty magnetic tape decks. Indeed, with removable units such as magnetic tape reels and exchangeable disc packs, the total capacity is virtually unlimited. It is very easy to remove one storage unit and plug in another, and most computer installations maintain large libraries of information – programs, data, compilers, etc. – on reels of magnetic tape or disc packs ready for use when needed. Because the access time of the magnetic stores is relatively long, data is usually transferred between them and the core store in blocks (p. 153) of several hundred words at a time as discussed on p. 139. Magnetic tape is by far the cheapest form of storage, but suffers from the serious disadvantage that it may take several minutes to search along a tape to locate a particular item. This is why large files of information, such as must be kept by insurance companies and some government departments, for example, are now commonly kept on magnetic discs instead of on reels of tape.

In the hierarchy of magnetic stores, the disc occupies an intermediate position, both as regards capacity and access time, between the drum and the tape. During the last few years, since about 1967, magnetic discs, in both fixed and exchangeable forms, have largely displaced drums and tape to become the dominant type of magnetic storage.

(iii) One or more card readers capable of reading between 600 and 1,600 cards a minute and a card punch capable of punching between 150 and 300 cards a minute. The two functions are sometimes combined in a single piece of equipment.

(iv) A high-speed line-at-a-time printer (or perhaps two or three of them), operating at a maximum rate of perhaps 1,200 lines per minute, with about 100 character positions across the paper. The printer is connected directly to the central unit, in contrast to the off-line printer of the 1956 computer. Some of the larger commercial installations where there is a great deal of printed output use even faster devices, known as Xeronic printers. They work in quite a different way from conventional electro-mechanical printers (*Xerography* is derived from two Greek words meaning 'dry writing') and can print more than 10,000 characters every second.

(v) One or more photoelectrically controlled paper tape readers capable of reading about 1,000 characters a second, and one or more paper tape punches capable of punching between 100 and 300 characters a second. The old five-track tape of Figure 77(a) is now being superseded by wider tape with eight hole positions across its width* (Figure 77(b)). This gives 256 different combinations – more than enough to represent all the characters we need including both upper and lower case alphabets, and still leave one spare track for parity digits to enable single printing or reading errors to be detected, as explained on p. 147.

(vi) An operator's desk or console containing an electric typewriter which can be operated either by a human typist or directly by signals from the central processor. A typewriter of this kind, which is similar to the teleprinter used for telegraphic communication, is called a *tele-typewriter*, or *teleprinter* for short. Its function, in the present context, is to enable the computer operator to communicate, both ways, with his machine. We shall see shortly that its role is being extended to perform this function not only for the operator sitting at his console but for the computer user sitting at the end of a telephone line.

A modern computing installation consists, then, of a group of interconnected units, most of which are concerned with either input, output, bulk storage, or communication to distant stations over telegraph or telephone lines. The heart of the installation, the central processor (p. 246) which tends to get smaller as electronic technology progresses, is surrounded by an ever increasing collection of peripheral equipment of one kind or another.

Plate 5 shows a large data processing installation of the Department of Health and Social Security at Reading. The central processor is an ICL 1906, manufactured by International Computers and Tabulators Limited – one of the larger models of the

* Seven-track tape is sometimes used, but is going out of fashion.

1900 family. The cabinet housing the central processor and most of the store can be seen in the back of the picture to the left, the magnetic tape units are along the far wall to the right, the operator is sitting at his console in the centre right, peripheral units are distributed throughout the room. Plenty of space has been allowed for the staff to move around and perhaps for future expansion of the installation.

Visual Display and Computer Graphics

The items of equipment discussed in the last section are to be found in nearly all installations; they represent the lowest common measure of the present 'state of the art'. During the last few years a number of new devices, mainly concerned with the input, output or transmission of information, have appeared on the scene. In this section we consider those that relate to what has come to be known as *Computer Graphics* – the technique of communicating with a computer (both in and out) by means of pictures.

It is not enough for a computer to calculate and print an answer: the answer must be presented in such a way as to be useful to somebody, in the sense of increasing his knowledge or providing him with new understanding. The conventional high-speed printer can churn out vast quantities of information but if only a small proportion is ever looked at, its industry is perhaps misplaced.

In scientific and engineering work, as we shall see in the next chapter, it is often more useful to plot computed results than to tabulate them. Ten years ago it was not unusual for teams of girls to spend laborious hours plotting by hand the results of calculations that had been performed effortlessly – and voluminously – by a computer in a few minutes. There is less of this sort of thing now that the automatic plotter has become generally available as a computer output device. The plotter is automatic in the sense that its operation is under program control: the computer is programmed to issue instructions to the plotting mechanism which cause the pen and paper to move relative to each other so as to trace out the diagram or graph that is wanted. Various mechanical arrangements are possible. In some instruments the paper moves in one direction (say x) while the pen moves across the roll of paper in the perpendicular direction (say y): a plotter of this type can be seen on the right of Plate 6. In the larger plotters the paper is fixed to a table and the pen is attached to a mechanism which can move it over the table in both the x and the y directions. In most instruments the position of each successive point to be plotted is not specified afresh by its coordinates. Instead, the program tells the plotter how to reach the next point from the last one. It is increments in position, rather than distances from a fixed datum, that are specified. Plotters that work in this way are called *incremental plotters*. Automatic plotters, like all mechanical devices, are extremely sluggish by electronic standards; it may take up to half an hour to plot a family of graphs derived from a single calculation.

The electronic counterpart of the plotter is the cathode ray tube (CRT) display, or *visual display unit* (VDU) as it is sometimes called. It basically consists of a cathode ray tube and some electronic devices to enable the computer to control it. When given a pair of coordinates (x,y) by a computer program, the VDU will cause a flash of light to appear on the corresponding spot on its CRT screen. Complete pictures, including letters and numerals, can be made up of thousands of individual spots. Some VDUs have electronic circuits that can 'paint' straight lines on the screen automatically given only the two end points, thus avoiding the necessity of having to compute coordinates for all the spots on each line. Others have special 'character generating' circuits whereby the outline of a complete character – a letter of the alphabet or a numeral, for example – can be made to appear on the screen in response to a single instruction.

This convenient and versatile device, now that it is becoming rather less expensive, is proving very popular with both scientific and commercial users. Being entirely electronic, it works extremely fast. Computed results can thus be displayed on the screen virtually instantaneously for direct viewing. If a permanent record is needed, the screen can be photographed, either manually or under program control.

To the business user, one of the main attractions of the VDU

251

is that it reduces the volume of printed output, much of which has no permanent value. Anything that can help to arrest the ever increasing flood of paper is certainly to be welcomed! He will usually be content with an alphanumeric display; that is, a display consisting of letters of the alphabet, numerals and a few special symbols. By not asking for diagrams or pictures the commercial user can get a much cheaper instrument which we shall call an *Alphanumeric Visual Display Unit* (AVDU) to distinguish it from the full picture display.

So far we have been treating the VDU solely as an output device. With suitable attachments it can also be used as an input device. The most straightforward way of doing this is by means of an alphanumeric keyboard with a direct input connection to the computer. The input function of the keyboard device is essentially the same as that of the tele-typewriter on the operator's console. The difference is that the output appears on a CRT screen instead of printed characters on a roll of paper. There is, to use the current jargon, no *hard copy* of the output. Plate 7 shows a typical AVDU of this kind.

The material to be input is composed on the keyboard and appears on the screen as it is typed. It can be checked and edited before being passed into the computer store. By providing a few extra facilities – a set of push buttons and the necessary electronic control circuits – an AVDU can also be used as an inquiry station. Information held in the computer store can be displayed on the screen as the result of an inquiry, which can be made either by typing a message on the keyboard or by pressing a sequence of buttons. The information so displayed can be amended or augmented by the operator before being returned to the store. The AVDU thus provides a convenient, economical and versatile means of alphanumeric communication between the man, be he operator or user, and his computer. In the next chapter we shall see something of how these devices are so used.

Alphanumeric input is inadequate for some purposes; a scientist or an engineer, for example, may wish to feed data into the computer directly in pictorial or graphical form by 'drawing' on the face of the CRT screen. He can do this by using a device called a *light pen*, which consists of a photoelectric cell placed in a small tube so that it can be held in the hand, as seen on the left of Plate 6. Communication between the light pen and the computer depends on the fact that a picture on a CRT screen is built up, point by point, by the action of an electron beam which scans rapidly and repeatedly over the area of the screen. Since the spots which make up the picture are flashed or 'painted' on the screen one after another, a photo-electric cell placed against the screen will respond only when the light from some part of the picture falls within its limited field of view. In this way the computer can tell which part of the screen the operator is pointing at by noting when the light pen responds. Temporal information can be converted into spatial information.

The light pen can be used not only to point, but also to draw. To do this we need a tracking program which causes a small cross – known as a *tracking cross* – to be displayed on the screen. When the light pen is pointed at the centre of the cross, it remains at rest. If the pen is moved slightly, the tracking program causes the cross to be re-centred. The effect is that the tracking cross follows the pen across the screen. The light pen can also be programmed to do other things, such as erasing, shifting or modifying parts of a displayed picture.

A full graphical input-output system depends, in short, on the provision of a set of special programs to enable the computer to interpret incoming signals as instructions relating to the display. The operator can generate such signals by pointing with or moving the light pen, by typing messages on a keyboard or by touching a sequence of push buttons. As this information is taken in, the computer constructs the growing drawing within its own store and displays it on the screen. The light pen does not make any direct mark on the display; the computer stands between the 'pencil' and the 'paper', so to speak. This means that the computer can actively assist in the drawing process. It can, for example, be programmed to straighten out wobbly lines, move or erase lines already drawn, or substitute true circles for poorly drawn ones. It is able, in fact, to replace a rough sketch by an accurate drawing in accordance with the user's intentions.

All this sounds very attractive, but is far from easy to achieve. Visual display equipment is now widely available, the problem is to make effective use of it. On the output side, it is not too difficult to produce programs for displaying simple graphs, but to add scales, labels and notes to the graphs or to produce contour plots, for example, makes quite heavy demands on the programmer, and each new format must be programmed individually. Effective graphical input requires more complicated programs than graphical output, and many possibilities are still unexplored. However, valuable results have already been achieved in some fields of scientific research, as we shall see in the next chapter, and in engineering design. The techniques of computer graphics are indeed becoming widely used in the design of computers themselves, particularly in the topological design of complicated electronic circuits. The range of engineering applications is steadily widening and during the next five or ten years we may expect to see major developments in what has come to be called *computer aided design*. Even so, graphical input and output, in the sense of communicating with a computer directly by means of diagrams and pictures, seems likely to remain an expensive and esoteric business, with the research scientist and the top class design engineer as the main practitioners.

Fast computing – slow input and output

During recent years the problems of input and output have commanded a great deal of attention from designers and programmers alike. There are two main reasons for this. The first is that more and more computers are being used in business offices where they do quite short and simple calculations, but repeat them over and over again on very large quantities of data. The second is that computing speeds have increased much more than input and output speeds.

Before 1958 computers were mainly engaged on scientific or technical calculations of one kind or another; nowadays most of them are employed on clerical tasks – on payroll or stock control calculations, for example. In this kind of work the essential role of the computer is to manipulate large quantities of digitally coded material – usually referred to as *data* – in a prescribed manner; an activity often referred to as *automatic data processing*

(A.D.P. for short). The amount of computation that has to be done on each unit of data is usually quite small. This does not mean that commercial programs are short and straightforward; their mathematical content may be trivial, but their organizational and logical content may be substantial. Some payroll pro. grams, for example, contain more than ten thousand instructions- Another feature of clerical computing is that several different kinds of input data may be needed simultaneously, and that the computed answers may be required in several different forms. We have already referred to this in the previous chapter when discussing COBOL.

The organization of the rapid input and output of streams of coded data is, in fact, one of the major problems of A.D.P. There is also the problem posed by the sheer bulk of the information to be processed. Large numbers of clerks spend a good deal of time compiling, amending, or consulting files of information. To mechanize this kind of activity, a clerical data processing installation requires a very large backing store. Nowadays this usually consists of a battery of magnetic discs and/or magnetic tapes.

The basic problem, however, arises from the ever widening speed gap between electronic and mechanical processes: between the high speed at which electrical signals can be manipulated and the very much slower speeds at which material objects (cards, tape, punching knives, print hammers, etc.) can be moved around.*

One way of tackling it has already been mentioned at the end of Chapter 8. It is to insulate, so to speak, the computational activities proper from the sluggish processes of input and output. All the input material – which may consist of source programs, numerical data, library subroutines, compilers, etc. – is first punched on to cards or paper tape and then read in, not directly to the core store, but to a special reserved area of the backing store – either magnetic tape or disc – which is called the *input well*.

When the central processor is ready to deal with the next job, it dips into the input well to get the new information it needs. The program for the new job is transferred from its temporary parking position in the backing store to the core store where the

* Some information on how this gap has widened is given on p. 272.

central processor can operate on it. Other items of information needed by the program, such as compilers, data or subroutines from the library, will already be stored on magnetic tapes or discs and can also be transferred into the core store when required.

The reverse process occurs at output. The computed results are parked temporarily on another area of magnetic storage (known as the *output well*) where they are stacked in order of arrival and then fed out in turn to the appropriate output unit – line printer, card punch, paper tape punch, graph plotter or visual display unit – at the rate at which they can be dealt with.

The installation at the Computer Centre of the University of Birmingham, to take a specific example, contains nine magnetic tape units. Two of these (A and B, say) are permanently reserved for the input well, and two more (C and D) for the output well. Input coming in from punched cards or paper tape can be read on to one tape (say A) at the same time as information on tape B is being transferred into the core store. When all the information on tape B has been so transferred, the roles of the two tapes are interchanged. The two tapes (C and D) forming the output well have similar roles in respect of the output units. Compilers, library subroutines and other organizational programs of general utility are kept permanently on a fixed disc store, which in this installation has a capacity of 32 million characters.

In some installations the input and output wells are accommodated on a magnetic disc or drum rather than on tapes. The scheme is illustrated diagrammatically in Figure 79.

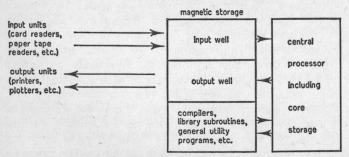

Figure 79. Use of input and output wells.

A parking and queueing scheme of this kind has obvious advantages when some jobs involve extensive calculations but little input and output, while with others it is the other way round. This is often the case when the computer is required to deal with a wide range of jobs, involving an admixture of technical, scientific and commercial work. At the Birmingham University Centre, for example, the high-speed printer which can print 1,000 lines a minute is in action for about twenty-five per cent of the total time (about 120 hours per week) that the computer is operating. However, the rate of generation of output is very uneven; sometimes there is a substantial queue of jobs waiting in the output well, at other times the printer may have little to do. Twenty-five per cent may seem a poor utilization rate but it represents a pretty formidable output of reading matter. This type of printer, working flat out, could print the whole of the Bible in less than an hour.

The important thing is not merely to even out fluctuations, but to prevent the main computing work being held up by input or output at all. This means that we must arrange matters so that several things can go on at the same time, so that the slower processes do not hold up the faster ones. To fix ideas, let us consider a single reading unit which can read punched paper tape at a maximum rate of 1,000 characters per second.* There is thus an interval of at least 1,000 microseconds (one thousandth of a second) between reading a character and reading the next one. This is a long time by electronic computing standards; long enough, for example, to add several hundred ten-figure numbers together. The problem is how to use this time to good effect.

Suppose we have a special little store which can hold just one character (of between five and eight binary digits). We shall call it the *buffer store*. When a character is read from the tape, it is immediately transferred to the buffer store (Figure 80). The tape then moves forward (comparatively slowly) to bring the next row of holes into the reading position. When the buffer store receives a character it at once sends a signal to the central computer. The effect of this signal is to interrupt the program that is being executed at the time (this will usually be an object program for

---

*A similar situation, but for magnetic tape transfers, was discussed from a somewhat different point of view on p. 195.

another calculation), and to switch control to a special subroutine which is held permanently in the main store. As soon as the transfer is complete, a signal is sent back to the buffer store, thereby putting it into a state of readiness to receive another character from the tape. At the same time the central processor is instructed to proceed with the main calculation until the next interrupt signal is received.

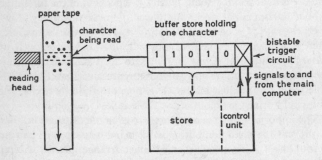

Figure 80. Use of buffer store for input.

The point is that these operations, being entirely electronic, take very little time – ten microseconds perhaps – while a very much longer period – 1,000 microseconds at least – must elapse before the central computer can be interrupted again by a signal from this particular buffer store. In fact, as we have seen, there are likely to be a number of input or output units, each with its own buffer store. Even so, they will require the attention of the central computer for a small proportion of the time only – not more than five per cent. This means that, even with many input and output units operating at once, the central computer is available for most of the time for its essential job of executing a program; the input and output processes do not reduce the effective computing speed appreciably.

Such overlapping of computing, input and output is a simple example of what is known as *time sharing*. We may think of three different problems being worked on at the same time: computing on problem *B*; reading in the data and program for problem *C*; printing or punching the answers to problem *A*.

With a multiplicity of input and output units, the situation could be even more complicated. The data for a fourth problem, *D*, might be read from a pack of cards at the same time as the program for problem *C* was being read from one paper tape and the data from another. Many of the larger computers are now provided with quite elaborate time sharing facilities, the organization of the many parallel activities being controlled by a *supervisory program*. This program looks after all transfers of data across the 'provincial boundaries' of the complete installation – that is to say, transfers between any of the input or output units and the store, between different kinds of store (e.g., discs and cores), and even between different sections of the same kind of store. It also looks after various other matters, such as *scheduling* the flow of work, including the communication between the computer and the human operator.

The reason why the interaction between the man and the machine must be dealt with by a supervisory program is that human actions take so long – much longer than those of tape readers and automatic printers, which as we have seen are sluggish enough by electronic standards. It would be intolerable if the central processor had to wait for an operator to load a deck of cards into a reader, supply the printer with a new roll of paper, or change a magnetic tape deck.

The supervisory program is designed to keep watch over the state of the constituent parts of the installation, and to send a message to the operator warning him in good time that one of them requires his attention. Such messages usually appear on a teletypewriter or visual display unit at the operator's desk. If the operator is unable to complete his task in time, the supervisory program causes the central processor to switch at once to some other task, such as compiling or executing another program.

To enable such switches to take place virtually instantaneously, several programs must be in the computing stage at the same time. This mode of working, whereby the time of the central processor can be shared between a number of different programs in various stages of execution, is sometimes known as *multi-programming*; it is an extension of the simple concept of input-computing-output time sharing that we have already discussed.

With multi-programming, precautions must be taken to ensure that one program does not interfere with another—by attempting to use one of its storage locations, for example. Such safety measures may be provided by electronic equipment or by special programs held permanently in the store – usually by a combination of both.

For many installations – but not all, as we shall see shortly – the main objective is to achieve the greatest possible throughput of work. This, as we have seen, demands a variety of sophisticated supervisory type programs to organize and schedule the flow of work to ensure that everything proceeds as smoothly and quickly as possible. The whole process, which is usually called *batch processing*, may be likened to an automatic production line in which decks of cards and lengths of paper tape are fed in at one end and reams of printed results emerge at the other.

We have mentioned only a few of the subtleties entailed in operating a large computing installation, but enough, we hope, to make the point that one requires a variety of organizational, supervisory and controlling programs (usually called *systems programs*), over and above the programs needed to enable the computer to execute specific tasks (called *applications programs*). The term *operating system* is sometimes used to refer to the complete collection of systems programs and procedures needed to operate a particular installation. On page 201 we introduced the term *software* in connection with compilers. The word is in fact used more widely to include compilers, systems programs and the general utility programs and subroutines which make up the program library of an installation.

We see, then, that modern computers must be supplied with four kinds of programs.

(1) Systems programs to organize the flow of work and deal with input and output, time sharing, man-machine communication, etc.

(2) Compilers for translating from high level languages into the machine language of the particular computer.

(3) A collection of commonly required general utility programs and subroutines (the program library).

(4) Applications programs for specific jobs.

Programs of types (1), (2) and (3) (the software) must be kept permanently in machine language form in some part of the computer store. As these programs may amount, in total, to many millions of instructions, most of them must be accommodated in the backing store (magnetic disc or drum) and be transferred temporarily into the core store when the central processor wishes to use them. The main supervisory program must, however, reside permanently in the core store, since it controls, among other things, the movements of all the other programs. The basic software is usually supplied by the computer manufacturer as an integral part of the machine and represents a very substantial fraction – more than fifty per cent in some cases – of the market price of the computer.

Multiple access and conversational computing

It is natural to try to extend the concept of time sharing from jobs to men; to seek to arrange matters so that a number of different people – not merely a number of different programs – can use the computer simultaneously. Indeed, during the last five years or so, this concept – the thoroughgoing embodiment of which is known as *conversational computing* – has come to occupy a central position in the computing scene. This type of time sharing, which we may call *multiple access* (or *multi-access*) operation, enables a number of people to use the computer at the same time, with each one being able to proceed as if he were the sole user – but of a rather slower machine.

A number of such schemes, of varying degrees of complexity, are now operating successfully. Many of them are quite modest, being designed to deal with fairly small problems programmed in one prescribed language. Their popularity shows that there is a substantial number of people who are not well catered for by conventional batch processing computing and who find it tedious to do their work on a desk calculating machine.

Some of the larger multiple access schemes offer much more comprehensive facilities. They provide each user with a filing system inside the computer in which he may keep programs in a variety of languages, tables of figures, lists of names and

261

addresses, anything else he pleases, in much the same way as he can keep files in a filing cabinet. He can make changes to a file without retyping the whole document, create new files or delete old ones. Since a file may consist of a program, he can use the file editing facilities to correct errors in a program while it is being developed, or to amend a fully developed program in the light of experience. One of the earliest and most famous of the larger multiple access systems was developed at the Massachusetts Institute of Technology between 1961 and 1963 and is known as the Compatible Time-Sharing System (CTSS). An essential feature of all such systems is the existence of a large number of direct connexions to the central computer from many different points, which may be in the next room or many miles away. At M.I.T. there are several hundred such access stations; some are in offices and laboratories of the Institute, and some in the private homes of members of the staff. Each station is equipped with a tele-typewriter device, often referred to as a remote access or 'on-line'* console or terminal. An authorized person can use any of these devices to send messages to and receive information back from the computer. Subscribers outside M.I.T. can also obtain direct access to the system by means of the telecommunication network of the Bell Telephone System and Western Union. A system of this size and scope demands a large, fast computer and a variety of sophisticated systems programs to organize and control the whole operation. At M.I.T. these programs occupy nearly a million words of store. A lot more storage space must be provided to accommodate the private files (for programs and data) of the many individual users.

A user who wishes to use the system must introduce himself by typing the word LOGIN, followed by his problem number and name. The computer replies by printing out the time and then asks the user to give his password. This feature was found to be necessary to guard the privacy and inviolability of the private files. If the password is not acceptable, or the particular user has exhausted his monthly allowance of time, or the machine is already being fully used, the machine prints a message stating that access is not available. Otherwise, the user can type some

*The meaning of the term 'on-line' will be explained in the next section.

further instructions to the computer. (These are usually called *commands* to distinguish them from the instructions that constitute an ordinary computer program.) If, for example, the user wishes to store some information (perhaps a program, a stock list, or some engineering design information) he gives the INPUT command and proceeds to type his material. When he has finished, he types the word FILE which causes the information he has just typed, suitably labelled with line numbers for easy reference, to be converted into a permanent file somewhere in the magnetic storage of the computer. Changes can be made to a file by typing the command word EDIT, after which additions and alterations can be made by using the line numbers. When editing is complete, the amended file can be stored away by typing the word FILE as before. Once a program has been placed in the store under a suitably chosen name, another command will cause it to be compiled, thereby creating a new file. The user may cause the compiled program to be executed by typing the command LOADGO, in which case the output from the program will be printed out on the tele-typewriter console of the particular user.

A feature of all multiple access time sharing schemes is that the program of a particular user does not remain continuously in the core store during the whole time it is being executed. In the M.I.T. system twenty programs can be 'active' simultaneously. All of them are being continually shuttled to and fro between the core store and the auxiliary magnetic store; at any instant of time only one of them is in the core store actually being executed. The user is, of course, not directly aware of this swapping although he may realize what it is that makes the computer appear to work more slowly than if he had it entirely to himself.

Another system that has had considerable influence on subsequent developments was developed at Dartmouth College in New Hampshire in 1964. The aims here were more modest than at M.I.T.: to provide facilities for performing fairly small calculations using a simple programming language (called BASIC) that a novice could learn in an hour or two by sitting at a typewriter console. All students of the College are now taught to use a computer in this way.

Electronic Computers

The Dartmouth ideas have been taken up commercially – by G.E.I.S. Limited, for example, who operate a very successful time sharing service in the U.K. The central installation consists of three main items: a computer designed for multi-access operation; a small separate computer which is used solely as a *communications processor* to sort out and schedule incoming and outgoing messages from the various remote users; and a large magnetic disc storage unit. All that a subscriber to the service needs on his premises is a tele-typewriter, which can be connected to the central computer through the public telephone network. To use the system, the subscriber dials the service, just as he would dial any telephone call, and is connected direct to the central computer. After identifying himself and his problem, and answering a few questions put to him by the computer, he waits for the message READY to appear on his typewriter. When he gets it, he can proceed to type in a new program, amend or run an existing program that is already stored on the disc, and so forth. Communication between the subscriber and the time-sharing system is established and controlled through commands to the system (e.g., RUN, SAVE, LIST); requests by the system for information (e.g., SYSTEM..., NEW or OLD...); the user's response to such questions (e.g., BASIC, NEW); and messages sent out by the system (e.g., READY, WAIT).

To convey something of the flavour of the kind of exchange that takes place, we will consider an extremely simple case of a problem we have already met in Chapter 6, namely that of computing and printing a table of squares of numbers from 1 to 10. Here, then, is the entire 'conversation' as it would appear on the user's typewriter. We have, for clarity of exposition, underlined those parts of the conversation that are typed by the user. Material not underlined represents messages from the computer. The notes on the right are, of course, explanatory only.

Notes

G.E.I.S. Ltd.
ON AT 14 : 11   LNDN A 18/09/68
  TTY 10
USER NUMBER – – P 63514
SYSTEM – – BASIC

	Notes
NEW ØR ØLD – – <u>NEW</u>	Ø to distinguish the letter from the number zero
NEW FILE NAME – – <u>SQUARES</u>	
READY	
100 PRINT 'X', 'X↑2'	Column headings
<u>110 LET X=1</u>	
<u>120 LET X1=X↑2</u>	
<u>130 PRINT X, X1</u>	
<u>140 LET X=X+1</u>	
<u>141 IF X=11 THEN 999</u>	Causes program to stop when required
<u>150 GØ TØ 120</u>	Arranges for program to cycle until X=11
<u>999 END</u>	
<u>RUN</u>	
WAIT	
SQUARES 14 : 13	Program name and clock time

```
     X      X↑2
     1      1
     2      4
     3      9
     .      .
     .      .
     .      .
    10     100
```

TIME: 1 SEC	Chargeable computer time
<u>BYE</u>	Switch off message
XXX ØFF AT 14 : 17	

This program has been written in the BASIC language developed at Dartmouth, but the system also accepts programs written in FORTRAN or ALGOL.

The G.E.I.S. time sharing system became commercially available in London in August 1967. By January 1968 the demand was such that the capacity had to be duplicated. A third system was added in Acton in October 1968, a fourth in Manchester in January 1969, and it is planned to install further systems in provincial centres during 1969. Each system has forty telephone lines and so forty subscribers can be serviced at any one time. The system can, of course, cope with a much larger number of terminals since most subscribers, like most users of the ordinary telephone service, only wish to use the service from time to time and usually only for short periods.

' *Real time*' and '*on-line*' computing

It will be convenient at this point to introduce the reader to two further pieces of jargon that have become too firmly entrenched to be ignored.

Both digital and analog computers are often used in the following way. What is called a 'mathematical model', usually a set of relationships expressed by equations, is set up of the situation being studied – the flight characteristics of a proposed aircraft design or the automatic control of chemical plant, for example. As it is usually impracticable or prohibitively expensive to study the behaviour of the real situation, particularly over a wide range of conditions, the computer is used to investigate the behaviour of the model instead; that is to say, the equations representing the model are solved over a period of time for a large number of different values of the numerical coefficients. It is usually convenient to arrange matters so that time in the real situation is also represented by time in the model, so that successive states of the real world correspond to successive states of the model. However, the time scale need not be one to one. If, for instance, the model technique were being used to study the evolution of a star over a period of millions of years, the calculations would need to be rather drastically speeded up. If, on the other hand, one was trying to predict the course of an atomic explosion, the significant part of which takes only a few millionths of a second, the calculation would almost certainly be slowed down so as to extend over several minutes. If, however, the time scale factor happens to be exactly unity, we can say that the problem is being solved, or the simulation is being carried through, in *real time* (c.f. p. 63).

Some computing must be carried out faster than in real time. In numerical weather forecasting, for example, where the movement of the atmosphere is simulated in a computer, we must do the job faster than nature does. Forecasting of any type in real time, whether we are concerned with the weather or the national economy, is not particularly useful.

So far the term 'real time', though ugly, is precise. The difficulty arises when the usage is carried over from situations where one is modelling a system to situations in which the computer itself is part of the system: where we are no longer simulating something else, where the computer *is* the control device. This means that here is no 'real speed' with which to compare the computing speed, so the term 'real time' is not applicable. Unfortunately it is to just this type of situation that this overworked term has come to be commonly applied.

The main characteristics of situations that are now usually, but regrettably, described as 'real time' are twofold. The first is that the time scale in which a computer must do its work is determined by external events over which it has no control. The second is the need for rapid response; the pattern of these events is changing so rapidly or is so erratic that the computer must respond very quickly – usually in a matter of seconds.

Although wages must be paid every Friday and forecasting must keep ahead of the weather, such work would not be regarded as being carried out in 'real time', since a computer has, so to speak, a considerable period of time in which to manoeuvre. Consider, by contrast, a computer-based system for booking air travel tickets, or for controlling road traffic lights. In these cases the computer must attend to and respond to each incoming message as soon as it is received. It is computer applications of this kind that are usually referred to as 'real time'; 'quick response' would be a more descriptive term.

Another piece of jargon that is now firmly established is *on-line*, which we have already mentioned in connexion with multiple access consoles. A piece of equipment is said to be 'on-line' to a computer if the two are linked directly by a physical connexion. There is clearly no need to stress the fact that the various items of peripheral equipment in a central installation are 'on-line' to the central processor in this sense, and the term usually refers to equipment that is some distance away.

The usage is sometimes stretched to refer not only to equipment, but to people. A person is said to be 'on-line' to a computer when he is communicating with it through an electrical link such as a telephone line, using some kind of keyboard instrument for the purpose. In this case, 'on-line' means that the communication link is directly connected to the computer, in contrast, for example, to an 'off-line' link which causes packs of cards to be punched automatically at the central location, with the cards then having to be loaded into the computer by hand.

Towards a national computer grid

It will be apparent from what has been said that the complex of new techniques and new ways of using computers that are loosely referred to by such terms as time sharing, multiple access, on-line and real time are closely interrelated.

The large installation of the 1970s may be envisaged as comprising:

(i) one or more central processors equipped with time sharing and multiple access facilities;

(ii) a large capacity backing store made up of a collection of magnetic discs, tapes, drums, etc.;

(iii) a battery of input-output devices – card and paper tape readers and punches, lineprinters, tele-typewriters and alphanumeric visual display units. Some installations will also have full graphical input and output facilities and/or automatic graph plotters;

(iv) a satellite computer operating as a kind of automatic telephone exchange for a large number of communication links of various types and speeds to terminal equipment at remote stations.

For 'conversational' time sharing of the kind discussed earlier in this chapter, all that is needed is a teleprinter, perhaps supplemented by an alphanumeric visual display unit. The data is transmitted over either telegraph type circuits or ordinary telephone circuits adapted to transmit digital signals at speeds of 50–100 bits per second.

Remote stations are also likely to become increasingly important with the more conventional batch processing mode of working. As operating systems become more efficient, *turnround time* (that is, the time between a user handing in his material and being able to collect his results) is limited neither by hardware nor software but by the sheer volume of cards, tape, paper, etc., that must be checked, collated, packaged and addressed by the reception and dispatch clerks. The solution of the difficulty is to spread the load; to set up a number of input and output sub-stations at which work can be fed into the main batch processing computing stream and answers can be taken from it. The basic terminal equipment at this kind of remote station consists of a card reader and a line printer, although slower models than those used at the central installation usually suffice. Some stations are likely to be equipped with a paper tape reader and punch, a tele-printer or a visual display unit of some kind. The communication link is normally a high quality telephone circuit, either public or private, capable of transmitting digital data at speeds of up to 2400 bits per second. (This is the fastest circuit that the G.P.O. is able to make generally available to customers for data trans-mission.)

Finally, as an example of a very different kind of remote station, we have a satellite computer linked to a central processor by a high speed link capable of transmitting data at rates of several hundred thousand bits per second. This performance can be achieved with broader band communications channels, such as coaxial cable telephone systems or microwave radio links. Such channels are not yet generally available in the U.K., but the G.P.O., given enough notice, can usually provide wideband circuits which can handle up to 48,000 binary digits per second. It is possible to hire still faster circuits (240,000 bits per second) between certain places, but it is usually an expensive business to extend such circuits from the G.P.O. main route terminal to the customer's premises. To keep these requirements in perspective, we would point out that an ordinary television channel transmits several million bits of information every second.

The trend towards quick response multiple access computing, with many distant users getting a share of the power of a central computer when they need it, is generally held to be the most significant development in computer utilization of the last five years. Many have hailed it as a second computer revolution created by the union of two technologies – of computing and tele-communications.

Our typical installation of the future – a time-sharing central processor with a very large backing store and numerous telephone lines radiating out to various input/output stations, some of them equipped with smaller computers of their own – may be likened to an electricity supply system. The analogy suggests the question: will computing power eventually be provided on a national scale over a network like the electricity grid? The answer is probably 'yes', but not for some time. The first steps will certainly be more modest; perhaps, on the one hand, the development of specialized services – for stockbrokers, or for users of numerically controlled machine tools, for example – that can be offered to all comers through a communication network, and on the other hand, the increasing use by large organizations of private networks.

In 1966 the National Physical Laboratory, in collaboration with the Post Office, began a detailed study of the technical problems of multiple access computing over long distances. Two years later it produced a design for a data communication network which, it is claimed, meets all the requirements, the most important of which is ability to adapt to a rapidly changing environment, with old and new equipment and usages having to coexist. The scheme envisages an hierarchical arrangement of subscriber terminals ('remote stations' in our terminology), multiplexor devices to concentrate and sort out incoming messages and so save data transmission costs, local area computers and regional computers, all linked together by a network of communication lines of varying data carrying capacity. It is proposed to make use of some of the long distance lines already provided for the telephone network, but to the users the system would appear as completely separate and self-contained.

The development and installation of a data communication system of this kind would undoubtedly occupy a number of years. The NPL-GPO proposals are now being discussed with the manufacturers and other interested parties. It is to be hoped that some positive decisions will follow.

The pace of development

Apart from the changes and new developments we have been discussing, there has been steady progress during the last decade in many rather more obvious directions – faster computing, larger storage capacity, greater reliability in operation, more powerful and convenient programming techniques. The general trends for the first two of these are illustrated in Figures 81 and 82, again with logarithmic scales. (We show broad bands, rather than lines, because of the considerable variation that exists between one computer and another.)

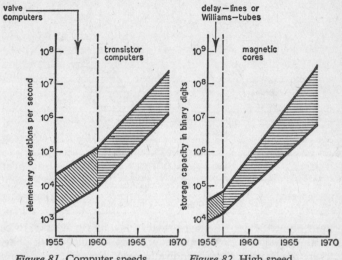

Figure 81. Computer speeds.

Figure 82. High speed storage capacity.

The quantity plotted in Figure 81 is the average number of elementary computing operations that can be carried out in a single second. A rough allowance has been made for the proportion of additions, multiplications, etc., in a typical calculation, and for the different times they take to execute. The quantity plotted in Figure 82 is the capacity of the working store, measured in binary digits.

Figure 83 has a rather different purpose; it tells you, in round figures, what you get for your money. A quantity we have called the 'utility index' is plotted against the capital cost of the computer, both scales being logarithmic. The utility index is roughly proportional to the product of the speed and the storage

271

capacity, but some allowance is made for other factors. Time does not appear explicitly; the figure relates to computers designed since about 1960. Once again, we can exhibit broad trends only. The fact that the trend-band goes up at a steeper angle than forty-five degrees means that a large computer is likely to be

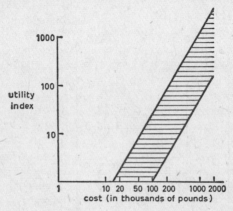

Figure 83. Computer utility index against cost.

more economical to use than a smaller one. By paying, say, twice as much, we can get three or four times as much work done. There are, however, many individual exceptions to this general rule, and a potential customer is advised to assess each computer on its merits in relation to his particular requirements.

Figure 78 (p. 245) shows how input and output speeds have increased during the same period – again on a logarithmic scale. Broadly speaking, the left hand end of any bar represents the state of affairs in 1954; the right hand, the best that can be done with 1968 equipment. Between these years input and output speeds have increased, on the average, by a factor of about 10. During the same period – and this is the significant thing – computing speeds have increased very much more – by a factor of more than 100 (Figure 81). This means that today it takes more than ten times as long, measured in the timescale of the computer itself, to get data in or out as it did a few years ago. The gap between fast electronic computing and slow mechanical input and output is, indeed, growing wider all the time. It is a worrying situation, presenting a continuing challenge to the designers of computing equipment and to the designers of programming systems. Both parties, as we have seen, are prepared to go to considerable lengths to meet it.

Providing a computing service

The rest of this chapter will be concerned with the computer in its human setting – as part of a computing centre, the object of which is to provide a service to people. How should such a centre be planned and organized? What range of services ought to be offered? What sort of people are needed to provide these services? What qualifications should they have and what training should they be given? Questions of this kind do not admit to general answers. It would be disastrous to attempt to run a university computer, for example, in the same way as a computing installation in the head office of an insurance company. It turns out, however, that most installations can conveniently be grouped in three broad categories, which we may call scientific, technical and commercial.

The scientific installations are to be found, typically, in universities and research institutes. The computers in the technical group are concentrated in the engineering industry, where they are mainly engaged on calculations relating to the design and development of the company's products; other work, such as stores accounting or production scheduling, may be done as well, but as a secondary task. Finally, we have the commercial group which includes all those installations where most of the time is spent on accounting or production control work of one kind or another.

The staff of any computing installation must include people having a variety of different skills. Some will probably be specialists in the particular class of work being done; crystallographers, structural engineers, accountants, or linguists, for example. Most of them, however, will be concerned with more basic computational tasks, such as writing programs, punching tape or cards, operating the equipment, or maintaining it in good order.

273

To see what is entailed here let us list the various stages in the complete process of doing a job on a computer.

(1) Identify and define the problem in precise terms.

(2) Choose the method of attack; decide what numerical procedures to use.

(3) Organize the calculation as an ordered sequence of steps appropriate to the particular computer being used; construct a flow diagram; decide on such matters as input and output arrangements.

(4) Construct the program; that is, write out the schedule of instructions describing the calculation. These instructions may be written in a computer-like language, but are more likely to be in some high-level language such as ALGOL or COBOL which the computer is able to translate.

(5) Prepare the input material – both the program of instructions and the numerical data for the particular calculation – in a form in which it can be read into the computer. This usually means operating a keyboard device to punch cards or tape.

(6) Check the behaviour of the program on a number of test calculations where the computed results can be compared with known answers. Correct any mistakes discovered.

(7) Execute the program – that is, carry out the computational job for which it has been written. This may mean running the program many times over, perhaps at regular intervals, such as daily or weekly. We shall call this stage *production computing*, to distinguish it from stage 6, *program testing*.

(8) Record the results in a convenient form – usually as printed characters, but sometimes as graphs on paper, or as displays on a CRT screen. Results that do not need to be looked at immediately, but are to be read back into the computer later on, would be recorded on magnetic tape, packs of cards or punched paper tape.

(9) Interpret the computed results.

(10) Inspect the computer and the ancillary equipment and do any necessary maintenance work. (This is not done at the end of each job, but at some convenient time, such as the first thing every morning – or every Monday morning.)

Now the person who is primarily concerned with stages 1 and 9 is the customer – the man for whom the calculation is being done. The programming staff is responsible for stages 2, 3 and 4; the machine operators for stages 7 and 8. Stages 5 and 6 may be regarded as border areas; stage 10 is the province of the maintenance technician.

Open shop and closed shop programming

In some computing centres all the programming is done by a central group of programmers who usually spend their whole time on the job (*closed shop* programming). In others, while there may be a few full-time programmers around the machine, most of the programming is done by people outside the central group (*open shop* programming). Such people may be termed 'occasional programmers'; they normally program only their own jobs and are primarily interested in getting particular results rather than in computational niceties as such. The open shop and closed shop methods of working represent the extremes; many centres prefer an intermediate arrangement with a central programming staff supplemented by some occasional programmers to deal with more specialized matters.

Now it so happens that most scientific installations are run on open shop lines, with a small central programming group, most of them mathematical graduates, and a much larger number of occasional programmers who deal with their own problems, from stage 1 onwards. The typical commercial installation, on the other hand, is organized as a closed shop, with perhaps ten full-time programmers and few, if any, part-timers. The typical technical installation occupies an intermediate position. Needless to say, the actual state of affairs is nothing like so tidy as this; the spectrum is continuous and extends over a very wide range. At one extreme we have the large scientific installation with several hundred programmers using it; at the other the small punched-card computer in a business office with two or three people writing all the programs.

In the world of real life, in contrast to that of examinations, the main difficulty usually resides in identifying and formulating a problem, not in solving it. What this means in the present context is that the first of our ten stages may well occupy the attention of a large number of skilled people for a longer period of time than all the remaining stages put together. With the closed shop mode of working, stage 1 is a combined operation involving, on the one hand, the customer – be he production manager, accountant, design engineer, or scientist – and on the other, a senior member of the programming staff. In a scientific or technical installation, this senior programmer would almost certainly be a university graduate; for business work more emphasis is placed on experience in the organization and knowledge of its procedures. The people who investigate the ways and means of applying computers to the data processing activities of a particular organization – governmental, commercial, or industrial – are called *systems analysts*. They are scarce, much sought after, and hence well paid; they form what is virtually a new profession created entirely by the impact of the computer on the business organization. A governmental Committee which reported in December 1966 estimated that by 1970 British industry and commerce would need an additonal 11,000 systems analysts as well as 19,000 programmers. To meet this demand, special 'crash' courses of training were worked out by the National Computing Centre, and are now being run at technical colleges and other institutions throughout the country. Systems analysts, with their probings and questionings and their addiction to new ways of doing things, are already having an unsettling effect on many time honoured business practices – and hence on many individuals whose working life has been fashioned within the framework of these practices.

The computer is a great disturber of cherished ideas. Lady Lovelace realized this in 1842, when she made the point that in recasting problems into a form suitable for solution by the Analytical Engine 'the relations and nature of many subjects . . . are necessarily thrown into new light, and more profoundly investigated'.

To return to our ten stages, the systems analyst would be responsible for stages 1 and 2, and probably for 3, but he would delegate stage 4 to a more junior person – sometimes called a *programmer* and sometimes a *coder*. Among scientists, where the term systems analyst is little used, the complete process is usually regarded as 'programming'. The reader is warned that there is no consistent terminology here.

With open shop working, on the other hand, the two parties to stage 1 coalesce; the customer *is* the programmer. He may consult the central programming group on stage 2, or he may deal with the whole of the first four stages himself.

Getting programs right

Although modern developments have made the task of the programmer much easier than it was, very few programs, even now, are written correctly at the first attempt. Before a program can safely be used on production calculations (stage 7), its behaviour must be thoroughly tested and proved to be correct (stage 6).

How is this done? In the early years the usual procedure was to run the program in slow motion, one instruction at a time, and observe what happened. Computers were provided with a number of visual indicators – rows of lights or cathode-ray tubes – which enabled the contents of some of the arithmetic, control or storage registers to be inspected. This practice – sometimes known as 'peeping' – was soon found to be intolerably slow. It can be speeded up by inserting stop instructions at suitable points, thus enabling the operator to restrict the slow motion to selected parts of the program. Those parts that are above suspicion can be run through at full speed. Even with these improvements this procedure is far too prodigal of valuable machine time and different techniques are employed nowadays.

The basic idea is to remove a faulty program from the computer as soon as a mistake is detected. Another program can then be put in right away and wasted computer time is kept to a minimum. To this end, most modern installations are provided with a variety of ingenious diagnostic aids. The most important of these consist of special diagnostic programs, some of which are usually held permanently in the computer store. Their function is to provide the programmer with information that is likely to help him detect, locate, and diagnose any errors in his program. Such information is usually printed as an error message on a line printer or electric typewriter so that the programmer can take it away and study it in his office. With the advent of multi-access operation from remote consoles, the position is being modified in that the programmer can correct minor errors in his programs while sitting at his console. This is a partial return to the early practice of 'peeping' but with the crucial difference that his corrective activities no longer hold up the central processor, which is doing other work while he is thinking and typing.

Diagnostic programs may be called into action in several ways: automatically when a mistake is found; at the request of the operator or user (e.g. when he presses a button on his console); or in response to special instructions embodied in the program being tested.

We have explained in the previous chapter how nowadays most programs are written in a source language which is translated, or compiled, into a set of equivalent computer instructions. There is, in fact, a wide gap between what the programmer writes down and the instructions that are actually obeyed. One might expect that the wider the gap, the more difficult it would be to find out exactly why a program was misbehaving. Fortunately, the makers of compilers are well aware of this danger, and have paid special attention to the problem of error diagnosis.

Two classes of error in source programs must be distinguished: those which are discovered during the translation process and those which are not detected until the object program is being executed. Errors of the first class occur when the programmer breaks one of the grammatical rules of the language he is using. The usual procedure is to arrange for a *mistake report* to be typed out for each such error detected by the compiler. The report usually consists of a number or phrase which serves to identify the kind of mistake, together with information on the position or nature of the offending items.

Errors of the second class – those which come to light during the actual computation – are harder to deal with, and the subject is too specialized to be pursued here. Even with all modern conveniences, the business of developing and testing new programs continues to occupy a great deal of time. On many scientific installations, where much of the work is always new, program testing accounts for more than thirty per cent of the total computing time, leaving less than seventy per cent for production calculations using programs already established as correct.

The operating team

While the main job of the operating team is, of course, to operate the computer (stage 7), they also have the task of maintaining the flow of work. This entails assembling the input material, both programs and data, which may be on punched cards, paper tape, or magnetic tape, and despatching the results to the various customers (stage 8).

Computer operators are not usually responsible for the actual preparation of the input material (stage 5), although in some installations they are required to spend part of their time on this kind of work. Commercial organizations, especially those in which a lot of data has to be prepared in accordance with a strict timetable, often find it convenient to have a separate card or tape punching department with a staff which may well be larger than that of the computing group itself.

To give an idea of how a computing service with a mixed load is organized, we give on the next page the current daily timetable for the main computer (an ICL KDF9) at the University of Birmingham Computer Centre. The machine is used to provide a largely open shop service to about 500 occasional programmers, mainly University staff or research students. Some ten to fifteen per cent of its time is occupied with administrative data processing or with testing and running small programs written by people under instruction. The computer is operated 'round the clock' (three shifts) – except at weekends when special arrangements must be made – but it is convenient to begin at 9 a.m., the start of the working day for most people.

For most of the time the computer is run under the control of a batch processing operating system known as 'Egdon'. The name derives from the fact that the system was developed by an atomic energy research establishment situated in Dorset near Thomas Hardy's Egdon Heath. The system can accept programs punched on cards and written in one of three languages – FORTRAN, ALGOL or a KDF9 machine language

Time	Programming languages	Nature of work
0900–1100	Fortran, Algol or Usercode	Short or medium length jobs, depending on demand.
1100–1145	„ „ „ „	Program testing. Customers queue up; maximum of 2 minutes per person.
1145–1300	„ „ „ „	Short jobs (i.e. taking less than 5 minutes).
1300–1400	—	Scheduled maintenance (p. 281) (operators go to lunch).
1400–1530	—	Systems development, etc., by staff of Computer Centre, followed by miscellaneous 'housekeeping' tasks.
1530–1615	Fortran, Algol and Usercode	Program testing (as at 1100 hours).
1615–1900	„ „ „ „	Short jobs
1900–2230	„ „ „ „	Medium length jobs (i.e. taking between 5 and 15 minutes).
2230–0200	„ „ „ „	Long jobs (i.e. taking between 15 and 30 minutes).
0200–0600	Other languages	All kinds.
0600–0900	Fortran, Algol and Usercode	Jobs taking more than 30 minutes. These must be booked in advance.

known as Usercode – or indeed, with certain safeguards, in a mixture of all three.

The division between long, medium and short jobs is arbitrary, but is related to the proportion of jobs of different lengths that are submitted to the Centre. The main facts are summarized in the Table below.

Time T	Proportion of total time spent on jobs taking less than T	Number of jobs taking less than T
1 minute	5%	50%
2 minutes	12%	65%
5 minutes	25%	80%
15 minutes	55%	93%
30 minutes	80%	98%

Thus we see, for example, that while fifty per cent of jobs *by number* take less than one minute each, they account only for five per cent of the total computing time. The Birmingham pattern is typical of that at many Universities and research institutes. About 300 different jobs go through the computer each day – an average of between four and five minutes per job. Short jobs are run during the daytime and longer jobs during the night in order to give a better turnround time for short jobs. The aim of the Centre is to give a six hour turnround (twice daily) for short jobs and a twenty-four hour service for the longer jobs. Daily fluctuations of demand have prevented this objective from being achieved at the time of writing; for the longer jobs a turnround of forty-eight hours is not uncommon.

Some twenty per cent of the work coming into the Centre is programmed in what we have called 'other languages'. The most important of these is a simple source language of the 'autocode' type which was developed some years ago and widely used at Birmingham before the Egdon operating system was available. New programs are no longer being written in these languages, so special testing sessions are not required. Systems development work, which is allotted about one hour a day during the week and extra time at weekends, is currently concerned with such matters as multi-access operation from remote consoles and computer graphics.

Computer maintenance and reliability

The electronic computer is a complex piece of equipment which must be able to maintain an extremely high standard of operational performance. We certainly expect it to work for periods of at least several hours without a fault; that is to say, assuming a speed of no more than 100,000 elementary operations a second (a very modest figure nowadays), to perform more than a thousand million (10^9) additions, multiplications, and so forth, without a single error. This is more than ten times as much as a skilled operator of a desk calculating machine can get through in a lifetime!

This standard of reliability can now be virtually guaranteed – but only at the price of eternal vigilance. Even the best computers need skilled and frequent nursing and the usual practice is to set aside a period each day for what is known as *scheduled maintenance*. This consists mainly of preventive measures – measurements, adjustments, and replacements intended to prevent faults from occurring subsequently, rather than to correct existing faults. The length of time that it pays to allocate to such maintenance must be decided by experience; about one hour a day, with occasional longer periods, is fairly typical. With the old computers, most of this time was spent on servicing the electronic circuits, particularly the numerous thermionic valves. The valve has now been superseded by the more reliable transistor, and electronic computer circuits have been made much less susceptible to external conditions. This has enabled scheduled maintenance to be reduced somewhat, and computers are certainly far more reliable than they were ten years ago. The main effect, however, has not been to reduce maintenance effort overall, but to change its character – from being predominantly electronic to being predominantly mechanical and electro-mechanical. The central processor needs less attention, but the ever increasing quantity of input, output and communication equipment needs more.

The technician usually starts his daily servicing by running a number of *test programs* on the computer. These are programs specially designed to probe the overall working of the computer and to check the functioning of its main units. To increase the power of these tests, and allow them to find incipient as well as actual faults, maintenance technicians make use of a technique known as *marginal testing*. The procedure is to check the computer with its electronic circuits working under artificially induced conditions which give a smaller margin of safety against faults than in normal working. In this way gradual deterioration in a circuit is noticed, and a new unit substituted before an operational fault occurs. If the computer correctly performs all its test programs in all the adverse conditions, one can be reasonably confident that it has an adequate margin of safety – at any rate for the next twenty-four hours – when operating in normal conditions. Even so, faults do sometimes occur during normal running and demand immediate *corrective maintenance*. In such cases the technician's problem is mainly diagnostic, once the cause of the fault is identified it is usually a fairly simple matter to cure it, either by removing and replacing the faulty unit or by effecting a repair *in situ*.

Most computers can now be maintained at a level of service-ability, if averaged over a long enough period to iron out the inevitable fluctuations, of at least ninety-eight per cent. This means that, on average, no more than two hours in every hundred are lost due to faults in the equipment. This does not include time lost due to faulty programs or operators' mistakes. It does, however, include not only the time spent in actually diagnosing and correcting the fault, but any time wasted in attempting to use a faulty computer before the technicians are called in and the time used afterwards in running test programs to check that the fault has indeed been put right. Where the utmost reliability is absolutely essential – as, for example, in a computer-based air traffic control system – twin or even triple computers may be installed. In such cases elaborate arrangements must be made either to duplicate the work or to switch over auto-matically to the back-up machine should a fault develop, or be suspected, on the primary machine.

11. SOME JOBS COMPUTERS DO

Scientific Research

The first digital computers were built in the laboratories of Universities and research institutes. Nowadays, most of the development and design of new computers, as well as actual construction, is done by the computer manufacturers, although they still look to the research people for new ideas. We have mentioned in the last chapter the pioneer work of the Massachusetts Institute of Technology and Dartmouth College on multi-access computer systems, and many other examples could be cited. In Britain the original pattern has persisted in the sense that the centres at which work started in 1946–47 are still in the forefront of research in computer science.

Universities, research institutes and the larger industrial research laboratories are now equipped with computing facilities as a matter of course. The number of published research papers which make use of results obtained on a digital computer now runs into thousands every year. While many of these deal with highly mathematical topics in astronomy, physics, chemistry or genetics, for example, an increasing number are concerned with less mathematical subjects such as medicine, linguistics or anthropology. The field is so vast that all we can attempt to do is to make some remarks of a fairly general nature and mention a few of the more striking or pioneer achievements.

We consider first the relationship of the computer to two fields of investigation which are generally held to have raised, during the last twenty years, some of the deepest and most fundamental questions in man's understanding of nature: elementary particle physics and molecular biology.

The physics of elementary particles is concerned with the fundamental building blocks of nature. To the physicists of thirty years ago, the universe was built up of no more than three basic particles: electron, proton and neutron. Several new particles, such as the meson and the neutrino, were then discovered; the trickle became a torrent and today physicists recognize more than a hundred so-called elementary particles, although it must be admitted that many of them spend their time being converted into others. The nature of these elusive particles and the interrelationships between them is one of the great puzzles of contemporary science. It seems that only intensive experimental work can give the theoretical physicists the material they need in order to have any hope of solving the puzzle in the sense of constructing a unified theory. Unfortunately the equipment required for this work is so expensive that it must be concentrated in a few very large research institutes; at the CERN Institute at Geneva, for example, which is jointly financed by a number of European Governments. These institutes use computers in a very big way; without them, research in high energy nuclear physics would be impossible.

We may distinguish three roles in which the computer has become an indispensable tool of particle physics research. The first is that of a 'number cruncher' to carry out lengthy calculations of extreme complexity. The second role is that of a data processor; to digest and analyse vast amounts of experimental information from a variety of sensing, measuring and counting devices. Nowadays such devices are usually connected directly to the computer, and the whole process is largely automatic. The equipment is 'on-line' to the computer which must operate in 'real time', to use the jargon explained in the previous chapter; the computer must respond very quickly to an erratic stream of external events. The third role is a non-numerical one; that of recognizing the tracks produced by elementary particles using an instrument known as a bubble chamber, the function of which is to make such tracks visible to the camera. What we mean by being able to 'recognize' a track is the ability to distinguish the genuine article from a spurious pattern of marks on a photographic plate or film. Once a track has been established as genuine it must be charted in three dimensions and recorded for subsequent analysis. The problem here is one of *pattern recognition*; something that humans are extremely good at (we can recognize a face or a voice after twenty years) but which is notoriously difficult to mechanize, as those concerned with air defence and air traffic control matters, for example, have known for a long time. The fact is that we do not know how the brain recognizes patterns so we find great difficulty in programming the procedure for a computer.

Molecular biology is one of the new 'inter-disciplinary' sciences in which the techniques of physics are applied to the study of living substances. During recent years there has been spectacular progress in our understanding of the structure of living matter, and in particular of the highly complex molecules which carry the essential genetic information that every cell must have. By enlarging our understanding of the structure and composition of these molecules and of the way in which the genetic information is encoded in them, the molecular biologist is bringing us closer to fundamental questions about the nature of life itself.

In molecular biology, as in particle physics, computers are used on a very large scale as tools of the trade, but in this case the nature of the subject itself puts it into a special relationship with the tool. Genetic molecules are essentially mechanisms for storing and reading out information. They thus present the computer designer with a unique opportunity to observe how nature handles one of his major problems. The genetic material in a human being contains something like a million million (10^{12}) bits of information; rather more than can be held in the magnetic disc storage units of the largest computers yet built. Nature's storage devices are incredibly economical and reliable. Each bit of information needs only a few hundred atoms of matter to store it and the information so stored is preserved with almost perfect fidelity through innumerable cell divisions. In the light of the findings of the molecular biologist, the computer designer has a very long way yet to go.

The aim of the molecular biologist, as we have seen, is to elucidate the structure of organic molecules. To do this they use the techniques of X-ray crystallography, which have been perfected by the physicists over some fifty years. Now the task of the crystallographer is to determine the spatial arrangements of the atoms in a molecule. His raw material consists of photographs of the patterns obtained when crystals of the substance being studied are irradiated with X-rays. Unfortunately the information contained in such photographs is insufficient to permit of a direct mathematical attack on the problem, so the crystallographer has to resort to a process of successive approximation. He must guess a molecular structure, calculate the resulting photographic pattern and compare it with his experimental observations, then try again with what he hopes is a better guess. The calculations are extremely lengthy and tedious; before the advent of the electronic computer it was by no means uncommon for the analysis of a single X-ray photograph of quite a simple molecule to take two or three years. Now the job can be completed in a few hours; calculation can keep pace with measurement. As Charles Babbage put it, with prophetic insight, more than a century ago: 'The whole of chemistry, and with it crystallography, would become a branch of mathematical analysis which, like astronomy, taking its constants from observation, would enable us to predict the character of any new compound.'

The more complex the molecule, the more complicated such calculations are. With the digital computer it became practicable to apply the technique to investigate the molecular structure of the substances produced by living organisms. The first notable achievement on these lines was the elucidation, between 1954 and 1956, of the molecular structure of vitamin B_{12}. It was discovered in 1926 that pernicious anaemia could be alleviated by administering liver extract. After twenty years work the chemists succeeded in isolating the active factor – a crystalline substance now known as vitamin B_{12}. Its chemical formula is $C_{68}H_{88}O_{14}PCo$; it is the only vitamin to have a metal in its molecule – in this case, cobalt (Co). The B_{12} molecule is far more complex than any molecule whose structure had previously been determined. To analyse it successfully called for a very refined experimental technique and a great deal of computation. In this instance the relative positions in space of all the atoms in this complex molecule were established to an accuracy of one thousand millionth part of an inch. The work was shared between scientists at Oxford, Princeton, and Los Angeles, the actual computation being carried out partly on a Ferranti Mark I computer at Manchester and partly on the National Bureau of Standards computer at Los Angeles.

Dr J. C. Kendrew, of the Medical Research Unit at Cambridge, carried this method of approach a stage further when he determined the three-dimensional structure of the myoglobin molecule, for which he was awarded the Nobel Prize for Chemistry in 1962. Myoglobin is a protein which occurs in animal muscle. Its importance derives from the fact that an oxygen molecule is able to attach itself loosely to a myoglobin molecule, thereby providing a mechanism whereby supplies of oxygen can be stored in muscular tissue. The molecule of myoglobin, like all protein molecules, contains many thousands of atoms – far more than the vitamin B_{12} molecule, for instance.

In order to understand the chemical behaviour of proteins and their functions in living organisms, it is necessary to discover not only their chemical structure, but also the way the atoms are arranged in space – what Kendrew has called the molecular architecture. Proteins form crystals, so once again the techniques of X-ray crystallography can be brought to bear. It is the great complexity of these substances that makes the task of unravelling their molecular structure so difficult and laborious. Complicated computing procedures are needed and the volume of data to be handled is very large indeed. Kendrew began his attack on myoglobin as early as 1950 with the aid of EDSAC 1, the original Cambridge University computer. After some years of massive computation, it became possible for the first time to see the three-dimensional structure of myoglobin – first in broad outline and then in more detail. The story since then has been one of progressive refinement of the picture, using ever more powerful computers as they have become available, with the eventual object of resolving individual atoms. We conclude this brief account by quoting Dr Kendrew's own words.

We feel confident that it will eventually be possible to discover the general principles on which these very complex molecules are built, and so to obtain a fuller understanding of the chemical processes taking place in all living cells. Such understanding of the basic nature and functioning of living matter will be of the greatest intrinsic interest, and will also find far-reaching application in the treatment of disease and in the development of industries concerned with the production of food and other natural substances.

One disease to which it is to be hoped that Dr Kendrew's words will soon be found to apply is cancer. At Roswell Park Memorial Institute, a cancer research centre at Buffalo, New York, an IBM computer is being used to unravel the complex three-dimensional structures of the molecule of ribonuclease, an enzyme which controls the growth of living cells. It does this by breaking down the molecules of ribonucleic acid (RNA) – the substance that controls the manufacture of proteins within the cells of the body. If RNA is not de-activated at the proper time, cell growth may get out of hand and the affected cells may become cancerous. This is why a knowledge of the structure of ribonuclease might help in the search for a cure for cancer.

The techniques of X-ray diffraction and computer analysis used at Buffalo are essentially those that were developed at Cambridge some fifteen years earlier. The ribonuclease molecule has about 1,000 atoms, and the volume of 'number crunching' needed to unravel its structure is immense. To begin with, it is necessary to obtain the distribution of density of the electrons throughout the molecule. The density at any one point is determined by measurements of up to 10,000 reflections of the X-ray beam from a single crystal, each of which must be separately computed. Having done 10,000 calculations for one point, 10,000 more are required for the next, and so on. To chart the three-dimensional structure, something like half a million points must be analysed. It is obvious that without the aid of a fairly powerful computer, the task would be utterly impossible.

Figure 84 shows a computer printout of the electron density in one plane of the ribonuclease molecule. The numbers indicate relative density only; the contour lines were drawn in by hand.

It is interesting to note that ribonuclease has recently been synthesized independently by two research groups in the U.S.A., using quite different methods. It is, in fact, the first enzyme to be built up in the laboratory from its constituent amino acids.

By way of contrast, we now give an example from botany – a field of science where computers have not been much used yet. A survey of plant distribution in the County of Warwickshire was begun in 1950 as a joint project of the Birmingham Natural History and Philosophical Society and the Birmingham University Department of Botany. The field work, shared by amateur and professional botanists, extended over some sixteen years. The

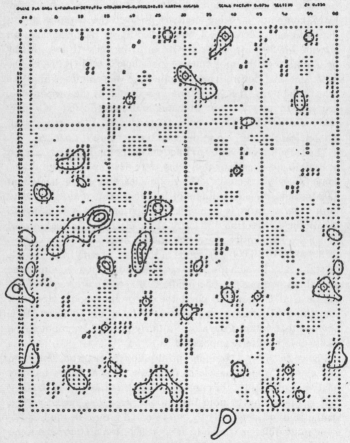

Figure 84. Computer printout showing where the electrons are most dense, and hence where the atoms are located, in one plane of a ribonuclease molecule. (The contour lines were drawn by hand.)

area covered by the survey was divided into squares of 1 kilo-
metre side, and one such square out of each block of four was
selected at random for detailed survey. For each species information was recorded on habitat (woodland, waterside, cultivated
land, etc.) and frequency (abundant, frequent, rare, etc.). This
information, suitably coded, was punched on paper tape, carefully checked for errors, and then processed in several stages on
the Birmingham University KDF9 computer. The final output
was a punched paper tape on which was encoded the necessary
instructions to an incremental graph plotter (p. 251). These
instructions enable a set of distribution maps to be prepared, one
map for each species. The plotter draws symbols in the correct
position on the map to indicate the habitat, or set of habitats, in
which the species has been recorded. One such plotted map – for
the Field Maple – is shown at Figure 85 (a). In this case the
county boundary, title, grid references, etc., have been added by
hand; the rest was plotted automatically from the paper tape. The
various symbols denote habitats as shown, while the frequencies
have been grouped into two grades (roughly 'frequent' and
'occasional') distinguished by thick and thin lines. In the published Flora, now being printed, the plotted map will be repro-
duced with an overprinting of another colour indicating the
features that have been put in by hand on Figure 85 (a).

The programs were also arranged to put out information on the
line printer at various stages of the work. This includes statistical
analyses of the data and a set of 'sketch maps' showing the distribution of each species. These interim maps were intended only
for internal use by the research group. Figure 85 (b), which
corresponds to Figure 85 (a), shows one example; the original
took three seconds to produce on the line printer of the KDF9.
Most of the mapping work was in fact done in 1965 and 1966
when the University computing facilities were very limited. Since
then the installation has been greatly extended and now includes
punched card equipment, an incremental graph plotter connected
'on-line' to the main machine, and a PDP8 satellite computer
with graphical display facilities. It is now possible to plot distribution maps directly or to display them on the screen of the
visual display unit for immediate inspection.

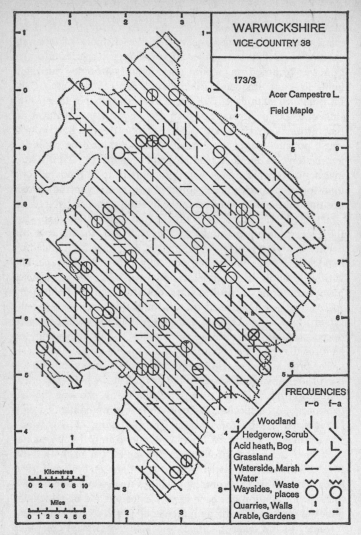

Figure 85 (a). Plotted map for *Acer campestre*. The county boundary, title, grid references, etc., have been added by hand. In the final publication these and other data will be overprinted in another colour.

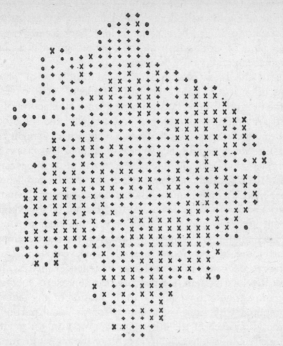

Figure 85 (b). Interim 'Sketch Map' for *Acer campestre*.
Printed on the computer's fast output line printer, this map took only
three seconds to produce.

+ Occasional to rare.
× Frequent to abundant.
· Indicates position of county boundary when no record exists.

We now turn to a very different topic – space flight. These lines
are being written within a few weeks of the three-man APOLLO 8
flight to the moon and the SOYUZ 4 and 5 docking manoeuvre
when two men transferred themselves in space from one vehicle
to another. There is no need to labour the point that without
computers – and indeed without a lot of extremely powerful and
reliable computers – space flight would be a sheer impossibility.
Very heavy calculations are needed at every stage – from the
preliminary design studies to the control of the motion of the

293

vehicle itself during its journey. The calculations themselves are too intricate to discuss here, so let us look back a few years to a pioneer piece of work which we can now recognize as a portent of the space age.

One of the most celebrated classical problems of physical science is known as the 'three-body problem'. It is concerned with the motion of three bodies in space under the action of their mutual gravitational attractions. Traditionally, the three bodies have been the Sun, Earth and Moon; nowadays they might be the Earth, the Moon and a space vehicle on a lunar trajectory. Since 1750 no less than 800 scientific papers, many of them bearing the names of the greatest mathematicians, have been published on this problem. The mathematical equations governing the motions are easy enough to write down, but they cannot be solved mathematically and their numerical solution is impracticable by pencil-and-paper methods. Fortunately, however, for the development of astronomy, it was found possible to develop approximate methods to deal with most problems of practical interest. In the case of the solar system, for instance, the sun exerts such a predominating gravitational effect that the motion of any planet can be computed with sufficient accuracy for practical purposes by assuming that each of the other planets exerts only a small perturbing effect on the basic elliptic orbit of the planet in question. There the matter rested until 1950, when Dr W. J. Eckert and his colleagues, using one of the early IBM computers, solved not merely the 'three-body' problem, but a 'six-body' problem. They calculated the position of the five major planets – Jupiter, Saturn, Uranus, Neptune, and Pluto – from A.D. 1653 to A.D. 2000 at intervals of forty days. The computations were based on some 25,000 observations, most of them made between 1730 and 1940, and the planetary paths were calculated to fourteen decimal places – that is to say, more accurately than they can be observed. About twelve million operations were performed altogether. Each one had to be carefully checked as part of the program, because a single error would have invalidated the whole of the subsequent work. The published results, containing $1\frac{1}{2}$ million figures, occupied a volume of 325 large pages. Many larger calculations have been done since, but to have carried through a task of this magnitude as early as 1950 was a notable achievement indeed.

So far computers have played a fairly limited role in pure mathematics, and most of the researches to which it has contributed are too specialized to be discussed here. One elementary – some would say trivial – example of some historical interest must suffice. It concerns our knowledge of a particular type of prime number, the 'Mersenne prime'. In 1644 a Franciscan friar named Marin Mersenne published a now famous conjecture on which of the first fifty-six numbers of a particular type* were prime numbers. Not until 1922 was this conjecture completely tested; the calculations are extremely laborious and increase rapidly in amount for each of the successively larger numbers tested. (Mersenne was right, taking the charitable view of a possible misprint, in fifty-three cases out of fifty-six.) There the matter rested until 1949, when the first of the Manchester University experimental computers was being put through its paces. Working all one night, when there was less electrical interference from the trams outside, the inventors of the computer checked all previous results and tested the next nineteen possibilities – without, alas, finding a new Mersenne prime. Since then several thousand further possible Mersenne primes have been tested, and eleven new ones had been discovered by 1964. (Compare this with the five much smaller – and so much easier to test – Mersenne primes that were discovered in the previous 300 years.) At that time the largest known Mersenne prime – and indeed the largest known prime number of any type – stood at $2^{11,213}-1$. This is a colossal number of more than 3,000 decimal digits; if written out in full it would occupy about one and a half pages of this book. Still larger such numbers may well have been discovered since.

Research in Economics

For our next illustration we turn to economics, where the processes we wish to study are much more complicated than in most of the natural sciences, and our knowledge of them is much less precise. We shall confine ourselves to a single example which, like

*Of the form 2^p-1, where p is a prime number.

Kendrew's research on myoglobin, goes back to the early days of the EDSAC 1 computer.

The research was conducted over several years by a group of mathematical economists at the Department of Applied Economics at Cambridge, under the direction of Professor Richard Stone. It entailed first, the construction of 'a computable model of economic growth', to use their own phrase, and then a study of its behaviour in order to examine the planning implications of various rates of economic expansion; in particular, to be able to make quantitative statements of the kind 'If you want to achieve such and such results, then you must do so and so.' They concentrated in the first place on the productive rather than the financial aspects of the British economy; on the goods and services it must deliver to achieve a specified rate of growth, and the resources of labour and capital it must absorb to make this possible.

The model itself is governed by three conditions. First, the anatomy of the system is represented by a *social accounting matrix*, which sets out the national accounts in the form of a table of annual incomings and outgoings for each constituent of the economy. The accounting matrix designed for the initial Cambridge model contained 257 separate accounts, giving a total of $257 \times 257 = 66,049$ separate elements. Many of them, fortunately, were zero.

Secondly, the physiology of the system is represented by a set of relationships which describe the functioning and balance of the economy. These relationships cover the processes of production, consumption, and capital accumulation within Britain, and between Britain and the rest of the world. Some of them depend on the technique of production and some on human behaviour, both of which are changing all the time. Their formulation and measurement is partly a matter of economic theory, partly of analysing published statistics, and partly of guesswork tempered by common sense.

Thirdly, the model must be convertible into a computer program, so that the sets of equations expressing the economic relationships can be solved, not once only, but many times over in accordance with the different assumptions to be examined. The first Cambridge model, which was developed between 1958 and

1960, was matched to the capacity of the University computer at the time. When the University acquired a more powerful computer (EDSAC 2) it became possible to analyse more complex – and hence more realistic – models of the economy.

A simplified version of the initial Cambridge computing model is shown in Figure 86 on page 299. To fix ideas, let us assume that the model relates to the year 1980. This means that certain assumptions must be made about future trends, both technological and behavioural.

The dotted lines in the figure refer to data, the solid lines to the calculations. The rounded blocks enclose relationships; the rectangles enclose variables. In fact most of the rectangles enclose a group of related variables set out in the form of a vector (p. 218). There are two loops in the model; a main one involving the requirements of the productive system for capital goods and a subsidiary one relating to foreign trade. (This latter loop is represented in Figure 86 only in the barest outline.)

To use the model we start by deciding what we want; that is to say, we specify the *output* of the productive system in goods and services of all kinds in 1980. We then calculate what *inputs* industry will need – what costs it will incur – in order to produce the final product required of it. A single prognosis of this kind would, clearly, be of little value. With a computer, however, one can trace the consequences of many different assumptions and so get a conspectus of alternative possibilities for the country's economic future.

We start, then, by setting a figure for the total consumption in 1980. This is denoted by C at the top left hand corner of the figure. Its value will depend on a number of basic assumptions about such matters as the rate of growth of consumption per head, and the rate of increase of the population. This consumption figure is then applied to a set of relationships which express the assumed pattern of demand in 1980 for the main categories of goods and services, both private consumption and government expenditure (health, education, defence, etc.). We shall not describe the subsequent stages of the calculation in detail; the annotations in the figure should enable the broad flow of the computation to be followed fairly easily.

Some items of consumption (cocoa and oranges, for example) can only be met by imports; these are diverted to the foreign trade loop as they do not contribute to the *final demands* made on home industry. Domestic consumption is, however, only one component – albeit the principal one – of this vector of final demands. The other components are *exports* (which in this simple model may be assumed to be estimated by examining world trends) and *investment*. It is convenient to divide this item into what we may call *industrial investment* and *community investment*. By the former we mean the new capital goods needed to maintain and increase the country's stock of productive equipment; by the latter such things as houses, hospitals, roads and schools, which, although indispensable, are not directly tied to levels of industrial production. At this stage both investment vectors must be estimated, although they may be modified later. The vector of industrial investment will in fact be generated automatically by the solution of the model itself, as we shall see shortly.

The set of input/output relations shown near the centre of Figure 86 expresses the fact that many intermediate products are required by the various industries in order to satisfy the final demand. Thus to produce a motor car we must have parts made of metal, fabric, glass, rubber, and so forth. The initial Cambridge model took account of thirty-one industries and thirty-one commodity categories, based on the Census of Production. By applying these input/output relationships – which must, of course, be estimated for 1980 – we get the vector of total *demands* on domestic industry, including both intermediate and final products. We now have to consider how far these demands are to be met by domestic production and how far by *competitive imports*. (By this we mean products which are imported, although they could be produced at home: bacon, cheese, and steel, for example.) Such imports must be siphoned off into the foreign trade loop, and there added to the non-competitive imports.

We thus arrive at the vector labelled *total domestic output*, which specifies the level of total outputs required from each industry. We can now compute what *inputs* each industry needs in order to produce the required output. To do this, we make use of a set of equations which express how industrial output depends

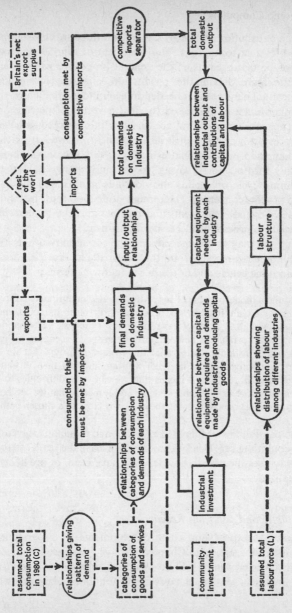

Figure 86. A model of economic growth.

on the contributions made by capital and labour, at some prescribed level of technology. The treatment of the labour factor will not be discussed here; the general procedure will be clear from the figure. Solving the 'production equations' tells us how much capital equipment is needed in each industry. Finally, this information can be processed to yield a vector of demands on industries producing capital goods. Now this is exactly what we have previously called industrial investment, so we have closed the main loop. Our original estimate of this vector will almost certainly turn out to be wrong, so we must change it, start the computing cycle off again, and continue in this way until the whole process converges. The foreign trade loop must be treated similarly; overseas payments and receipts must be brought into balance by a process of successive adjustment.

What, we may ask, is the value to the community of this kind of econometric research? In the early 1960s Professor Stone expressed his beliefs and hopes in the following terms:

To build a model capable of supplying detailed quantitative information remained an idle dream of economists until the high speed computer was born. Now we have a tool fit for the task. . . . A modern computer can produce a new version of the social accounts within a few hours. We should realise what this means. It means that we can explore alternative policies in detail without suffering their unwanted consequences in real life; it means that we can trace difficulties to the weak points of their economic system; and it means that we can begin to think seriously about keeping the economy close to a chosen path.

The possibilities of this kind of economic modelling, given the right conditions, are clearly immense. We leave the reader to form his own assessment as to how far they have been, or are likely to be, realized.

Linguistic and Literary Research

Some of the most important developments in programming technique – the subject of Chapter 9 – have been based on the fact that a computer can be told how to translate a set of instructions from a language that is convenient to human beings into a language that is convenient to itself – what we have called computer language. Is it possible to go further in this direction? Can a computer be programmed to translate from one human language to another – say, from Russian into English?

No one expects a computer program to produce a translation having any pretensions to literary quality. Indeed the practical emphasis up to now has been mainly on scientific and technical material with the modest aim of producing a fairly crude translation that will be intelligible to a specialist in the subject. The work carried out so far has certainly established the practicability of producing programmed translations at this level; it is proving difficult to go much further.

The difficulties are almost entirely linguistic. Real languages are illogical, capricious, untidy, and ambiguous. Idiomatic expressions provide obvious hazards; most people have heard stories like the one about the computer that translated 'out of sight, out of mind' into the foreign language equivalent of 'invisible imbecile'. The meaning of a word may depend on the context – consider, for instance, the last word of the sentence 'the students are revolting', while such a simple statement as 'I shall lose no time in reading your book' is likely to defeat most translation programs.

The basic problem of 'automatic' translation is to specify a set of precise rules which must be followed in order to translate from language A to language B. The simplest approach is to give a word-by-word translation, perhaps supplemented with grammatical annotations and alternative renderings in cases of doubt. The result, in the words of Booth and Richens, two of the earliest workers in the field, is 'a sequence of words and grammatical directives with a vague approximation to a stereotyped form of pidgin English'. In fact, of course, there is nothing like a one-to-one correspondence between the words of one actual language and those of another, so a word-for-word translation must necessarily be very imperfect. To do better it is necessary to take the sentence, rather than the individual word or phrase, as the linguistic unit. The good human translator does this as a matter of course, and much else besides, but to embody in a computer program his 'feel' for the nuances of language is a different matter altogether. How far, we may ask, is it worth improving the quality of programmed translation at the cost of greatly complicating the program and slowing down its execution? It is argued, on the one hand, that any 'computer' translation, however sophisticated, needs some editing to turn it into standard idiomatic English, and that quite a crude translation enables such editing to be done without much difficulty. Furthermore, the specialist can nearly always get what he wants from a crude translation; in exceptional cases he can call for a human translation of an important text. It is pointed out, on the other hand, that the specialist in programmed translation has a professional interest in continually improving the quality of his product, and that research, however esoteric, may well yield practical returns eventually. Both lines of argument are valid and there is no necessary conflict between them.

Here, to give some impression of the linguistic quality produced by a fairly sophisticated general purpose program, is a computer translation of the first paragraph of a speech delivered on 7 May 1960 by Mr Khrushchev to the supreme Soviet of the U.S.S.R., as reported in *Pravda* on the following day.

Comrade deputy!

All appearing on session expressed full consent with/from positions, advanced in reports, and unanimous supported offer Soviet government about cancellation taxes with/from worker and employee and other measures, directed on increase welfare Soviet people, and about completion in 1960 year translation all worker and employee on abbreviated worker day. In own appearances deputy unanimous approved inside and foreign policy Soviet government.

A human translation of the same passage is:
Comrade Deputies!

All those who spoke at the session expressed complete agreement with the positions advanced in the reports, and unanimously supported the proposals of the Soviet government for abolition of taxes collected from industrial, office and professional workers and for other measures directed at improving the welfare of the Soviet people, and for the completion in 1960 of the transition of all industrial, office, and professional workers to a shorter working day. In their speeches the deputies unanimously approved the internal and foreign policy of the Soviet government.

On 16 May a computer translation of the complete speech (from which the above excerpt is taken) was submitted by the IBM Corporation to a Sub-Committee of the U.S. Congressional Committee on Science and Astronautics.

This, it may be objected, was in 1960, a long time ago in computer history. The fact is, however, that not much practical progress has been made since then. Indeed the main lesson to be drawn from the experience of the last twenty years is that 'automatic' language translation is far less economically attractive than was previously thought. The nature of existing languages is such that any attempt to go much beyond a straightforward word-for-word translation soon leads to programs of quite astonishing complexity. During the 1950s a very large effort – in the Soviet Union especially – was devoted to computer translation projects. In the U.S.A. there was a rapid expansion in the early 1960s. The results in both countries fell far short of expectations and activity in this field has declined during recent years – certainly relatively to work on many other computer applications, and probably in absolute terms as well.

This recession may, however, only be temporary. The computer has presented a formidable challenge to linguistic scholars: the challenge has been accepted and may well be met. It is more than ten years since Professor Noam Chomsky, of the Modern Languages Department at M.I.T., published a small book which started something of a revolution in scientific linguistics. Chomsky distinguishes between the surface structure and the deep structure of a language. The former is, roughly speaking, the kind of grammar – parsing, sentence analysis and so forth – that we all suffered from at school; the latter is a more abstract way of representing inherent grammatical relationships which allows us, for example, to recognize the different semantic relationships involved in the two sentences 'John is going to London' and 'John is going to pieces'. It is, of course, the existence of an underlying deep structure in all languages that makes word-for-word translations so inadequate.

By the age of six a child can understand and generate a potentially infinite number of sentences – many of them new to him. Within a few more years he is able to recognize, intuitively, those that are grammatically acceptable and those that are not. He has, in fact, constructed for himself a thoery of the grammar of the language which takes account of its deep as well as its surface structure. Now clearly the child does not invoke a special rule for each sentence; there must, therefore, be a finite set of rules. The implications for computer translation are far reaching. If languages – all languages – can be described by a finite set of rules, then such rules can, in principle at any rate, be embodied in a computer program. The way is thus open for accurate translations from one language to another – idioms, puns, ambiguities and all – by means of a computer program of finite, but no doubt considerable, length. While the practical realization of the Chomsky thesis in computing terms is a long way off – at present little more than a gleam in the eye of a few academics – modern scientific linguistics certainly offer a reasonable hope of eventual success.

Fortunately, however, the usefulness of the computer to the student of language and literature is not confined to its dubious ability as a translator. It can, for example, be programmed to analyse textual material for stylistic features, and so provide a more objective basis for examining such questions as disputed authorship, the chronology of an author's works or the location of textual fragments.

In this kind of work the most difficult part of the job is usually the preliminary stage, that of creating an accurate version of the literary text – not only the actual letters, but punctuation marks, accents, literary annotations, etc. – in a computer-readable form; that is to say, on punched cards or paper tape in the first place. One of the leading workers in this field has pointed out that to produce an error-free tape of 50,000 words of Greek text it is necessary for the tape to be checked five times by at least three different people. 50,000 words may seem a lot of writing, but the Homeric poems – the *Iliad* and the *Odyssey* – run to about 220,000 words, or one million characters. In any case, if statistical techniques are to be applied to textual analysis, large amounts of material are needed in order to get reliable results. Once a 'good' text has been created on paper tape, say, it can easily be transferred to magnetic tape or a magnetic disc. In this way millions of words of textual material can be stored in what is, for practical purposes, a perfect memory, any portion of which can be easily recalled.

The next stage is to examine the contents of the text by means of *word lists*. These are ordered lists, usually in alphabetical order, of all the word-forms in the text. There are two main types: the *glossary*, in which each word-form in the list is associated with a count of the number of times it occurs; and the *concordance*, which gives the position reference – usually the page of the printed text – of each occurrence of every word-form in the list.

The best known concordance is Cruden's Concordance of the King James Version of the Bible, London and Edinburgh, 1736. It took Cruden three years to compile, working an estimated nineteen hours a day, and left him 'subject to intellectual infirmity, to overloading of the mind'. The poor man had to write each word and its context on a separate slip of paper and then sort the slips. Although Cruden confined himself to the more important words, it is not surprising that the early editions contained many errors and omissions. Nowadays, by contrast, once a text is in computer-readable form, word lists of any desired kind can be prepared painlessly and quickly, almost as a matter of routine.

Armed with a battery of word lists, the scholar can then embark on a critical study of the integrity or authorship of his texts. What he needs at this stage is a set of computer programs each of which, when executed, will cause some kind of statistical exercise to be performed on the words of the coded text; for example, to evaluate the frequency of occurrence of certain words or pairs of words, or the distribution of sentence length or some other linguistic pattern.

One of the earliest, most widely known and most hotly debated study of this kind was made in 1961–2 by two Biblical scholars – the late Professor G. H. C. Macgregor of Glasgow University and the Rev. A. Q. Morton of Culross, Fife. The main aim of the research was to investigate the problem presented by the Pauline epistles. Of the twenty-one epistles in the New Testament, the first fourteen, from Romans to Hebrews, have been commonly attributed to the Apostle. The question has, however, been debated for centuries. Macgregor and Morton based their work on the the principle that authors have certain habits of style deeply engrained. The problem is, therefore, to identify some unconscious literary mannerisms that can be traced in everything an author writes. With the aid of a Mercury computer they analysed about 400 samples of Greek prose texts – some 600,000 words in all – drawn from more than a dozen different authors. They claimed to have established no less than seven reliable tests of authorship, most of them concerned with the frequency and mode of use of some of the commoner words in the Greek language, such as *kai* and *de* (meaning approximately 'and' and 'but').

Morton describes (*Observer*, 3 November 1963) how he and Macgregor returned to the problem of the Pauline Epistles after three years spent on other things. 'We discovered,' he writes, 'by applying with the help of our computer the seven tests of authorship, that each one gave the same result. Five of the fourteen Epistles were indistinguishable: Romans, first and second Corinthians, Galatians, and Philemon. The remaining nine came from at least five other hands.' Now since Paul is universally accepted as the author of Galatians the conclusion is that these five are the genuine Pauline epistles.

More recently Morton has applied these techniques to a number of early Greek texts, including Homer. His findings in this case, in contrast to those for the Epistles, are that almost the whole of the *Iliad* and the *Odyssey*, as they have come down to us, are the work of a single hand.

Among the many other problems to which computer-aided textual analysis has been applied we may mention the chronology of the works of Plato and Xenophon; or coming to the eighteenth century, the authorship of the disputed 'Federalist' papers, all of which were apparently written by James Madison, and of Swift's doubtful *Letter of Advice to a Young Poet*.

A similar approach has been used by some Cambridge prehistorians, although in this case the raw material is not words, but certain measurable characteristics of pottery from a number of excavated sites. Indeed, an increasing number of scholars in the humanities are now using computers as a matter of routine.

Computers can also be used to solve logical problems: to prepare school or examination timetables or to check legal documents for consistency, to mention but two examples. Indeed, the fact that the digital computer works in the binary scale makes it specially suitable for such tasks. In logic, too, we are concerned with binary elements. There is an immediate correspondence between the two possible values of a logical propostion, true or false, and the two possible values of a binary digit, 1 or 0. We have seen in Chapter 8 how close is the link between symbolic logic and computer design.

To program a computer to solve logical problems we must be able to operate on the individual binary digits of a computer word, the normal carry from one digit to the next being suppressed. Nowadays computer designers always provide facilities of this kind and the elementary logical operations (such as the 'and', 'or' and 'not equivalent to' operations explained in Chapter 8) form part of the basic instruction set of most computers (p. 113). This is why special-purpose 'logical machines', of which quite a number were built during the last century, no longer excite much interest. The general purpose computer can be programmed to do the job.

All computer programs for numerical computations contain both arithmetic and logical instructions. A simple example of the latter is the conditional jump instruction of Chapter 6 (p. 119), the logical form of which is: 'If some proposition A is true, do this; if A is false, do that.' The more advanced computing languages provide comprehensive logical facilities. In ALGOL for example, one can declare logical variables and use logical expressions. These are analogous to real or integer variables and expressions, but have the distinguishing feature of taking only two different values, namely, true or false. (They are not mentioned in Chapter 9 solely in the interests of brevity.)

Engineering design and production

In the life cycle of many industrial products, from aircraft to synthetic fibres, there are four main stages: research, design, production, and use. We have already emphasized the importance of computers in research, and shall mention applications connected with the use of a product at the end of this chapter. Computers are also very valuable in engineering design and production.

In the aircraft industry, for example, a vast amount of what is called 'stress calculation' is necessary to check that a new design of aircraft is strong enough for various extreme conditions that it may meet, yet not unnecessarily massive. Before the advent of computers these calculations were done by large numbers of girls using mechanical desk calculators, or junior 'stressmen' using slide rules. The aircraft firms, acting through their collective organ, the Society of British Aircraft Constructors, set up an Electronic Computing Panel as early as 1952, when there were less than a dozen working computers in the country. Within a few years computers were installed in all the main centres of aircraft and aero-engine design and development. The electrical, civil, and chemical engineers followed hard on the heels of their aeronautical colleagues. In nuclear engineering, where the computational load is especially heavy, the aid of the electronic computer has been enlisted from the outset. A substantial proportion of the world's largest and most expensive computers is to be found in atomic energy establishments.

An engineering article, whether it be an aeroplane or a bridge, a transformer or the wiring arrangement of a computer, must be designed so as to do a particular job at a specified level of performance. We may think of these requirements as being embodied in a technical specification. It is usually possible, however, to meet the specification in many different ways; the job of the design engineer is to select the 'best', which usually means the cheapest. Now the engineer must keep his eye on both the clock and the cashbox. He is not able to try every possible combination of design features, but must strike an economic balance between the information he would like to have and the time and cost of getting it. The computer, by making calculation cheap and easy, moves the point of balance in the direction of more information. It enables the engineer to extend both the range and depth of his design studies: not only can he examine a greater number of alternative designs; he can examine each of them more thoroughly.

In fact the design of some things, such as electrical power transformers, is very stereotyped. There are various quantities, which can be chosen by the designer, which determine how the article will be made, and what its performance will be. These are called the *design parameters*. For a transformer they include the size and shape in plan of the iron core (which must be one of a range of standard sizes and shapes), the thickness of the core, the thickness of the wire used for each different winding, and the number of turns on each winding. The designer can calculate the performance of the transformer from the values of these parameters, and finding the best set of values is sufficient to determine the design more or less in its entirety.

It is seldom possible to arrive at the best design by orthodox mathematical methods because the equations used to calculate performance are too complex and are subject to too many overriding restrictions. The designer has to proceed by cut and try methods, as indicated in the flow diagram of the process, Figure 87. If this work is transferred to a computer, not only is expensive human effort saved, but more accurate (and more laborious) performance calculations can be done, and can be repeated more often. This results in a better design than if the calculation had been done by a man.

Many production processes, too, can be improved with the aid of computers. A prerequisite for this is a certain degree of automatic control, such as has been introduced in so many industries since 1801, when Jacquard first exhibited the card-controlled looms which so excited Charles Babbage. An important principle of many automatic devices, beginning with James Watt's steam-engine governor, is closed-loop control, as exemplified also by the position-control servomechanism described on page 97. The essential feature here is that actual achievement is continually compared with desired performance, and any discrepancy is used to cause continual corrective action. Thus, in a chemical engineering process, the temperature of a solution may be kept approximately constant by adjusting a steam valve automatically, compensating for varying amounts of heat generated in the chemical reactions which are going on. In another example, the thickness of steel strip produced by a rolling mill may be

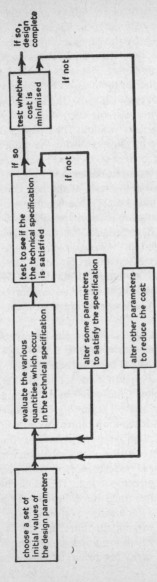

Figure 87. Flow diagram illustrating a stereotyped engineering design process.

automatically maintained constant, with much smaller errors than under manual control, irrespective of variations in temperature, ductility, and so on, of the input material.

The early automatic controllers had a knob by which a man was able to set the desired value of the controlled variable, just as a housewife sets her oven temperature. The man knew the process thoroughly, and from experience and rule of thumb was able to set all the controlled variables to values which were suitable for the output required, and to the quality of the input.

Nowadays it is possible to set the controlled variables to their optimum values by means of signals sent from a computer – in a chemical process, for example. A computer has been applied to a well-known chemical process by the Pleasant Valley Wine Co. in New York State which 'has installed an electronic system to handle all processing from the time the grape juice leaves the presses. It controls temperatures, blending, fermentation, racking, clarification, filtering, storing, and bottling.' ('Vin automatique', *Electronics*, 11 November, 1968.)

A computer is, in fact, able to take account of a large number of external conditions which affect the process – such as, for example, the market prices of the raw materials, the primary output, and the by-products, as well as the more obvious things such as the physical characteristics of the input materials. Using the best available mathematical model of the process, it can calculate optimum conditions to any nominated accuracy. It can even be programmed to search for an optimum empirically, when some of the parameters of the process are not known very accurately. It does this by making successive small adjustments to the controlled variables, and observing the effect on the output.

Steel production is a fruitful source of examples. A hot-strip mill rolls a red-hot steel ingot into a coil of steel sheet in a continuous process, and a digital computer controls the setting of each of the several rolling mills. After this, the steel is in the form of a strip, several thousand feet long, still nearly red-hot, and moving very rapidly as a result of the successive reductions in thickness. Before the strip is ready to be coiled up, it must be cooled, and the rate of cooling affects the physical properties of the final product. A hybrid computer (p. 72) can control the cooling process, to ensure a uniform product independent of the speed at which the strip moves, which can vary from 10 to 35 miles per hour even during the processing of one ingot.

Numerous nozzles, spread over a distance of a hundred yards, squirt powerful jets of water at the upper and lower surfaces of the strip, at total rates of the order of 50 gallons per second. The analog portion of the hybrid computer receives, as input signals, the measured speed, temperature and thickness of the strip, the temperature of the cooling water supply, the desired final temperature of the strip as selected on the control console, and the measured final temperature. It computes the required total flow rate of cooling water, and supplies this to the digital portion of the computer. This is responsible for choosing the pattern of nozzles to be used, in accordance with metallurgical requirements for the particular product, which are specified from the console. Within this constraint, the digital circuits also turn on sufficient nozzles to achieve the required total flow; the quantum of this amount is the flow from one nozzle.

A digital computer can also coordinate a sequence of production processes in which one batch of the product may take several days to be dealt with. For some processes no more is required than to display the computed information to the workpeople; to tell them, for instance, in what order the ingots are to be marshalled for the mill, when to start reheating an ingot, and so on. One job in particular to which computers have been applied is that of choosing a set of sizes, from among orders as yet unfilled, into which a steel billet can be cut without odd fragments being left over as scrap. This can be made completely automatic. As the billet approaches the finishing mill to be rolled out thinner, its length is automatically measured by photo-electric cells. As the leading end of the billet emerges from the mill, its speed is measured and the computer calculates what the new length will be, by reference to the speed of entering the mill and the old length. By the time the rolled billet starts to pass through the travelling shear, the computer is ready to control the cutting to size, without the need to wait until the billet is completely rolled to see how long it is.

The automatic transfer machine, such as is used to make motor car cylinder heads, for example, typifies automation for many people. In many industries, however, such as the aircraft industry, production quantities of any one item are too low to justify a heavy outlay on elaborate and highly specialized machinery. The prime need is to be able to produce a variety of components in quite small quantities at a reasonable cost. Indeed, this problem is a very real one in the mass-production industries as well; for instance, during the tooling-up process and when prototype models are being built.

Some progress has been achieved in recent years by exploiting various precision casting and moulding techniques; in many cases, however, components of complex shapes must be machined from the solid for reasons of strength. Within a few years the wings of high-speed aircraft, for instance, will probably have to be made in this way. In the research stage, the problem is with us now. Before an aircraft can be designed, very accurate scale models must be made and tested in a wind tunnel. Such models, if they are to stand up to tests at supersonic speeds, must be extremely strong. This means that they must be cut in one piece from a block of high-tensile steel. Such operations, when the cutting machines are controlled by hand, are slow and expensive. This is because so much time is spent in such tasks as interpreting drawings or altering the settings of the machine or the position of the workpiece, compared with the time spent in actually cutting the metal. Furthermore, the cutting itself usually has to be done quite slowly to enable the operator to control the tool movement by hand with sufficient accuracy.

What is needed, then, is some way of reducing the thinking time, the setting time, and the machining time without sacrificing accuracy. A high degree of flexibility, so that one machine can deal with a variety of jobs, is also desirable. This is, of course, just the kind of situation where the versatility of the digital computer can be exploited to good effect. A number of schemes for controlling machine tools from the output of a digital computer are now in regular operation. In all of them the role of the computer is that of a middleman between the designer and the machine tool. The input to the computer consists of data, in the simplest possible form, about the work to be done. The computer digests this data, and generates from it an output which instructs the machine tool as to the path it must follow in order to cut the desired article from the solid to the required accuracy. This output is recorded, on paper tape or magnetic tape, and thereafter used as input data to the automatic machine tool. This is done more than once if more than one article is required to the same design. Depending on the batch size, and on the nature of the article, the production time may be up to twenty times less; perhaps five times less would be a fair average.

Commerce and Administration

When digital computers started to appear in business offices in the mid 1950s, they were put to work on some of the bread-and-butter jobs that had been dealt with up to that time by armies of clerks. It is indeed the relentless growth of the clerical army which provides one of the main incentives for the business man's interest in computers. There are more than four million clerks in Britain and the number is increasing by about a hundred thousand a year. Many of them are engaged on routine, repetitive tasks which are clearly susceptible to mechanization.

There is, of course, nothing new in office mechanization; we need only mention the typewriter, the telephone, and the adding machine. Hollerith made his basic invention about 1890 and punched-card machines – either mechanical or electromechanical – have been widely used for half a century. Electronic techniques invaded the office-equipment industry about twenty years ago. The first result was the development of special purpose punched-card machines called *electronic calculators*, which were the electronic counterparts of the tabulators and collators discussed in Chapter 3. The introduction of the fully automatic stored-program electronic computer into the business office was a logical next step.

We have already mentioned the pioneer work of the catering firm of J. Lyons & Co.; the preparation of a departmental payroll was entrusted to the first LEO computer in 1953. The project was so successful that parallel work in the wages office was stopped a month later. By 1957 LEO was producing a weekly payroll for about 15,000 people, together with a detailed analysis for costing and accounting purposes. All the pay calculations, including PAYE and other deductions, right through to the printing of the pay-slips, were carried out automatically in one operation, the complete job taking about six hours each week.

Another of LEO's early jobs was to deal with the daily orders on the central bakeries and kitchens at Cadby Hall from about 150 teashops in the London area. Under the old system each shop manageress had to fill up – no doubt in triplicate – a formidable wad of order forms each day. Under the new system, which came into operation in November 1954, she placed a standing order based on normal requirements and only needed to report any daily revisions that might be necessary in the light of current sales. She did this by ringing Cadby Hall during the afternoon. The calls were received by a group of girls who punched the information direct on to cards which were then fed to LEO in batches. Within a few months about 8,000 revisions of standing orders covering some 250 different items of goods were handled in this way each day. Less than an hour after receiving the last telephone call, LEO was able to produce the total production orders and the detailed information and documents required for the assembly, packing, and despatch of the goods to each teashop. The necessary cost accounting, stock control, and management statistics were produced at the same time, and the whole exercise was completed each day by five o'clock.

These two examples give some indication of LEO's early activities. Nowadays the Lyons' computers handle much of the clerical work of the company: stock control, job costing, production planning, invoicing of goods to dealers, to mention only a few of their tasks.

The calculation of wages and salaries was the first, and remains one of the most popular, of the computer's commercial jobs. The preparation of a payroll program can be a formidable task; some of those now in regular operation contain more than 10,000 separate instructions. On the other hand, a comprehensive automatic payroll scheme can offer very substantial advantages in flexibility of operation. Such things as changes in rates of pay or income tax, the Christmas bonus, the pension scheme, or the contribution to the sports fund can be dealt with quite easily. One company has stated that the ability to calculate on the basis of minutes worked, in place of the three-minute intervals formerly used by the pay-clerks, has saved about £4,000 a year. Whether this is to be regarded as an argument for or against computers will no doubt depend on the point of view. A less contentious benefit has been to reduce the number of queries. Employees 'paid by computer' receive more information on their pay-slips and have less cause to complain of incorrect arithmetic.

Here is a rough analysis of the main jobs that were being done on a representative sample of 100 computers used in commerce in 1961. The general position has not changed much since then, although the vanguard has certainly moved forward to occupy quite a lot of new ground.

Payroll	50
Stock control	35
Invoicing	20
Sales accounting and analysis	15
Costing	14
Production control	13
*Operational research	12
Revenue accounting	9
*Production scheduling	7
*Budgetary control	5
Distribution of supplies	3

The figures add up to more than 100 because many computers are used for more than one job – as they should be to give full value. All the items, except those marked with an asterisk, form part of the traditional procedures of the business house; they would no doubt be familiar to Antonio and Shylock. In the larger offices computers have now taken over many of the more tiresome clerical chores; with cheap time sharing services becoming widely available, they ought soon to be doing the same in the smaller ones as well.

One field of commerce where the introduction of computers has already led to changes in long established office procedures is banking. Most people are familiar with the rather odd looking symbols at the bottom of bank cheques. They usually define three numbers: the serial number of the cheque, the code number of the customer's bank and the customer's account number. The characters are printed in a special magnetic ink and in a stylized form based on thick and thin vertical strokes so that they can be read into a computer automatically, like a magnetic tape. The general problem of the automatic reading of printed or hand-written characters will be briefly discussed in Chapter 13. Suffice to say here that the banks, after much experimentation, chose a magnetic rather than an optical method of reading, mainly because the magnetic process is unaffected by the presence of (non-magnetic) dirt or superimposed marks and stands up well to folding and the kind of rough treatment that cheques are likely to be subjected to.

When a cheque is received at the branch office of a bank, one of the first things that happens is that the amount of the cheque is printed on in similar magnetic characters, special typewriters being used for the purpose. The cheques can now be 'read', listed, sorted and checked automatically. Each day the cheques and other documents relating to each account are fed into the computer and the account is brought up to date. The computer also contains a number of items of more permanent information – dates on which standing orders are to be paid, overdraft limits and the like. These are examined in conjunction with each account and if any action needs to be taken, the appropriate message is printed out. Interest charges are also calculated and the balance of each account is printed out for the information of the branch manager.

In addition to handling the accounts of its customers, a bank also needs a variety of information for management purposes. Even so, a computer of the size required to do the job cannot be kept busy by a single branch. This is why most installations are to be found in large towns with many branch offices. The banks operate a simple form of time-sharing in which a postal or courier service is used to transmit information between the local branches and the central computer of the town or district. A natural extension is to use the public telephone network for this purpose. In fact this method of working is becoming increasingly popular, not only in banks but in insurance companies, building societies and many of the larger commercial or governmental organizations. It is not 'real time' (that is, quick response) operation in the sense explained on page 266; each participant in the shared service can be instructed to transmit his prepared material at a prescribed time. For example, a central banking computer in a large town might accept data from each branch once in the morning and twice in the afternoon. The work would be processed overnight and for each branch the state of all accounts would be printed out at the branch ready for the manager's use by nine o'clock the next morning.

Airline seat reservation

An example of a commercial application which embodies both multi-access and quick response features is the booking and control of seats on scheduled airline flights. Most of the major airlines have installed computer-based systems to do this job, and those used by the two British national airlines are fairly typical.

The British European Airways system, known as BEACON, came into operation in 1965 at a capital cost of some £5 million. The heart of the system is a pair of computers specially designed for multi-access operation (UNIVAC 494 models) and a very large magnetic store which the two computers share. The installation occupies one floor of BEA's West London Terminal Building. On the floor immediately above is a large booking office occupied by some 200 reservation clerks (Plate 8). Each clerk is equipped with a push button control-typewriter desk instrument known as a *Uniset*, two of which can be seen in the foreground of Plate 8.

Incoming telephone calls are handled by the BEA switchboard operators (using 420 lines) at a rate of about 10,000 calls a day. Those concerned with sales enquiries are routed to the reservation clerks who are deployed in groups according to the geographical area concerned. A clerk deals with an inquiry by interrogating the central computer, which she does by pressing the appropriate buttons on the control panel of her Uniset. Full information on sales and timetables on all flights for a year ahead is stored in the central BEACON store, so information on the seats available on any of these flights can be obtained by the clerk in a fraction of a second. To make a booking, the clerk uses the teleprinter keyboard on her Uniset to type the passenger's name, flight details, etc., which are immediately read into the central store. For checking or cancellation, information can be immediately recalled by similar press-button action. When a booking is made, the number of seats recorded in the store as being available on the flight concerned is automatically reduced in readiness for the next inquiry.

In addition to dealing with telephone enquiries, the BEACON computers also process up to 14,000 incoming teleprinter messages every day, and may send out several thousand more over the BEA teleprinter network. In the spring of 1967, the information in the central computer store was made available by direct line to the main British regional offices outside London. This facility is now being extended to the major BEA offices overseas.

The advantage of an automated system of this kind to the air traveller is obvious; the value to the Company is that the more precise control of bookings enables it to increase its operational load factor – the average percentage of seats sold per flight. Airlines operate on narrow economic margins and BEA estimates that a one per cent increase in load factor is equivalent to an extra income of over £1 million per year.

The other British national airline – the British Overseas Airways Corporation – has invested in an even more ambitious scheme which goes by the name of BOADICEA. It went into operation in November 1968; its total capital cost is put at £42 million. The central installation consists of three large IBM computers (Model 360/65), several high capacity magnetic disc storage units, 20 magnetic tape units, 4 line printers and the usual facilities for handling punched cards and paper tape. The main difference between BOADICEA and BEACON, apart from size, is that the former is used not only for passenger seat reservation, but for a great many other tasks as well. The most important of these are illustrated diagramatically in Figure 88. BOAC has been bold enough to install a comprehensive computer-based system covering virtually every aspect of its operations as a world airline. Conventional batch processing, which is suitable for many of the tasks shown in the Figure, is interleaved with quick response multi-access working for seat reservation and similar tasks.

A notable feature of BOADICEA is its global coverage. BOAC has offices in more than 200 cities in seventy countries, each directly linked to BOADICEA in London. Some 350,000 messages are transmitted over the two BOAC communication

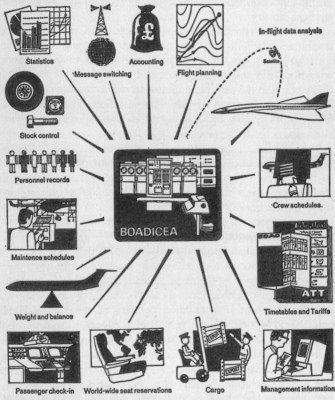

Figure 88. Some of BOADICEA'S many jobs.

networks every day. The faster network serves Britain, the Continent of Europe and North America. The busier offices in this area are equipped with visual display and keyboard desk instruments; the less busy offices use high speed printers instead of visual display devices. Offices in the rest of the world are equipped with standard teleprinters instead of desk sets and are linked to BOADICEA by the second network – BOAC's private telegraph network. Four computers – in London, New York, Sydney and Hong Kong – are used to concentrate on incoming messages and pass them forward automatically. The two systems work essentially in the same way, but with the telegraph system response times are usually a matter of minutes rather than seconds.

BOADICEA's other tasks, as indicated in the Figure, are too numerous to discuss individually; a few remarks on one of them – flight planning – must suffice. Let us consider, by way of illustration, planning a flight on the busiest route, that between London and New York. Now on most occasions a 'straight line' path between these two cities would not be the best route to fly, neither the quickest nor the most economical in fuel. (A 'straight line' on the surface of a spherical earth means a 'great circle' path.) The main reason for this is the variation in the wind over the area: strong winds, continually changing in strength and direction, blow above the North Atlantic nearly all the time. The best path has therefore to be recalculated several times a day, whenever a new weather forecast is available. Account must also be taken of the effects of height and temperature, both of which affect flying speed and fuel consumption.

A flight plan must be prepared for each flight before departure and submitted to the appropriate Air Traffic Controller for his approval. He examines it from the point of view of safety and good traffic management. The airline, for its part, is concerned to ensure that its aircraft always take the fastest and most economical route in the conditions prevailing at the time, subject, of course, to any restrictions the Air Traffic Controller may impose. Preparing a flight plan is a complex trial and error task: it involves computing a whole set of flight paths in three dimensions and then selecting the 'best', in the sense just explained. It takes a skilled flight planner about forty-five minutes to do the job; the BOADICEA computers can polish it off in a few seconds.

The weather information – provided in fact by another computer at the Meteorological Office at Bracknell – is transferred to punched paper tape and fed directly into the store of BOADICEA. The computer contains a set of 'shortest path' programs which operate on this information to work out the best path. (A note for the mathematically minded: the technique used is that of dynamic programming and works by progressively extending a 'time front' outwards from the departure point.) Tests have shown that a machine-computed optimum track is usually between 5 and 10 minutes faster than a manually calculated one, and sometimes a good deal more. It is the aggregate of comparatively small savings like these, taken over BOADICEA's many tasks, that explains why BOAC has been prepared to invest so heavily in an integrated computer-based system.

Operational research

During the last few years the commercial exploitation of computers has become more adventurous. Computers are being used not only for doing old jobs better, but to do things that have never been done before. The first stage is to provide the managerial staff with better information; that is to say, with information that is more comprehensive, more thoroughly digested, and more up to date. This leads on to the exciting part – the use of computers not only to process data, but to solve business problems; to *use* information, not merely to provide it. This means that the computer must be programmed not only to manipulate the data supplied to it in order to produce certain results, but to go on and make deductions from those results. The computer is beginning to take part in the business of decision-making – the traditional prerogative of those exalted beings we call managers, directors, or executives. There is an analogy here with numerical weather forecasting, in which the computer is programmed first to derive the current state of the atmosphere from the observational measurements and then to deduce its future behaviour – a task formerly reserved for human beings. The starred items in the list on p. 316 fall broadly into this category. We shall focus attention on the first such item – the one labelled *operational research*. This, roughly speaking, means the application of scientific procedures to the formulation and solution of executive problems; that is to say, to situations in which it is necessary to take decisions – usually on insufficient information – that will lead to some kind of action. Such situations arise all the time in industry, commerce, and public affairs – and also in the military field, where operational research first became respectable during the Second World War. The operational research scientist has a number of problem-solving techniques at his disposal. For these to be useful, he may well need a computer to do the numerical work. We shall discuss only one of these techniques here.

Most business decision-situations exhibit two characteristics. First, they are extremely complex, involving a large number of continually changing factors which interact with each other. Secondly, one is seeking what is in some sense the 'best'; the most favourable solution in the context of the many constraints imposed by the situation itself. These may be due, for instance, to shortage of labour or materials, or to contractual obligations to customers.

Problems of this kind can sometimes be formulated – usually after some simplification – in such a way that they can be solved by a mathematical technique which has the somewhat unfortunate name of *linear programming* but is better termed *linear optimization*. Programming here is not used in the computing sense, but as a synonym for 'planning'; the significance of the adjective 'linear' will appear shortly. We shall illustrate the kind of problem to which the technique can be applied by a simple example for which we are indebted to Professor S. Vajda, a leading authority on the subject.

A cloth manufacturing problem

Consider a company which manufactures two types of cloth (L and M) and uses three different colours of wool. The material required for a length of one yard of each type of cloth is given by:

Type of cloth			Wool available
L	M		
4oz.	5oz.	of red wool	1,000oz.
5oz.	2oz.	of green wool	1,000oz.
3oz.	8oz.	of yellow wool	1,200oz.

The right-hand column shows how much wool of each colour is available. Now the manufacturer can make a profit of 5s. on one yard of type L cloth, and 3s. on one yard of type M. How shall he use his available material so as to maximize his total profit? Let x and y be the number of yards of cloth L and cloth M respectively that are produced. Then, since only 1,000 oz. of red wool are available, we have

$$4x + 5y \leq 1,000.$$

Similarly, considering the available green and yellow wool, we must have

$$5x + 2y \leq 1,000$$

and

$$3x + 8y \leq 1,200.$$

(The symbol '$\leq$' means 'less than or equal to'.)
The profit, P, in shillings is given by

$$P = 5x + 3y.$$

We want to choose x and y so as to maximize P, subject to the constraints represented by the above inequalities and to the fact that neither x nor y may be negative.

Let us set out the problem in graphical form. Any pair of values of x and y corresponds to a point in the plane of Figure 89 whose coordinates are (x,y). The point O is the origin; Ox and Oy are the axes of coordinates.

The first thing to note is that we may confine our attention to the part of the plane corresponding to positive values of x and y, since negative amounts of cloth do not mean anything. The three full lines correspond to the three constraints due to the limited availability of the three colours of wool. Consider, for instance, the first constraint. The graphical interpretation of this is that we must exclude that part of the plane which lies further away from the origin than the straight line whose equation is $4x + 5y = 1,000$. We can see which side it is by noting that the origin (where $x = 0$ and $y = 0$) is on the admissible side, since 0 is smaller than 1,000. The effect of the two other constraints can be derived in the same way, and we reach the conclusion that the only region which remains admissible, after satisfying all the constraints, is the pentagon whose vertices are O, A, B, C and D. All points within this region, including the boundary lines, are admissible. All other points are inadmissible. All that remains now is to find the point in the region whose coordinates (x,y) make $5x+3y$ as large as possible. Now all lines whose equations are $5x+3y=P$ are parallel to each other: the greater the value of P, the further the lines from the origin. (Two such lines are shown dashed in Figure 89.) We must therefore go as far as we can in the direction of the arrow without leaving the admissible region. This takes us to the point B, whose coordinates are $176\frac{8}{17}$ and $58\frac{14}{17}$. This point corresponds to the solution of our problem. The maximum profit will be obtained by producing about 176 yards of cloth of type L and about 59 yards of type M.

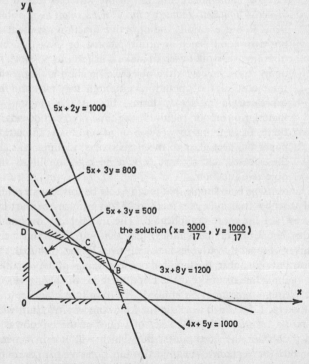

Figure 89. A linear optimization chart.

Most problems that can be solved by the techniques of linear optimization have the following features in common.

(i) We have a number of variables, or 'unknowns', which can take only positive or zero values; they may be further restricted to whole numbers.

(ii) The mutual interaction of these variables can be represented by a set of linear equations or inequalities, called *constraints*.

(iii) We wish to choose, from among all those solutions which satisfy the constraints and the non-negative conditions, the particular solution that produces the best result. By the 'best result' we normally mean the one which makes the value of some linear function of the variables (called the *objective function*) either as *large* or as *small* as possible. If, as in our example, the objective function represents a positive 'good', such as profit, income, or some measure of utility, we would wish to make it as *large* as possible. In many cases, however, the objective function is simply the total cost of the operation, although this may not be expressed in monetary terms, but as the amount of material or labour required, the time taken to do something, or in terms of wastage of material – as in cutting paper or sheet glass to meet customers' requirements. In these cases, clearly, we would seek to minimize the objective function.

Our example is so simple that it can easily be solved with pencil and paper by 'trial and error' methods. Most problems of practical interest are far more complicated. The number of constraints (either equations or inequalities) may run into thousands; the number of separate variables is usually even larger. Although the constraints are linear, the fact that negative values of the variables are inadmissible means that the usual methods of solving sets of linear equations cannot be applied. We have to use an iterative method (p. 125), which works in the following way. We start with an *initial solution* – that is, a set of values of the unknowns – which satisfies the constraints, but which will not in general minimize (or maximize) the objective function. We then examine the situation systematically and make a series of adjustments which have the effect of progressively improving the value of the objective function until eventually the optimum solution is reached.

Linear optimization is a new subject. The development of general methods of solution did not begin until 1947, although some special problems, now recognized as being of linear optimization type, were posed – but not usually solved – a few years earlier. Thus a paper by F. L. Hitchcock entitled *The distribution of a product from several sources to numerous localities* appeared in 1941. The movement of railway wagons, mentioned in Chapter 1, is a simple example of a problem of this kind – usually called the transportation problem.

In 1945, J. Stigler wrote a paper called *The cost of subsistence* in which he discussed the cheapest diet which would suffice to meet some prescribed minimum nutritional standard. He considered seventy-seven food items and arrived at the cheapest combination by trial and error methods. 'The procedure,' he said, 'is experimental because there does not appear to be any direct method of finding the minimum of a linear function subject to linear constraints.' This was true in 1945, but ceased to be so soon after. When Stigler's problem was solved subsequently by linear optimization methods it was found that he had got very near to, but had not quite reached, the 'optimum' (if the word may be allowed in so sombre a context).

We have seen that most linear optimization problems must be solved by an iterative process of successive approximation. A large number of steps may be needed, and each step may involve a lot of arithmetic. Fortunately, however, the procedure is highly systematic and repetitive, so is well suited to being programmed for a computer. We shall not go into computational details here; suffice to say that the process of solution entails the manipulation of matrices (p. 217), that is, of ordered sets of numbers arranged in rectangular arrays.

Why, we may ask, have the techniques of linear optimization become so popular in management planning? The answer is twofold: first, the variety of practical problems that can be expressed in a suitable linear form, and secondly, the fact that the heavy arithmetic can be turned over to computers. It is no accident that linear optimization and electronic computers were born at almost exactly the same time and have grown up side by side. The applications of linear optimization are legion: from the routing of aircraft or tankers to the mixing of fertilizers or animal feeding stuffs; from the blending of aviation fuels to the planning of ice cream production; indeed to any 'linear' situation where limited resources have to be allocated so as to achieve a desired objective. The 'linear' proviso is, in fact, no longer essential as mathematical techniques are now available to deal with non-linear situations of various kinds.

The first successful solution of a linear optimization problem on an electronic computer occurred in January 1952 on the SEAC machine of the National Bureau of Standards at Washington. Nowadays a set of linear optimization computer programs are to be found in most computer libraries; some of them can deal with problems containing several thousand separate constraints. In practice, the purely computational aspect rarely presents much difficulty. The crux of the problem lies in constructing a sufficiently realistic model of the situation one wishes to analyse, and then in deciding on suitable numerical values for the various coefficients.

Computers in Medicine

Hospitals, like many large organizations, need to collect, record and disseminate large amounts of factual information, with the inevitable result that the staff are burdened with a fearsome load of paper work. Recent American studies, for example, have shown that the hospital nurse spends from forty to eighty per cent of her working time performing clerical tasks.

In the U.K. most Regional Hospital Boards, who are responsible for managing the hospital sector of the health service, have installed computers during the last few years. They were used initially for accounting and administrative tasks of the traditional kind: most of them still are. Computers are also to be found in specialized service departments – pathology, pharmacy, biochemistry, radiotherapy, and so forth – in many of the larger hospitals, and they have been an essential tool of medical research for many years.

As an example of a specialized medical application, we consider a computer-based patient monitoring system in an Intensive Care Ward or Unit. Patients in such units require constant attention; they must be kept under observation twenty-four hours a day so that any critical condition may be promptly detected, diagnosed and treated; a few minutes may be a matter of life or death. As soon as a patient enters such a unit, the usual procedure is to attach to his body a number of sensing devices. These are connected to instruments which measure the action of his heart, and his respiratory system, blood pressure, body temperature, and so forth. Before the advent of the computer, information from these instruments, most of which were of analog type (p. 73), was displayed, usually as wavy lines or 'wave forms', on oscilloscopes or strip chart recorders. The records had then to be observed and interpreted ('monitored' in current jargon) by a physician or nurse in order to detect any change in the patient's condition that might require immediate action. Most of the instruments, being analog devices, can handle simple functions only and each measured quantity must be displayed separately, essentially in the form in which it is measured. Unfortunately, however, the factors which are critically important for diagnosis are not determined by simple inspection of a number of separate physiological signals, but involve the mutual interaction of several such signals. This is where the computer comes to the rescue, with its ability to analyse large quantities of data rapidly, accurately and tirelessly.

In the Cardiopulmonary Intensive Care Unit of the Presbyterian Hospital in San Francisco, to take one example of many, the signals from patients' sensing devices are continuously and automatically transmitted to a computer. Other data – on the patient's blood, for example – is entered manually by laboratory technicians using a keyboard instrument near the patient's bed. The computer is programmed to calculate the current values of twenty-five physiological factors that a physician can use for diagnosis. Some of these are monitored continuously for alarm conditions, while some are calculated and displayed on the screen of a visual display unit, either at regular intervals or when called for. In short, then, a computer in an Intensive Care Unit can, if suitably programmed, provide the medical staff with up-to-date information in the right form and at the right times. On the one hand, it can 'boil down' the incoming data and suppress irrelevant details; on the other hand, it can store and analyse full historical information on the patients' condition and so detect slowly changing trends that might otherwise be overlooked.

We have already remarked that nearly all computers in medicine have been employed hitherto either on conventional data processing tasks or in a specialized medical role in a particular department. However, during the last two years there has been a significant change. With the advent of quick response multi-access operation from remote terminals equipped with visual display units, the medical world is becoming interested in a much more radical concept: that of the computer as the centre of an integrated information system covering all the activities of a hospital, perhaps of a regional group of hospitals, and closely associated with the other parts of the health service.

One of the first hospital authorities to go into action on these lines was Stockholm County, which is developing an integrated system which includes every aspect of medical management, control and treatment, and also the County's administration and financial control. The computer selected for the first stage of the project is the UNIVAC 494, with a store of 260 million characters capacity in which all medical records will be kept. This was the model, it will be remembered, that was chosen by BEA to handle its seat reservations because of its suitability for quick response multi-access working. The initial system is now being installed (1969) in one of Stockholm's large hospitals (1,500 beds); in 1972 it will be expanded to include a 1,750-bed hospital that is now under construction near Stockholm at a cost of $150 million. Indeed, the project is regarded as a pilot scheme for all the fifteen hospitals of Stockholm County (13,500 beds).

In the U.K., the Department of Health and Social Security has given a modest lead on similar lines by promoting about a dozen experimental computer projects aimed at exploring different aspects of the problem of handling medical data in hospitals, in general practice and in public health, and also in various situations involving more than one of these parts of the health service. They will all receive financial support from the Ministry until about

1973, when the more promising schemes will be selected for further development and eventual adoption for more general use.

The most advanced of these projects is at King's College Hospital, London, where the first stage of a comprehensive multi-access system based on an ICL 1905E computer is now being installed (1969). The project arose from a detailed study by the Department of Clinical Medicine of the general problem of how best to record and organize clinical data for easy processing and retrieval. All patients' records, and much else besides, will be held on the magnetic disc store of the computer. When a member of the hospital staff needs some item of information, he (or she) will interrogate the store by using a keyboard device, either a visual display unit or a tele-typewriter terminal, connected 'on line' to the central computer. Six visual display units and seven typewriters are included in the initial installation – sufficient for two wards and three service departments of the hospital. The system will be expanded in stages and it is planned to go up to sixty visual display units as soon as possible. Some of them will be mounted on specially designed mobile units that can be pushed round the wards.

The project planning team took the view that doctors and nurses would not take kindly to being asked to become amateur typists, so they developed a system whereby the user is able to select the information he requires – the pathology laboratory report on a particular patient, for example – by pressing the appropriate buttons on the console of his visual display instrument. A 'key word' is associated with each button to remind him of the various available choices. Selection of a particular key word, or group of key words, leads on to a new choice of messages designated by another set of key words. In this way the particular item of information required can be selected by making a series of choices; by following a path along a tree-like structure, the route to be taken at each branch point being specified by the simple action of pushing a button.

The next project in order of time is at Stoke. In this case the system will be based on an ICL 4/50 computer due to be delivered in 1970, and will serve the town's two main general hospitals and also its central out-patients department, which handles most of the out-patients work for the sixteen hospitals in the area. The equipment proposed is similar to that at King's College Hospital, but the problem is being approached more from the administrative side with less emphasis initially on clinical data. Visual display units will again be a prominent feature of the scene. Computer programs and operational procedures are being developed for a number of tasks: for out-patients, appointments and recording of visits; on the in-patient side, the management of waiting lists and admissions and the control of medical records; and the various statistical analyses of hospital activities that are required by the Regional Board.

Seven other projects for large 'real time' systems – at teaching hospitals at Manchester, Birmingham, Cambridge, Liverpool and three in London – are in the feasibility study stage. To complete the story, we must mention two research projects, at Oxford and London, that are directed towards other parts of the health service – group general practice and the community health records of the local government authorities. Computer studies are also being made of a number of specialized medical services, such as blood transfusion, radiotherapy and drug prescriptions.

All this activity – and there is much else – is certainly to be welcomed, albeit most of it is in an early stage. Few comprehensive medical computer systems are actually in operation in any part of the world and many people believe that the scale of effort is far too small. This view was well put by a speaker at a Conference on Medical Computing Problems held in January 1969 who pointed out that the total value of National Health Service computing equipment actually installed in Great Britain was about £1¼ million, while a sum of £30 million had been spent by one of the banks.

Tailpiece

In this chapter we have, as it were, brought to the surface a few fish from a very large pool, but sufficient, we hope, to establish the ubiquity of the electronic computer in the contemporary scene. We conclude with an example of how a computer has impinged on the affairs of one of the most isolated communities in the world – the people of Tristan da Cunha. When the population of this remote island was brought to England in 1961 following the eruption of the local volcano, the Medical Research Council set up a Working Party to investigate their physical and psychological condition. The islanders unexpectedly returned to Tristan in 1963, but the scientists continued their work and so were able to study the problems of resettlement. Computers are playing a large part in these studies; a short account which appeared recently (*Listener*, 16 January 1969) gave three examples of their use.

The first was to process the very full dental records that were collected by Mr John Fisher of the Birmingham University Dental School. His investigations established all too clearly that the dental condition of the islanders had deteriorated from excellent to poor in a period of thirty years, following the first arrival of sugar and sweets from the outside world.

The second example brings us to human genetics, to studies of the incidence of certain diseases to which the islanders are particularly prone. The first task was to assemble good genealogical records for the whole population. Dr A. Edwards of Cambridge then produced a set of programs based on the genealogical data which enabled the flow of genes from one generation to the next to be simulated on the computer. By running these programs it was possible to establish the extent to which a disease like asthma may have an environmental background or a genetic basis, or both.

The third example is concerned with the spread of infectious diseases, most of which were infrequent in Tristan before 1961. However, when the islanders arrived in England they suffered severely from respiratory infections such as colds, bronchitis and pneumonia. Since their return to Tristan, the frequency of these infections has reverted to the low pre-1961 level, but epidemics of colds are still likely to occur after a ship arrives. The staff of the Clinical Research Centre of the Medical Research Council have been able to construct mathematical models of the spread of viruses in the community. With the aid of a computer they are able to study the behaviour of these models – that is, to solve the equations constituting the model – in various situations. The validity of the models is tested by fitting the results predicted by the equations to the actual course of the epidemics observed on the island. The situation is extremely complex, and many features have still to be accounted for. If, by further study, explanations for these can be found, it is probable that they will remain true in other parts of the world. It is only the combination of a small, simple, community like Tristan and a large, complex tool like a computer that offers a real chance of solving such difficult problems at all.

Such, then, are a few of the many applications for which digital computers have proved eminently useful. Versatile as they are, they do not always provide a completely satisfactory answer to a problem. Neither, of course, do analog computers. Indeed, there are some jobs for which neither a digital nor an analog computer by itself is suitable. Such jobs pose new problems, some of which we discuss in the next chapter. We must point out that the material of this chapter is cognate with that of Chapters 5 and 8, and it is difficult to find a place in this book to put it without interrupting one or another sequence of ideas. We put it next, in the penultimate chapter, as being the least inconvenient place.

12. MIXED ANALOG AND DIGITAL COMPUTING

A natural role for the analog computer is in simulating a product or a process that an engineer is designing – an aircraft, a chemical plant, an electricity supply network, and so on. The engineer uses the computer to investigate how his proposed design will behave; or more often, he finds out what combination of the design parameters that he has under his control, such as the size of a mechanical component or the working temperature of a liquid, will give the best results. He usually makes repeated computing runs, changing the initial conditions each time, so as to investigate the behaviour of his device in different environments or in response to different stimuli, and making changes also to co-efficients in the set-up to optimize his design. In this process he is interpreting his design policy into simple detailed steps.

It is in fact possible for him to specify his strategy to a digital computer, and then leave it to work out the tactics for the analog computer. For this purpose, the analog and digital computers need to be in constant communication, and granted that this can be arranged, it is found that the two computers can readily reinforce one another. A striking example of such hybrid computation is the simulation of the flight of a spacecraft with on-board control of its trajectory. Here, the digital computer is responsible for simulating the position of the spacecraft to an accuracy of say 1 mile in 200,000 miles (for a Moon mission), the movement of the sight lines to radio stations on the earth, and the on-board guidance computer. The analog computer accepts computed steering demands from the digital computer and simulates with realistically rapid response time the action of the thrusters, and the rotational response and deflections of the spacecraft structure. It can thus supply the digital computer with simulated angular positions and velocities of the spacecraft.

Hybrid computers (Plate 3) need means of conversion between

analog and digital representations, and indeed such converters are widely used in many other fields as well. For example, in the control of machine tools or chemical processes, the quantities which are to be controlled – positions of mechanical parts or rates of flow of fluids – are analog in nature, since they vary continuously. They must be converted to digital measure if a digital computer is to take control. Furthermore, the controlling signals from the digital computer will usually need to be converted back to analog form in order to energize motors or hydraulic rams, or to open and close valves.

Conversion between analog and digital representations

A digital word (p. 113) can only represent a finite number of different magnitudes, so any process of converting from analog to digital representation (known as *digitizing*) must include quantization (see p. 70 and Figure 90(a)). It is often useful to combine this with *sampling* of the analog quantity – inspecting it only at predetermined intervals, and ignoring it between sampling instants. This allows time between these instants for the conversion process. Sometimes, indeed, a number of analog quantities are sampled in turn in a regular cycle, and the same conversion circuit is used to digitize each in turn. In this case the successive digital outputs are either recorded or put into the store of a digital computer. Sampling instants must be close enough together for the analog quantity not to change too much between samples. This quantity is often thought of as constant between consecutive sampling instants (Figure 90(b)), in which case sampling is equivalent to quantization of time.

If the sampling instants are not close enough together a substantial error can occur, which is best illustrated by considering an analog quantity that contains a regular oscillation. Figure 90(c) shows such a quantity sampled at six regularly spaced instants, and not assumed to be constant between sampling instants. The figure also shows the completely erroneous reconstruction of the original quantity that is obtained by drawing a smooth curve through the six sample points. Of course, it may be that the oscillation of the original quantity is spurious, i.e., that it is in fact a steadily increasing quantity (dotted line in Figure 90(c)) contaminated by high frequency noise. It may be known that the six samples are quite close enough together to give a good picture of the quantity. The quantity reconstructed

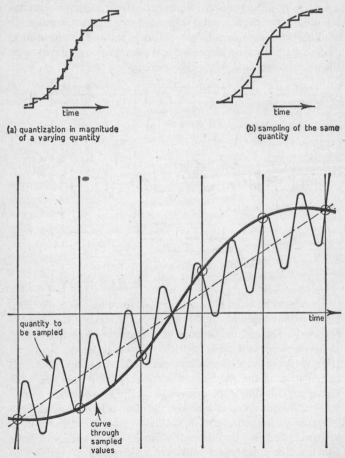

(a) quantization in magnitude of a varying quantity

(b) sampling of the same quantity

(c) sampling too slowly (the vertical lines denote sampling instants)

Figure 90. Quantization and sampling.

from the samples, however, is still considerably in error, compared with the original straight line. The conclusion is that before sampling, rapid oscillations must be removed (or *filtered*) from the quantity to be sampled.*

In the opposite process, conversion from digital to analog representation, the converter does not usually perform a number of different conversions in turn. This is because analog storage of each output would be needed to keep its value constant while the other conversions in the cycle were taking place.

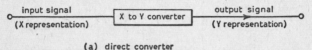

(a) direct converter

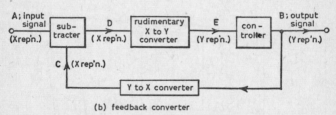

(b) feedback converter

Figure 91. Direct and feedback converters.
(X denotes Analog and Y denotes Digital, or vice versa.)

There are two types of converter; one in which the conversion, either from analog to digital or vice versa, takes place directly (Figure 91(a)), and the other in which negative feedback is used (a *feedback converter*, Figure 91(b)). In the latter type, a signal (B) is generated in the opposite representation to the input signal (A), that is, in the representation to which this signal is to be converted. Signal B feeds a converter of the opposite type to that required for the direct conversion, the output of the converter (C) being compared with signal A. The discrepancy (D) then serves to drive signal B in the direction which brings C and A towards equality. The rudimentary converter, which operates on signal D,

---

*Expressed in mathematical terms, if T is the time interval between samples, all components of higher frequency than $1/2T$ must be removed. The frequency of the original oscillation in Figure 90 (c) is 3.6 times this limit.

usually distinguishes three values only of D – positive, zero or negative – and is therefore much less complex than a direct converter.

This feedback principle is of very general utility. The mathematical reader might like to know that it enables a function generator, connected in the feedback path of an amplifier, to serve for the generation of its inverse function. In particular, it is used in the position-control servomechanism (p. 97) to do electrical-to-mechanical analog conversion with the aid of a mechanical-to-electrical converter.

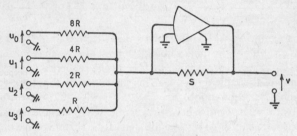

Figure 92. Direct digital to electrical analog converter.

In practice, conversion in either direction between analog and digital is best classified according to the analog representation involved, either mechanical or electrical. The digital representation is almost invariably electrical, so mechanical digital representation need not be considered.

Conversions between electrical analog and digital representations

Direct conversion is possible from electrical digital representation to electrical analog representation, using basically a network of resistors. To simplify the explanation, we assume that it is required to convert a four binary-digit number in parallel form (p. 162) to analog form. The circuit is shown in Figure 92; each of the signals u_3 to u_0 takes the value $+10$ volts with respect to earth if the digit it represents has the value 1, and 0 volts for the value 0. These voltage levels must be maintained much more accurately than in normal binary digital representation. The circuit is, in fact, that of page 91, with further input signals, and it forms a weighted sum of these. The current flowing from the input terminals to the virtual earth at the amplifier input terminal is

$$\frac{u_3}{R} + \frac{u_2}{2R} + \frac{u_1}{4R} + \frac{u_0}{8R}$$

and, as before, this is equal to the current in the feedback resistor, $-v/S$. Thus we get

$$v = -\frac{S}{R}\left(u_3 + \frac{u_2}{2} + \frac{u_1}{4} + \frac{u_0}{8}\right). \qquad (1)$$

If we put $S/R = 4/5$, say, then v varies from 0 to -15 volts in steps of 1 volt as the binary number represented by the four digits $u_3\,u_2\,u_1\,u_0$ varies from 0000 to 1111 in the sequence of the first column of the table on p. 143. This shows clearly that the circuit is doing the required job.

To deal with negative numbers represented by complements, all that is necessary is to reverse the sign of the signal voltage of the most significant digit, so that 0 volts still represents 0, but -10 volts represents 1.

For more than, say, six bits, the disparity in this simple circuit between the largest and the smallest resistance becomes more than sixty-four times, which is unsatisfactory for good circuit design. In this case it is better to use more elaborate networks of resistors (for example, the type known as a ladder network), and it also becomes necessary to take extreme care with the signal voltage levels. The input signals are, in fact, used only to operate electronic switches made from diodes, which connect a highly accurate constant voltage supply to the appropriate point in the network. By this means, errors in the analog output can be kept down to perhaps 0.01 per cent, that is, a tolerance of plus or minus one ten-thousandth of the maximum value of the output voltage, which can go positive or negative with respect to earth. It is justifiable to make the quantum of the digital representation about the same size as the error in the circuit, so this means that a word of up to fourteen bits may legitimately be allowed for. There would be no point in designing for more than this number of bits, as the accuracy of the analog output would not thereby be increased.

This type of direct digital-to-analog converter can be used as part of a feedback analog-to-digital converter, such as is used in a digital voltmeter. All modern analog computers incorporate a digital voltmeter because its accuracy is much higher than that of a normal voltmeter, which indicates by a pointer moving over a scale. The feedback voltage analog-to-digital converter can be implemented in several different ways, of which it will suffice to mention only that which gives the fastest conversion. In Figure 91(b), the Y to X converter is the direct digital-to-analog converter, X denoting analog and Y digital. Signal B is a parallel representation of, say, twelve bits, and signal E takes one of two values, according to whether signal D is positive or negative. The controller includes a parallel register (p. 174), from the outputs of which comes signal B, and circuits for altering the register content in a fixed sequence of operations. This sequence is started every time that the analog input signal, A, changes to a new value. First, the register is cleared, and then the most significant digit is set to 1. (We assume that A and B represent positive numbers only). If E now indicates that C is bigger than A, the most significant digit is reset to 0; if E indicates that C is less than A, this digit is left at 1. The next most significant digit is now set to 1, and reset or not according to the value of E, then the next digit is treated similarly, and so on until all twelve have been dealt with. Since, in this process, no use is made of the result obtained in the previous sequence, the input being digitized *de novo*, the method is suitable when a number of analog signals are sampled and digitized in turn.

There is another method of conversion, to or from electrical analog form, which is basically different from the foregoing. It makes use of an intermediate quantity in a type of analog representation which we have not mentioned before, namely the duration of an interval of time. The starting instant of this interval is usually defined by a signal changing from its resting level (say 0 volts) to its active level (say +10 volts), and the end of the interval by the change back to 0. These two changes take place repetitively, the regularly-spaced starting instants being further apart in time than the maximum permitted duration of the time interval which is being defined. The representation is therefore inherently a sampled one; the magnitudes of the time intervals can be taken to specify the value of a variable at the starting instants.

Direct conversion is possible either way between time-interval analog and digital forms. In both cases, an oscillator is used, generating short, closely spaced pulses, of which the repetition rate must be accurately constant. These pulses are counted digitally, either for the duration of the time-interval for the conversion from time-interval to digital form, or until they amount to the number specified in digital form for the opposite conversion. The duration of the counting process specifies the time interval in the latter case. Unfortunately, these conversions are bound to be rather slow, and the higher the accuracy needed, the slower they are.

Direct conversion is possible from time-interval analog to almost any other conceivable analog. This is done by making the desired analog (for example, the quantity of a liquid) accumulate at a steady rate during the time interval, the quantity accumulated at the end being proportional to the duration of the interval. An integrator (p. 92) serves the purpose for conversion to voltage analog. The output voltage is made zero before the start of the interval, and the two-level signal (0 or 10 volts) which defines the interval is connected to the integrator input. After the end of the time interval, the integrator output voltage remains constant at a value proportional to the time interval. The opposite conversion, from voltage to time interval, uses the same circuit with the feedback principle.

The conversion from electrical analog to digital form, by first converting to time-interval analog, is again suitable for dealing with numerous analog inputs, using a fair amount of equipment in common.

Conversion between mechanical analog and digital representations

With mechanical analogs, direct conversion is usually from analog to digital form. This is the opposite of the situation with electrical analogs, as exemplified by the direct converter of

Figure 92. This time it is conversion from digital to mechanical-analog which uses feedback, either with a direct mechanical-analog to digital converter, or (after conversion to an intermediate electrical analog) by means of a position control servo-mechanism.

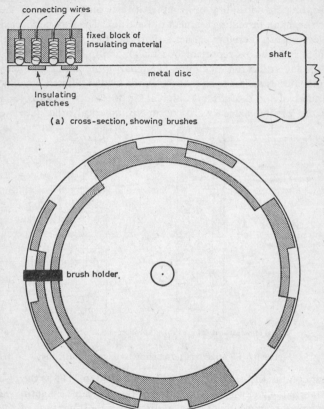

(a) cross-section, showing brushes

(b) pattern of insulating patches on disc

Figure 93. Direct digitizer for shaft position.

Figure 93 shows a converter which generates a digital version of the angular position of a shaft (a *shaft digitizer*). It consists of a metal disc, mounted on the shaft, carrying a pattern of patches or segments, of insulating material, and also a fixed assembly of 'brushes'. These are ball-bearings, forced by springs into contact with the disc. Each touches the disc at one point on its individual concentric circular track, and is connected to earth through the disc, or not, depending on whether it rests on the metal of the disc or on an insulating segment of the track. The wire connected to each brush therefore carries a signal (earthed, or open circuit) which is taken to represent one bit (1 or 0). The set of wires carries a parallel representation of a binary word, and the pattern on the disc is arranged so that the words read at different angular settings of the disc are all different. In the four-bit example in Figure 93, the sixteen words occur in numerical order (see the

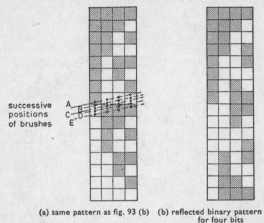

successive positions of brushes

(a) same pattern as fig. 93 (b)   (b) reflected binary pattern for four bits

Figure 94. Digitizer patterns shown diagrammatically.

first column of the table on p. 347) from 0000 to 1111 as the disc rotates anticlockwise. The position of the disc can be determined within one sixteenth of a revolution, i.e., the quantum of the representation is $22\frac{1}{2}$ degrees. The maximum error in the digital output is thus plus or minus $11\frac{1}{4}$ degrees. In a more elaborate system, by providing up to perhaps ten more brushes, and hence more bits, the error can be made about a thousand times smaller than this, but constructional tolerances prevent errors being reduced below this level.

Something more is needed, however, than is shown in Figure 93, for a reason which is explained by Figure 94(a). This shows the same pattern as Figure 93, but in a more convenient diagrammatic form. It also shows five successive positions of the brushes on the pattern, separated by very small rotations of the disc. Because of a slight error in mounting the brush assembly, the line joining the brushes is assumed to be not quite radial on the disc, and this is exaggerated for clarity. Other constructional errors have a similar effect on the working. When the brushes are in position A, they correctly read the number 0111 (seven); and in position E, which is very close to A, although the distance is exaggerated in the diagram, they correctly read the number 1000 (eight). However, at intermediate positions, they read at B, 1111 (fifteen); at C, 1011 (eleven); at D, 1001 (nine). These intermediate readings are of course completely wrong; the resulting gross errors are called *ambiguity errors*, because they make the true position of the disc uncertain. They occur whenever changes in more than one digit place occur together. Ambiguity errors are transient as long as the disc is rotating, and, in this case, greater manufacturing accuracy could reduce their duration. However, the disc may well come to rest at just the wrong place, so the error could continue indefinitely. To avoid this, one can conceive of a spring mechanism, which would cause the brush assembly to jump slightly, to avoid the bad spot in the pattern as it came round. This would substitute a small, tolerable error (due to the movement of the brush assembly) for the ambiguity error, which can be as much as 180 degrees, as in position B.

One practical way of avoiding ambiguity errors is to provide just such a jump, but by electrical means. A way of doing this, for example, is to provide two complete sets of brushes, spaced half a quantum apart ($11\frac{1}{4}$ degrees in Figure 93). They are used alternately, the changeover being made, back or forward, every time the disc advances half a quantum. Since the spacing of the two sets is half a quantum, at least one set is always clear of the boundaries in the pattern where ambiguity errors occur, and it is possible always to use this set. An additional track and brush control the changeovers, and the ultimate accuracy of the digitizer is in fact determined by this track.

There is an alternative, more radical, way of avoiding ambiguity errors, with none of the complications just mentioned. These errors can occur only when more than one digit, in the binary word read by the brushes, changes at nominally the same point in the pattern. The pattern is therefore rearranged so that only one digit changes at a time as the disc rotates. Such a pattern represents what is called a *unit-distance code*. The particular example shown in Figure 94(b) is the most useful of these, and is called the *reflected binary code*; it exists for any number of bits. Of course, the brushes now read numbers in the wrong order [0, 1, 3, 2, 6, 7, 5, 4, 12, 13, 15, 14, 10, 11, 9, 8, 0, . . . in Figure 94(b)], but this is quite a different matter from the wrong order obtained due to ambiguity errors, because it is always the same, and there is no doubt about what it means. Simple circuits can, in fact, convert the reflected binary code numbers to numbers in the correct order.

Instead of a metal disc and insulating patches, a glass disc and opaque patches can be used. In this case, the disc is illuminated and photo-cells replace the brushes. The advantages are that there is no friction on the disc, and that the light can be focussed into a narrow radial line. These points are important for the highest possible accuracy. For lower accuracies, the electrical contact method is cheaper.

There are many variants of these methods of conversion in widespread practical use, but we shall conclude this chapter by mentioning a method of digitizing the position of a shaft that depends on a quite different, and less well known, coding principle. Instead of marking the disc with a separate coded track for each binary place, as in Figure 93, only one coded track is used, and all the brushes contact this track at different points on its periphery (Figure 95).

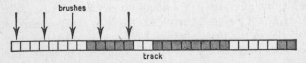

Figure 95. Diagram of unit-distance chain-code digitizer. The track is intended to be arranged in a circle.

In the position shown the brushes are reading the five-bit word 11100, and as the pattern moves to the left under the brushes, the sequence of words that is read is as follows:

11100	00011
11101	00010
11001	00110
11000	00111
11010	00101
10010	01101
10000	01111
10100	01011
00100	11011
00000	11111
01000	10111
01001	10110
00001	11110
10001	01110
10011	01100

It will be noted that this list contains thirty of the thirty-two possible five-bit words, corresponding to the thirty quanta of the track, and that they are arranged in a unit distance code. A code devised in this way from a single string of bits has been called a *chain* code, where the string of bits marked on the track is the chain. Clearly a digitizer based on this pattern would be smaller and simpler than one based on a reflected binary code. It would, on the other hand, have the disadvantage that no simple way is known of converting from this unit-distance chain code to orthodox binary numbers, other than by an operation of looking them up in a table like the one above. This is, however, perfectly possible in a computer. Furthermore, no general method is known of generating these codes, although it is known that the number of words in the code must be an exact multiple of twice the numbers of bits used.

13. FUTURE COMPUTERS

In this final chapter we allow ourselves a look into the future. In doing so we must remember that the electronic computer is a very recent addition to man's kit of tools and that many of its applications remain almost entirely unexplored. Our present achievements, impressive as they may look to us, are in fact extremely limited. Fortunately, however, the potential importance of computers is becoming generally recognized and a very large research and development effort is being directed to their design and to effective ways of using them – for good or ill!

Present-day computers are much more elaborate than ENIAC; they have several thousand times the storage capacity and work several thousand times as fast; they are a lot smaller and use a good deal less power; they give a choice of input and output devices and of programming systems; they are much easier to use than ENIAC and can do bigger jobs. There will be further improvements in all these things in the future.

Of course, similar generalizations can be made about the next generation of any product; to succeed, it must outdo its predecessor in all respects that are thought to be important. With computers in particular, these advances are interlinked. To do bigger jobs, programming languages and compilers must be improved, otherwise there will not be enough programmers available. This improvement will make computers easier to use on all jobs, not only on the bigger ones. For more efficient compiling, as well as for faster execution of bigger object programs, one wants a larger high-speed random-access store arranged on one level, in the sense explained on p. 139.

To finish large jobs in a reasonable time a computer will have to work faster and will have to provide more elaborate facilities. Furthermore, there will be less tolerance for errors, so that checking facilities will need to be more elaborate. At present, error correction usually implies crude replication of apparatus, or repetition of operations, the correct result being obtained by majority vote. In the future, we may expect to see more subtle methods of applying redundancy in structure and functioning; the correct result will probably be obtained by assessing the serviceability of a particular channel or a particular run, and giving its vote greater weight the more reliably it seems to be working.

Component developments

In spite of the fact that computers will comprise more apparatus – bigger stores and more logic elements – their physical size will have to be no larger, if they are to work faster. There is a fundamental reason for this. Electrical signals are propagated along computer wiring at nearly the speed of light – about a thousand feet per microsecond. That is, using a unit which is convenient for modern computer research and development, one foot per *nanosecond*. A thousand million nanoseconds make a second, or about the same number as there are seconds in thirty years. A signal would therefore take fifty nanoseconds to go from one end of a large present-day computer to the other. Already designers consider this effect when laying out the computer; in future they will have to reduce its magnitude by reducing the size of the constituent units. This will have another beneficial result – less power will be needed.

The word *miniaturization* was coined about twenty-five years ago to describe the process of reducing the size of the early radar equipment. If the reader dislikes this piece of jargon, let us warn him now; worse is to follow. The advent of transistors and *printed wiring* about ten years later allowed a spectacular advance in miniaturization. Both of these developments are exemplified by portable radio sets. Printed wiring is a general name for several techniques, using photography, etching, and printing with conducting ink, for producing a flat pattern of strip conductors on an insulating card. Another big advance has recently taken place, described by a further debasement in terminology as microminiaturization. The main stimulus for this originally came from

349

military needs and from requirements for space vehicles, but now the techniques have developed to be better and cheaper in some circumstances than older methods. The technique that can without exaggeration be termed a 'break-through' is the manufacture in a single process of a complete circuit, or many circuits (such as a parallel adder or a computing amplifier), in one piece from one lump of raw material (called a *chip*), instead of wiring them up from individual transistors, diodes and resistors. Such circuits are called *integrated circuits* (I C). A useful measure of miniaturization is the number of components that can be packed into a cubic inch. As long as valves were used, this number remained considerably less than one. It rose to about one component per cubic inch in the first transistor radio sets, to ten or more during the early 1960s in computers made from discrete components, and higher still in deaf aids. Integrated circuits are at present available containing several hundred components mounted on the surface of a silicon chip 0.3 inch by 0.05 inch, which would correspond to between 10,000 and 100,000 components per square inch, and at least several hundred thousand per cubic inch. But with such minute integrated circuits, the printed wiring necessary to interconnect them forms the main bulk of any practical embodiment, and this considerably reduces the density. Since a small digital computer, including store, only needs about 20,000 components, a vest-pocket general purpose computer will soon be feasible if the problem of making suitable input and output units can be solved.

One British firm, incidentally, has significantly increased the efficiency of the process of preparing an integrated circuit for production. To allow him to lay out the components and their interconnexions, the designer naturally has to work with drawings that are scaled several hundred times larger than the resulting circuit. A subsequent photographic reduction process is not only time consuming, but can cause dimensional errors because the photographs can shrink during development and fixing. In the improved method a set of computer programs accepts coded information specifying the position of components and interconnexions, and first draws a diagram of the integrated circuit. The designer checks and modifies this, and when he is satisfied, the computer programs generate punched tapes, each of which specifies one photolithographic mask, or template, to be used in the deposition of one of the successive layers of insulator or conductor that make up the integrated circuit. These punched tapes control a special machine tool that makes the masks directly in the correct size, using a laser beam to cut transparent slits in an opaque film; these slits can be as narrow as 2 ten thousandths of an inch (0.0002″). Not only does this method avoid a photographic reduction process, but it automates the making of drawings which is a rather routine and partly repetitious process, thereby improving the dimensional accuracy and reducing the number of mistakes.

Further changes will take place in stores. We can expect that, by the mid 1970s, thin-film stores of 100 nanoseconds cycle time and one million bits capacity will be available. If a capacity a hundred times larger is required, this should not increase the cycle time above 1 microsecond. By using longer words in the store to suit the 2D arrangement, thin-film stores will probably become cheaper than core stores. However, they will probably be displaced later on by integrated circuit stores, in which each bit is stored in a bistable trigger, or some equivalent active device. Already, such stores of relatively small capacity and very rapid access have been used in some large computers to supplement the main core store. Simpler integrated circuits, with perhaps one diode per bit, will come into use for read-only stores. The diodes will be disconnected in manufacture, or perhaps after manufacture using a laser beam, in those bit positions where a zero is to be stored.

For one-level high-speed stores of really vast capacity, say, a thousand million bits, there is the promise of an extremely exotic technique, at present working on a small scale in several research laboratories throughout the world. It is an application of the phenomenon of *superconductivity* by which the electrical resistance of many metals and alloys vanishes at temperatures near absolute zero (−273.7°C.). At the temperature of liquid helium, for example, 4.2 degrees above absolute zero, it is not possible to detect any resistance in a tin wire (we mean tin in the scientific sense). If a current flows in a loop made entirely of superconducting wire, it will continue to flow until it is disturbed – perhaps for years. The persistent current in a superconducting loop can therefore be set to flow either in one direction or the other, and so can represent a binary digit. Tin has the further useful property that a sufficiently strong magnetic field above a threshold value will destroy its superconductivity. This provides a means of controlling the persistent currents, and can also form the basis of logic elements.

Stores embodying these principles are called *cryogenic stores* and again use thin films and strip conductors to constitute a co-ordinate store. Superconductivity seems to be a delightfully absolute phenomenon from the designer's point of view; he is less troubled by secondary effects than with core stores, and this, together with the possibilities for miniaturization and integrated fabrication, suggest that very large cryogenic stores will be feasible. In the first instance, only the largest computers will be able to justify the cost of the refrigeration. Eventually, however, cheaper closed-cycle liquid-helium refrigerators may be developed and cryogenic stores may come into general use. All the same, the core store is a highly developed product and there is a considerable investment in its commercial fabrication, so in the words of one American expert, it will be some time before the core store is only a memory.

At the same time as these developments in the physical principles of storage, we can expect changes in access methods. Many jobs demand some sort of searching process in the store; to determine, for example, the desired entry in a stored dictionary, or the clock numbers of all employees who have worked on a particular job, or the significance of a symbol denoting a jump destination in an ALGOL program. With this sort of stored data, each item is formed from two or more distinct, but linked, parts. The address where the desired item is stored may be completely unrelated to the part of the item that is known. It may be out of the question to generate and maintain copies of the data in separate files, each sequenced according to a different part of the items. It is here that what is called an *associative* or *content-addressed* store will help. The programmer will nominate a value for a particular part of an item, and all items which meet his specification will be obtained from the store in one operation. For such a store, destructive reading would be a disadvantage, and an integrated circuit, or possibly a cryogenic store, will probably be the answer, since either type will permit fabrication in one unit of both the storage elements and the required logic elements.

Another method of store access which is sometimes useful is always to put a new item of data into a fixed address in the store, and arrange for this to displace (or 'push down') previous items to make room. This is ideal for jobs which require the records to be recovered in inverse order; reading a record destroys the stored data, and causes the next previous record to 'pop up' into the fixed position. Such a store is called a *push-down store*, and has the obvious merit, for the programmer, of not requiring him to specify an address. It is very useful, for example, to the writer of a compiling program. At present, such stores are usually provided by a subroutine which makes an ordinary store look like a push-down store. In the future, however, the storage equipment may behave in this way directly.

There will, of course, be many other developments in equipment and components. Indeed, our predictions may well be made ridiculous by some unforeseen and far-reaching invention which might concern not the computer itself, but the way in which its programs are written and operated.

Programming developments

The biggest problem facing nearly every computer user today is programming. Indeed, the situation is almost certain to get worse before it can get better. Thus, in the United States, programming costs in the 1950s accounted for a mere five per cent of total computing costs (equipment, programming, operation and maintenance). By 1965 the proportion had risen to about fifty per cent and is expected to reach about eighty per cent in the early 1970s. This trend becomes the more striking when it is viewed in the context of the substantial advances in programming techniques that have been made during the period. The most important of these, the invention of high level programming languages, formed the main subject of Chapter 9.

The reason for the programming bottleneck is the rapidly widening range of computing applications. Programmers are continually extending their activities into new fields; they are writing ever more complex programs and designing ever more sophisticated operating systems. This applies equally to all types of software (the programs that are usually supplied by the manufacturers and regarded as part of the capital equipment, as explained on p. 201) and to applications programs (usually written by the user). Computer designers are well aware of the problem and future computers will almost certainly contain additional equipment and other features to make programming easier. Developments in the design and organization of integrated circuits are making it more economically feasible to replace software by hardware than it has been in the past.

With high level languages, as we saw in Chapter 9, it is possible to standardize programming so that the same technique, and indeed even the same program, can be used on different types of computer. It is unlikely that there will ever be just one universal programming language, but some standard features will emerge, in the same way as motor cars, for example, have developed standard features. In spite of recent attempts to design a 'universal' language – for example, the PL/1 language mentioned on page 207 – the existing bifurcation into mathematical and commercial languages, typified by ALGOL and COBOL respectively, is likely to persist for some time yet; an economic combination of sports car and delivery van is rather unlikely.

Some of the existing compilers for advanced programming languages are gargantuan affairs, containing several hundred thousand separate instructions. This emphasizes the fact that compiling is one particular type of data-processing job, as opposed to a computing job. Data-processing programs, as typified by programs used in commerce, are characteristically rather long. This is usually because they have to make provision for dealing with a large number of exceptional cases, each of which occurs very rarely, and this is certainly true of present compilers. Present computers were not, in most cases, designed for the convenience of the compiler writer. They have all kinds of special features, all occasionally very useful for a particular job programmed directly in computer language, but usually a source of irritation to the compiler writer.

In the future we may expect the logic designer to listen to the compiler writer more and more: 'No fancy facilities, please, and above all, absolutely no exceptions to the rules.' We can hope, if this plea is answered, that compilers will not get longer and longer, as source languages become more flexible, concise, and powerful. Indeed, some computers are already being designed *ab initio* to accept programs written in ALGOL and COBOL.

Nowadays the greater part of computer software consists of the collection of supervisory and organizational programs that make up the operating system of the particular installation (p. 260). The need for such programs arises from the availability of faster hardware, better data transmission equipment, and a wider range of input and output devices: improved equipment creates a demand for improved means of using it. This is a recurrent theme in computer history, ever since, twenty-five years ago, the advent of the fast electronic arithmetic unit made it necessary to invent the stored program to take full advantage of it.

More ambitious computer applications, as well as the need for better compilers and more efficient operating systems, will lead to many developments in the technique of programming itself. Most of these, in so far as they can be foreseen, are too esoteric to discuss here. Suffice to say that advanced programming research is much concerned with questions of structure: the structure of artificial languages, that is with the rules that determine whether a sentence is properly formed; and the structure of the data on which the program is to operate. In much of this work the items of data are not numbers but what are called *list structures*, and so this type of programming is often called non-numerical programming.

Some of the main advances during the next few years will almost certainly be in such fields as quick response multiple access computing, long distance data transmission over large networks, and computer graphics, all of which were discussed in Chapter 10. The main obstacle to the more rapid spread of these techniques is the cost and time it takes to produce the necessary software to enable them to be utilized efficiently. It is to be hoped that this obstacle will be largely removed within a few years by improved methods of programming, using among other things new techniques for handling structured information of the kind mentioned in the previous paragraph.

So much for future computers, and methods of programming and operating them. What sort of jobs will they be used for?

Future applications

The experts on business efficiency attach much importance nowadays to channels of communication; they recognize that a manager can only make good decisions if he knows exactly what is going on. In one school of management science, such matters are reduced to charts, of which there are typically four. There is first the 'official' family tree of responsibilities. This, of course, is always out of date, and is distinguished from the rather different structure (the second chart) which managers *think* represents the true state of affairs. The third chart represents the *actual* organization and so must take account of information spreading by unofficial methods. The Chief Engineer's secretary, for example, always sits with the Supervisor of the Sales Typing Pool in the canteen, and manages to pass on to her boss the more scandalous of the gossip she hears. There is, lastly, and different again, the best organization for the purpose – optimum possibly, and optimistic certainly. It is here, in the pattern of the fourth chart, that computers can have a decisive influence, because they make it possible to obtain much better information, much more quickly, about the activities of the firm. In the years B.C. (that is, Before Computers), the dozens of departments in a big firm kept independent records, the essentials of which filtered very slowly up to top management. Now where a computer is used effectively in a particular department, which is certainly not always the case, information flows fast and freely inside the department, and top management receives what is sometimes an embarrassing number of accurate factual reports about the situation. The next step, clearly, is the universal use of a computer to permit the centralization of records and the consolidation of reports from all departments. Changes in the internal structure of the organization are usually necessary before this can take place, but there is no technical difficulty thereafter in having much tighter control of the firm's activities, at less cost in clerical effort.

In this new environment many technical innovations can become effective. One of these is the transmission of data over a distance, to link the firm's several computer installations. For this to be feasible on a large scale it must be possible to transmit digitally-coded information very rapidly over considerable distances. In this matter the G.P.O. was in the forefront with its high speed data transmission lines (48,000 bits per second), which are switchable in the same way as ordinary trunk telephone lines (cf. p. 269).

Another such innovation is the automatic reading of printed or written data by a computer input device (usually known as *character recognition*). This can reduce considerably the labour of transcribing source documents, such as invoices, on to punched cards or tape. When the document is printed in a uniform style of type designed for the purpose, it can indeed be read automatically, as we have mentioned on p. 317 in regard to bank cheques. If, on the other hand, different styles of type must be catered for, the task becomes much more difficult, and at present there is no economical equipment for doing the job. Automatic reading of handwriting – even good handwriting – is more difficult still. However, the general problem of character recognition is attracting so much research and development effort that we may reasonably expect substantial progress within the next decade, probably by using a mixture of analog and digital techniques.

Two methods of automatic reading are now in use. The first is known as *optical character reading*, in which the document is illuminated and the reflected light is focussed on to a photoelectric cell. The cell is arranged to scan the document and so is able to convert the space-pattern of light and dark areas on the surface of the document into a time-pattern of electrical signals which can be passed directly into a computer store.

The second method is *magnetic ink character recognition*, which is used by the banks (p. 317). Although it needs stylized characters and special 'magnetic' typewriters, it stands up much better than optical methods to the presence of dirt or extraneous marks on the document to be read. Once we have effective reading machines, the logical next step is to design devices that are able to recognize spoken words; a limited number of words – probably numerals and a few basic commands – would suffice for most purposes. Such devices are not yet in general use, but again we may expect progress during the 1970s.

Character recognition is a particular case of the more general problem of *pattern recognition*. We have already mentioned (p. 285) how difficult it is to mechanize this process. Although humans – and many animals – can recognise patterns, both visual and aural, so astonishingly well, we really have no idea how the trick is done. It is thus not surprising that we find it extremely difficult to program the task for a computer.

Many schemes for character recognition make use of a self-adaptive computer program; that is, in less neutral language a program which learns from experience, like the draughts program in Chapter 1. Learning from experience is one of several criteria of intelligence that have been put forward. Others are ability to generalize, to create new concepts and to act on general data when it becomes relevant. These rather sharper tests have, in present day debate, replaced the question 'Can computers think?', to which the short answer is 'Yes' and the longer one 'It depends on what you mean by thinking'. There are two extreme points of view which are both sterile. One is that a man is, after all, merely a biological machine working in accordance with the laws of physics and chemistry, and therefore it would be unreasonable to suppose that sufficiently elaborate electronic machines could not think also. The other is that thinking is defined as what a man does, and therefore computers can't do it; in other words, gentlemen may perspire, but horses can only sweat.

Clearly in the type of thought where a long chain of inferences must be followed correctly, as in doing arithmetic, computers perform better than men. If doing simple arithmetic counts as thinking, then the answer to our question is clear. The matter cannot be disposed of quite so easily, however. We must meet the critic who says that all the thinking has in fact been done beforehand by the programmer; that the computer, to paraphrase Lady

Lovelace, can do only what we know how to tell it to do; that the answers it delivers are all derived from the input data by the strict application of a set of known rules that have been written down in advance.

Now many mental processes cannot be reduced to a set of rules – or at any rate, have not been so reduced. Playing draughts or chess is an obvious example. In such a situation, one adopts an exploratory, trial-and-error approach, searching for clues as to whether or not one is on the right track. This method of solving a problem is known as the *heuristic* approach, in contrast to the use of a completely specified procedure which can be guaranteed to give an answer. (Such a procedure would be called an algorithm, as explained on p. 205.) The significant thing – and the answer to our critic – is that we are beginning to use computers to solve problems heuristically. Many people are attempting – with increasing success – to write programs to enable computers to perform non-routine, incompletely specified tasks – the kind of tasks which, if done by human beings, would be generally accepted as demonstrating mental abilities of a high order. Once again we may cite the draughts program of Chapter 1.

Indeed all the intellectual abilities mentioned earlier have already been demonstrated by particular computer programs, admittedly piecemeal, and in some cases in a rudimentary form. Thus for example, computers act on programs written in generalized languages, such as ALGOL, interpreting them to suit the equipment available. Again, computers have shown creative ability, of which we will cite three examples among many:

(a) In 1956 Hiller and Isaacson of the University of Illinois, using a program which specified rules of harmony and composition and applied them to notes specified by random numbers, were able to produce a computer-composed piece of music, the famous *Illiac Suite for String Quartet*, which was subsequently published. A good deal of programmed music has been produced since then, and indeed nowadays no large gathering of computer people is complete without a concert at which a selection of computer compositions is performed.

(b) A computer in California has been programmed to write poems by fitting words from a 3,500-word vocabulary into one of

359

128 patterns of simple sentences. Here is an example, followed by an extract from a review from the magazine *Time*.

> Few fingers go like narrow laughs.
> An ear won't keep few fishes,
> Who is that rose in that blind house?
> And all slim, gracious blind planes are coming,
> They cry badly along a rose,
> To leap is stuffy, to crawl was tender.

Faced with this poem, any competent modern critic could easily go to work. He might first allude to its use of alliteration ('few fishes', 'few fingers'). Clearly the poem deals with the plight of modern man reaching out for love and innocence but mocked by impending death. Love is the rose stifling in the blind house of modern technology. Note the repeated theme of blindness, and the plane that will bring annihilation to the world. Like the world, human love has no future. And little religious comfort. (The fish was an early symbol of Christian faith, now reduced – hence 'few fishes'.) Mirth, too, has shrunk to 'narrow laughs' though the poet, like Western man himself, fondly recalls the lost gentleness of childhood ('to crawl was tender').

The review concludes by saying that the computer cost 100,000 dollars, so the output cannot be called free verse.

In 1968 the Institute of Contemporary Arts mounted an international exhibition of computer art at Nash House in London, with the object of exploring and demonstrating some of the relationships between technology, particularly computer technology, and creativity. The exhibition ranged over a wide field – music, poems, graphic design, both still and animated, and even computer-programmed choreography. In most cases computers either produced the art form or were themselves part of it.

(c) Programmed to search for heuristic proofs of theorems in elementary geometry, a computer proved the equality of the base angles, B and C, of an isosceles triangle, ABC, by showing that triangles ABC and ACB are congruent. This method, although familiar to Pappus (third century A.D.), was not known to the programmer.

It seems, then, that computers can be made to give a surprisingly good imitation of intelligent thought, to take the minimum interpretation. In fact, it is unwarrantable to deny that the computers of the future, with their greater flexibility, bigger stores, and higher speed, will be able to think. What we do not know is whether 'electronic thinking' will ever be more than rudimentary; whether it will resemble the thinking of an earthworm rather than that of a man. The human brain is immensely complex – perhaps as complex as ten thousand present-day computers linked together. In the future, if and when this degree of complexity is attained by a single computer, we shall perhaps be able to find out if it can be made to match the power of thought of the human brain.

The problem of programming such a super-computer will still remain, however. The limitations of man as a programmer will always, in the end, set a limit to the intelligence that can be simulated by a machine. A computer's 'artificial intelligence' is prescribed by man, and a higher intelligence is demanded for the prescription than for the execution. Man, as the originator, will always be on top.

SUGGESTIONS FOR FURTHER READING

Awad, E. M. (ed.), *Automatic Data Processing: Principles and Procedures* (Prentice Hall, 1966).

This comprehensive exposition of business data processing was prepared under the auspices of the American Data Processing Management Association by representatives of six of the leading computer manufacturers under a Professor of Business Studies as general editor.

Babbage, C., *Charles Babbage and his Calculating Engines* (Dover reprints, 1961).

Selected writings by Babbage, Lady Lovelace, and others, edited and introduced by P. and E. Morrison. Much of the material deals with Babbage's project for a universal automatic computer, but his autobiographical and more general scientific writings are also well represented.

Bowden, B. V. (ed.), *Faster than Thought* (Pitman, 1953).

A collective work dealing with automatic digital computers and the jobs they do. One of the earliest, and still one of the most lively and entertaining general accounts. Part II is devoted to individual British computers; Part III to applications. The discussion of Babbage's Analytical Engine by Menabrea and Lady Lovelace is printed in full as an Appendix.

Bowles, E. A. (ed.), *Computers in Humanistic Studies* (Prentice Hall, 1967).

A collection of papers delivered at Conferences in U.S.A. in 1964–65. There are groups of papers on anthropology and archaeology, history, language and literature, and musicology.

Feigenbaum, E. A., and Feldman, J. (eds.), *Computers and Thought* (McGraw Hill, 1963).

A comprehensive collection of research papers in the field of 'artificial intelligence'. Topics covered include heuristic programming, game playing and learning, pattern recognition and theorem proving.

Fink, D. G.. *Computers and the Human Mind: an introduction to artificial intelligence* (Heinemann, 1966).

A popular introduction to the subject that is treated in depth in the preceding book.

Korn, G. A., and Korn, T. M., *Electronic Analog and Hybrid Computers* (McGraw Hill, 1964).

This comprehensive book treats components as well as complete computers and practical methods of using them. Although the authors introduce some mathematics and electronic technology, the book will be helpful to a non-expert who has to use these computers.

Levison, M., and Sentance, W. A., *Introduction to Computer Science* (Oldbourne Mathematical Series, 1968).

This book was written primarily for university students taking a first course in computer science at a University or College of Technology. Little mathematical knowledge is assumed, and the book will be useful to the general reader who wishes to gain further insight into the programming of computers in high level and machine languages.

Sisson, R. L., and Canning, R. G., *A Manager's Guide to Computer Processing* (John Wiley, 1967).

The object of this short book in the 'Manager's Guide' series is to explain in non-technical, business terms how computers and computer-based information systems can help managers and business executives to make better decisions.

Vajda, S., *Readings in Mathematical Programmnig* (Pitman, 1962).

A crisp, concise introduction to the application of mathematical techniques, such as linear optimisation, to planning problems. The study of a representative set of specific problems occupies much of the book.

Wooldridge, R., and Ratcliffe, J. F., *Introduction to ALGOL Programming* (English Universities Press, 1963).

A clearly written account, intended to be used as a self-instruction manual by a reader with no previous experience of computer programming. This book provides a convenient amplification of the brief account of ALGOL in Chapter 9.

Information: a Scientific American book (W. H. Freeman, 1966).

A collection of authoritative articles, first published in the September issue of *Scientific American*, on the general theme of the computer as a machine for processing information. The topics discussed include time sharing, data transmission, information storage and retrieval, and artificial intelligence. There are four chapters on the applications of computers in science, technology, organizations and education.

INDEX

Index

Index

Index

Index

MORE ABOUT PENGUINS AND PELICANS

Penguinews, which appears every month, contains details of all the new books issued by Penguins as they are published. From time to time it is supplemented by *Penguins in Print*, which is a complete list of all books published by Penguins which are in print. (There are well over three thousand of these.)

A specimen copy of *Penguinews* will be sent to you free on request, and you can become a subscriber for the price of the postage – 30p for a year's issues (including the complete lists) if you live in the United Kingdom, or 60p if you live elsewhere. Just write to Dept EP, Penguin Books Ltd, Harmondsworth, Middlesex, enclosing a cheque or postal order, and your name will be added to the mailing list.

Some other books published by Penguins are described on the following pages.

Note: *Penguinews* and *Penguins in Print* are not available in the U.S.A. or Canada

A DICTIONARY OF COMPUTERS

Editor: Anthony Chandor
Associate Editors: John Graham and
Robin Williamson

This is a glossary of some 3,000 words, phrases, and acronyms used in connexion with computers. It has been designed to assist both technical readers and the increasing number of non-specialists whose work is to some extent affected by a computer.

Exactly what computer men mean when they talk about 'graceful degradation' or 'garbage', about 'truth tables' or 'crippled leap-frog tests', about the 'flip-flop' or the 'output bus driver' is helpfully explained here in an alphabetical list of definitions with cross-references.

The entries are interspersed, too, with seventy general articles which cover, more fully, the major computer topics and such business processes as 'budgetary control' and 'systems analysis', which are more and more being handled by computers.

A DICTIONARY OF ELECTRONICS

S. Handel

So rapid has been the growth of electronics that you will not find the word in any English dictionary published before 1940.

Automation, radar, television, computers, artificial satellites, guided missiles, communications, and navigation – all these, with their profound effect on everyday life, are dependent on electronics, and each application contributes its quota of new words. Hence we have a serious problem of language.

This dictionary has been prepared by a consultant electrical engineer, with twenty years' experience in electronics, as a concise, accurate, and up-to-date reference work both for those who are professionally concerned with electronics and for those who are simply moved by a healthy curiosity about our complicated world. In the definitions provided, such words and phrases as may be unfamiliar to non-technical readers are all related, by systematic cross-reference, to 'standard dictionary' words. Specialists in electronics will find this a useful source of short, authoritative descriptions and, when they exist, standardized definitions.

THE ELECTRONIC REVOLUTION

S. Handel

Electronics can alter our world even more profoundly than the Industrial Revolution. Yet most people would be hard put to it to say what the word means.

Electronics might be defined as the technique of marshalling free electrons for the transmission of images, the recording and reproduction of sound, the storing and treatment of information, and the automatic control of industrial processes. It has become the nerve system of modern power and the brain of modern society. It can free us from drudgery in the factory, office and home, and enrich the leisure we shall then enjoy.

In this popular introduction to a complex subject the author describes, very simply, not only the scientific basis and the technical devices of electronics, but also its impact on our daily lives. After outlining the story of the electron's discovery and the swift growth of the electronics industry, he explains how scientific and industrial research in electronics revolutionized communications, transport and medicine; gave birth to television, radar and tape-recording; and produced high-speed computers and full-scale automation. On the debit side we see electronics sharpening the weapons of war, invading the privacy of the citizen, corrupting the mass media. And a chapter on cybernetics shows how this new technique may be applied to the science of government.

COMPUTERS, MANAGERS AND SOCIETY

Michael Rose

Computers, Managers and Society is an account, part technical, part sociological and part philosophical, of the computer revolution.

After a general survey of the development of computer-controlled data processing, Michael Rose examines the complex effects of the computer upon the clerical worker – the new opportunities, the dangers of alienation, the threat of technological unemployment. He then focusses upon the fast-developing problems of managers. Many of the standard managerial functions can already be programmed. But should executives delegate qualitative decisions to a machine? And if so, how far can and should these changes go?

'Computerization' presents managers with new opportunities on a structural scale unmatched since the Industrial Revolution. Do they really understand the new situation? Can they, when it is transforming itself so rapidly? And are we enough aware of the effects of the computer upon an even larger social group – society itself – now faced with the need to clarify its whole attitude to technological change?